"Michael Leach dreamed of becoming a Yellow[...] his wish and, with his memoir *Grizzlies On My Mind*, [...] personal journey, traveling with an unguarded heart into the mystery and beauty of the Yellowstone backcountry. He passionately and correctly speaks his outrage against the "barbaric" trapping of the park's wandering wolves, and of the inhumane bison slaughter by Montana's livestock department. Above all this is a personal odyssey; Leach shares his lusty interest for women in uniform, his faith in the power of wild nature, and the spiritual paths of healing.

—DOUG PEACOCK, author of *Grizzly Years* and *Walking It Off*

"Three and a half million people see Yellowstone National Park every year, but few people see as clearly and deeply into the park as Michael Leach. Yellowstone's combination of natural attributes and human oddities makes it a truly weird and wonderful place. Leach lifts a curtain, lets you see a layer of the park the casual visitor would never know. He writes with equal admiration for the subtleties and splendor—and the understanding that sometimes the subtleties are the splendor. Leach provides glimpses of the people—from biologists to law enforcement staff to astonishing gym rats in the border town of Gardiner—and the animals that make Yellowstone a world unto itself. Whether writing about famous wolves, dinosaur bones, arrowheads, marmots, or grizzly bears, Leach writes with a passion that is as inspiring as his subject. His journey of discovery through Yellowstone is both public and poignantly personal. Treat yourself to this unique and passionate perspective on America's greatest national park."

—JEFF HULL, author of *Pale Morning Done* and *Streams of Consciousness*

grizzlies *on* my mind

ESSAYS OF ADVENTURE, LOVE, AND HEARTACHE FROM YELLOWSTONE COUNTRY

MICHAEL W. LEACH

WESTWINDS
PRESS®

The essay "Bison and Bigotry" was previously published in *NewWest.Net* (online magazine) February 10, 2011 and the essay "Respect for Senor Blanco" was published in *Outside Bozeman* (magazine), Summer 2011.

Library of Congress Cataloging-in-Publication Data

Leach, Michael W.
  Grizzlies on my mind / by Michael W. Leach.
    pages cm
    ISBN 978-0-88240-995-5 (paperback)
    ISBN 978-0-87108-317-3 (hardbound)
    ISBN 978-0-87108-316-6 (e-book)
  1. Yellowstone National Park—Description and travel. 2. Natural history—Yellowstone National Park. 3. Animals—Yellowstone National Park. 4. Outdoor life—Yellowstone National Park. 5. Leach, Michael W.—Travel—Yellowstone National Park. 6. Leach, Michael W. 7. Park rangers—Yellowstone National Park—Biography. 8. Yellowstone National Park—Biography. I. Title.
    F722.L33 2014
    978.7'52—dc23
                          2014004306

Editor: Jen Weaver-Neist
Cover design: Brad Bunkers and Vicki Knapton
Interior design: Vicki Knapton
Map: Ani Rucki

Published by WestWinds Press®
An imprint of

GRAPHIC ARTS
BOOKS®
P.O. Box 56118
Portland, Oregon 97238-6118
503-254-5591
www.graphicartsbooks.com

For Kamiah, who inspires me each day with her big heart, sense of wonder, and little-person integrity: you are my source. May you always embody the strength, health, audacity, and wild spirit of the place from which you come. And to my mom and dad, April and Steve: without the two of you, my Yellowstone dream would be just that, a dream. Your love and unwavering support is a gift I will cherish as long as the waters sing their enchanted song.

Contents

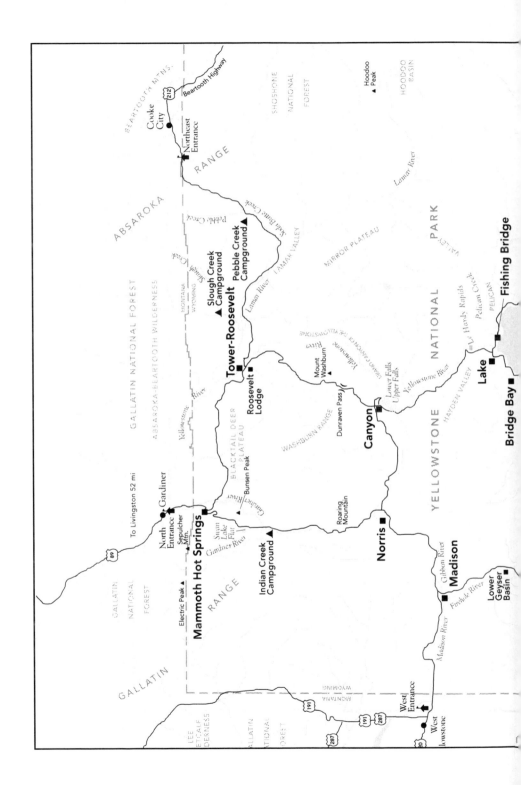

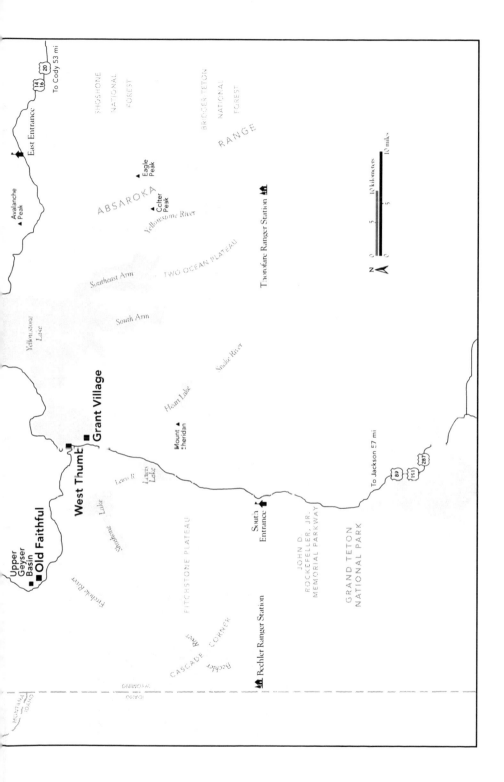

*If you know wilderness in the same way that you know love,
you would be unwilling to let it go. This is the story of our past,
and it will be the story of our future.*

—Terry Tempest Williams

Foreword

It was moments before dark when we arrived at our Hoodoo Basin campsite. A lava sunset welcomed us, helping in the final stretch of well over ten, tough miles for the day. But at the moment we could finally rest our exhausted bones, Michael raised the alarm. Mounded in a tidy pile near our campfire was a large bear scat. Full of cone scales, it appeared the bear had been eating whitebark pine nuts and passing the chaff—lots and lots of chaff. Probably a big bear, we both thought, as we glanced wide-eyed at each other.

Sitting at timberline in the Absaroka Range, the campsite was surrounded by whitebark pine stands. And there was a second, larger scat directly beneath the food pole, one of the only structural improvements of the campsite designed for keeping campers' food safe from marauding bears. Clearly, our long-sought destination had also recently been chosen as a foraging site by a bear. "No need for alarm," I said, and began again to focus on my weary body. As a professional wildlife biologist, I have spent countless days in the wild among bears.

Michael went on feeling the gratification I often find in exploring Yellowstone—discovering the presence of myriad flora and fauna uniquely suited to this wild place. There is a rejoicing in finding the signs of the truly wild places—in places that few roam. These are readily found deep in the backcountry, where animal tracks far outnumber human tracks, in the furthest corners of the mountains. But before I could focus on my fatigue, a marked change in Michael's manner grabbed my attention. Along with his gratification, there was fear. For him, as for many, the grizzly bear will either attract or repel a person from the wilderness based on a feeling—the feeling that one is at risk of becoming a real link in the food chain.

While finding fresh bear droppings can be unsettling for anyone, there was far more racing through Michael's mind. I wouldn't call it dread but, rather, a potent combination of respect and anticipation. He loved these bears, and finding one living so close was ultimately thrilling, despite the sleep he might lose during the night.

I describe his emotion then, looking back, as a celebration of the great bear. To feel their presence so deeply, without a direct encounter, had never been so fully poignant or stimulating. Channeling the wild in such a way is one of Michael's great gifts.

Two years have passed since then, and thirteen since I first met Michael in Yellowstone's iconic Lamar Valley. Most memorable about my first encounter with him, among many others in the group at that time, was his youth. Everyone there had assembled with the rising sun to pursue a common goal: the expectation of viewing the park's premier wildlife—perhaps a wolf, or maybe a grizzly bear. As a wildlife guide and wolf tracker for several decades in Yellowstone, I have led many groups through the park, and they are typically middle-aged, retired folks. But then here was Michael, in his earliest years of college, dedicating time to the discovery of Yellowstone's wonders. This new friend demonstrated an eagerness and dedication I had found very few to possess at his age, or any age.

Conversation is easy with Michael. Being outgoing, full of curiosity, and hungry for interaction with both people and nature are the hallmarks of his character. So, it was no surprise that I saw him many more times afield, out among our favorite haunts in the park, his enthusiasm for Yellowstone growing with each visit. There was great promise in his purpose. And I felt then, as much as I do now, that his goal was not just to have the Yellowstone experience but to share it. To live within the flow of nature, share his love for its wild places and creatures, and ignite in others some of the white-hot passion he felt would be his life's work.

Early on, Michael asked me if he had any chance of one day becoming a park ranger. I saw this as a role in which he could flourish, and where he could use his skills to convey the value of Yellowstone to its visitors. No doubt, he would be a motivating leader in this capacity, and I strongly encouraged him to pursue it. Not long after, I encountered him among the chaos of a "bear jam" (the traffic associated with a bear sighting), working as a park ranger. This is a challenging job in which the ranger manages an ever-flowing, overexcited crowd clamoring to see a roadside bear. Few rangers can keep their cool, and those who can seem supernaturally endowed with great patience. In Michael's case, he had it, and additionally embraced the prospect that allowing visitors to have an authentic (but safe and respectful) experience with bears in Yellowstone can be crucially pivotal to both the individual and the future of the park's bears.

The years since his rangering days have seen many other outgrowths of his passion. As Michael honed his craft, ever-sharpening his communication skills to impart the meaning of Yellowstone, I retained him as a naturalist guide for my wildlife tour company, Yellowstone Wolf Tracker. Once again, he excelled—especially in front of a group. With resonant voice and purpose, he delivered an enthralling Yellowstone sermon that had evolved from presentations he gave for years as an interpretive ranger, when he regularly gathered would-be converts around the campfire to hear "The Word." Among colleagues and friends, Michael became known as "The Rev," befitting his magnanimous ability to transform so many visitors into disciples of Yellowstone. Far from a simple exposition of interesting information and pretty pictures, Michael creates the backdrop of a spiritual home ground through his narrative, replete in personal experience and emotional growth. He weaves inspiration throughout by provocatively establishing the inspiration he has won from his many explorations and encounters.

It wasn't long before our roles reversed, and I joined the board of Yellowstone Country Guardians (YCG), a one-man show dedicated to fostering passion for the wild places of Yellowstone. The one man was, of course, Michael, who was concerned that young people were being left behind, and I shared that concern. For the area's youth, participating in YCG programs was nothing short of transformative.

Having grown up in the Yellowstone community myself, I had always felt that living in its shadow was not enough; young people needed better access to programs that make real and lasting connections with the landscape. I was fortunate to find this connection on my own, and with the direction of family and a handful of friends. But with Michael at the helm of YCG, there was no better mentor or outdoor experience for attending youth. Participants emerged more inspired and with higher regard for the value of where they lived.

Unfortunately, even though YCG's board sought to support Michael's vision with whatever means we could muster, we could not keep the organization afloat financially. Not having this organization through which Michael could work his magic for these kids was a profound loss, and I continue to search for a way for him to return to this vocation; because our youth—and our park—have never needed it more than now.

On the flip side, without the heavy YCG responsibilities, Michael had the time to write—for him, an equally compelling medium for advancing his mission. All admirers of nature will find the essays in *Grizzlies On My Mind* a masterful accounting of great and harrowing adventure, made tangible by skillful portrayal, and flowing with love for a place and the people who share that love.

Just as Michael would profess in his sermons, a new environmental approach is afoot. These essays describe this new approach, at first dividing sharply the ranks of the inspired and uninspired, but then lifting all from the latter to the former to build a united outcome. In this way, readers will find this collection to be Yellowstone's *Desert Solitaire*. It is the long-awaited narrative of how our most famous national park and its marquee bear inspired a refreshing new movement for nature's preservation and the nourishment of the human spirit.

—Nathan Varley

Nathan Varley holds a PhD in ecology and has studied the wildlife in Yellowstone for most of his career. He and his wife own a park wildlife tour company located in Gardiner, Montana.

Introduction

Visceral excitement pulsed through my scrawny eight-year-old body as I gazed into the eyes of a beast more massive than any I had ever witnessed. Welcome to God's theme park, Yellowstone. My earliest memories of Yellowstone stem from the perspective of a young boy enamored by our first national park's glory and by the spirit of adventure. Growing up along the shores of a small mountain lake in North Idaho, I cherished our annual pilgrimage to my grandparents' birthplace—Wyoming—and to my family's beloved Yellowstone. I can still vividly remember that nervous, Christmas-morning-like anticipation when we awoke at dawn to the song of the Madison River in Ennis, Montana—our launching point for each Yellowstone adventure. Even in August, the air would be crisp, with wispy waves of fog rising from the waters of the fifty-mile riffle, as the sun literally burst forth, illuminating the Madison Range to the west. To a young boy, it seemed they must have been the birthplace and spine of the continent.

Romping the mountains and forests near my home, it was easy for one childhood season to blend into the next without my recognizing the significance of their passing. Perhaps this explains how our family sojourns to Yellowstone ultimately came to mark the life-affirming milestones in my own personal journey—from curious boy to earnest young man, striving to uncover meaning in pursuit of living a life that matters.

Such is the raw power of Yellowstone. While its natural wonders, wildlife, rivers, and biodiversity are most celebrated, I have come to believe Yellowstone's greatest gift is its ability to inspire two-leggeds to uncover purpose, meaning, and goodness in our lives. As much as we are awed by the scenery and inhabitants that make the Greater Yellowstone Ecosystem one of the most important places on our planet ecologically, Yellowstone has always been first and foremost a people's park. Since its beginning, the wild spirit of Yellowstone has inspired countless visitors to strive for a more meaningful existence—one often intertwined with and based upon their love for nature and their desire for adventure.

My parents always fostered my sense of place. As a boy, I took great pride in my Wyoming and Idaho roots, four generations deep, but it wasn't until I first donned the green-and-gray Park Service uniform as a Yellowstone National Park Ranger that I fully appreciated the unmatched power of pursuing a dream. Working on Yellowstone's behalf has become engrained in my life's mission ever since. The very rhythm of my life has ebbed and flowed with the seasons of Yellowstone.

I began writing this book for one very simple reason: a deep and burning love for a place like no other. *Grizzlies On My Mind* is also a coming-of-age story about living our passion and chasing our dreams. The essays are mostly chronological, leading you through my experiences in hopes of fostering your own Yellowstone story. Though some facts and statistics may have changed, this book is a celebration of the wild heartbeat of a region that has captured the hearts and imaginations of people from all over the globe. With each essay, I hope to harness that boundless spirit via the perspective of someone who has had the privilege of living and working there, and to inspire a commitment to its future.

This is a book about love, heartache, and adventure written from a place of awe, vulnerability, and passion. These essays amount to snapshots of where I have been and how far I have come. During this journey, my writing, voice, and life may have changed, but through it all, I believe these essays tell the story of who I am, and how—and perhaps more importantly, why—Yellowstone and the surrounding country have served as my foundation and bedrock. Yellowstone has remained my constant.

From my struggles with a sometimes debilitating autoimmune disorder to my pre-fatherhood explorations and journey through fatherhood; from my life as a husband to my struggle with divorce and the challenge of being a newly single dad—a saunter along the Blacktail Deer Plateau, a view from atop Electric Peak, a quiet afternoon spent wading the waters of the Gardner River have served as my refuge; my place of solace; my reminder that life is a beautiful gift, and that each day spent in Yellowstone has the potential to remedy a broken heart and calm a racing mind.

For over a decade, I've had the opportunity to uncover and experience Yellowstone and its workings on an intimate level. I've been a ranger naturalist and bear education ranger, a fly-fishing and wildlife guide, a director of a Yellowstone-based nonprofit, a park and wildlife advocate, a high school basketball coach, and a motivational speaker; and through it all, I've breathed Yellowstone's essence. I love Yellowstone. I've come to appreciate and respect both the beauty and the heartache of this wondrous and often perilous landscape. And I love witnessing people becoming inspired by it. Yellowstone has been the greatest source of inspiration and goodness in my life. I owe Yellowstone for a life I love.

I have traveled from coast to coast—from Farmville, Virginia, and Longwood University to the shores of the Pacific and the California Academy of Science—sharing my Yellowstone "sermon"; it's a sermon that people of all ages and from all walks of life seem to want to hear. And I always start the same way. "Yellowstone. Just that word has something sacred to it, something sacred in its meaning. Just the word *Yellowstone* evokes powerful emotions—fuels the imagination and spirit—for people all around the world. Yellowstone is a holy place for those whose temples are the mountains and the wilderness; a place like no other on earth, one that fills the soul with excitement and energy."

I believe a sense of place is one of the greatest gifts we are offered as human beings, and there are few places as profoundly impactful as Yellowstone. During my time as a ranger naturalist there, I had the good fortune to give presentations about preserving wilderness within the Greater Yellowstone Ecosystem. Traveling up to five nights a week to the biggest venues in the park, I shared my love and passion for it. And I saw firsthand that same passion reflected back at me in the eyes of US and international visitors alike. As a fly-fishing guide, I observed clients falling in love with Yellowstone over the course of a day spent in pursuit of cutthroat trout on one of its rich rivers. As a wildlife guide, I watched the delight of clients from the United Kingdom, Europe, South Africa, Asia, Russia, Australia—all awed by the sight of their first wolf or bear in the wild. As a nonprofit director, I saw the hearts and minds of at-risk local youth transformed by a wilderness retreat or a fly-fishing school, inspiring desperately needed guardians for the future.

I recently received a note from an audacious eighteen-year-old with whom I had the pleasure of working through the nonprofit I founded in 2007, Yellowstone Country Guardians (YCG). Like so many of today's youth, this young lady has gone through more than any person her age should have to endure. As she participated in YCG programs, however, I literally watched as Yellowstone made a positive impact on her self-confidence and sense of purpose. I witnessed her eyes opening to a new world: a world of hope and possibility. Her entire letter moved me to tears, but for me, these simple words at its conclusion sum up the power of Yellowstone: "Every time I set out my line or tie a fly to my rod, I lose myself in the river. I am more connected to my surroundings and always remember to give back. You showed me the qualities of who I really am. YCG will be in my blood and branded on my heart."

Yellowstone has the raw power to touch and change lives.

I will never forget that brilliant August day when I walked more than forty inner-city teens from Boston, Massachusetts, to Artist Point, overlooking Lower Falls and the Grand Canyon of the Yellowstone— the same spot where legendary painter Thomas Moran created one of his most impactful Yellowstone masterpieces, *The Grand Canyon of the Yellowstone*. Awestruck, the students gazed in wonder. And then, a sixteen-year-old African American girl with tightly woven braids walked up to me and gave me a hug. "I never knew beauty like this existed in the real world," she said, tears streaming down her cheeks.

As a high school basketball coach, I took twenty teenage athletes in the middle of winter to sit on the banks of the longest free-flowing river in the lower forty-eight, utilizing the power and roar of the Yellowstone River as a metaphor for our team's philosophy and mission (with grand results, I might add). And as an advocate, I have stood arm in arm with another team—other lovers of Yellowstone—to lay my heart on the line with theirs at Montana's state capital in an effort to stop the senseless slaughter of Yellowstone's bison.

Yellowstone inspires us to be resilient and steadfast in our quest to uncover our own beauty and grace.

One of the people I admire most in this world, the beautiful Terry Tempest Williams, once wrote, "If you know wilderness in the same way you know love, you would be unwilling to let it go." If you know wilderness the way we do here in Yellowstone Country, you'd know that what separates this wilderness from just about any other part of the contiguous United States is its wildness. And for most of us, it is animals like grizzly bears, wolves, and bison that represent wildness at its most authentic level. More than science, ecology, geology, or any other discipline that studies Yellowstone's biodiversity, the intangibles are what make Yellowstone "Yellowstone."

This book is ultimately a story of love: love for place, love for wildness, and love for people who weave the fabric of Yellowstone's powerful story. In the following pages, you will be introduced to some of the most noble, dedicated, and inspiring Yellowstone characters I know—two-legged, four-legged, winged, and finned. Those of us who already know and love the park have experienced firsthand the unmatched ability of this iconic landscape to inspire that which we may one day become. And for those of you just becoming familiar with her beauty and grace, prepare yourselves for a transformative journey!

It is my hope that your journey through the pages of this book will in some way imprint Yellowstone in your mind and on your heart. Regardless of your physical state, I want to inspire you to get out and explore the most enigmatic, powerful, and magical place I know— a place known by a single word: Yellowstone. And what is humanity without the spirit of adventure? At its core, adventure is the nutrition and spiritual sustenance that feeds the soul.

The preservation of Yellowstone resides in the most important single piece of habitat left on our wild planet: that of the human heart. We only fight to save what we love, and we only love what we know. In the end, the fate of a wild Yellowstone is in your hands. The wild heartbeat of Yellowstone; its scenic rivers, valleys, and mountains; its grizzly bears, wolves, bison, elk, trout, and countless other species of plant and wildlife will only be here in the future if we want them here badly enough— if we are willing to advocate and be a champion on their behalf. I believe the symbolism represented by the integrity of the Yellowstone Ecosystem extends far beyond its boundaries. If we can't inspire a commitment to Yellowstone, I fear we won't find the audacity to preserve the last of our world's iconic wildlands. The fate of our wild planet is intertwined with the fate of a wild Yellowstone.

The rugged vastness of the Northern Rockies transforms the soul of those who know its wild splendor. Its harshness and magnificence inspire a gritty determination and burning desire to explore all that we may become.

When you experience the raw power of wilderness, your soul awakens to the essence of love. Wilderness, my friends, is a love worth fighting for.

For a wild Yellowstone. . . .

With nothin' but love,
Michael W. Leach

1

Grizzlies On My Mind

The long drive from Missoula showcased the reason early fall is my favorite time of year. On this resplendent October evening, the cottonwoods lining the Clark Fork River—at the height of their golden display—waved gently. The closer we got to West Yellowstone and the higher the elevation, the deeper into autumn we moved; so much so, that by the time we entered the Madison Valley, the colors began to fade. Farther down the road, along the shores of Hebgen Lake, the aspen stood naked. It would be another six months before their delicate leaves again danced in the wind.

Midterms may not be a good time for two college students to leave for five days, but as a dedicated seasonal ranger, I couldn't pass up an opportunity to walk the length of the Bechler River, and that's just where we were headed. After camping along the banks of the Madison River our first night out, my wife, Crystal, and I awoke to a cool morning, looking forward to the hour-long drive to Ashton, Idaho. I had dreamed of this trip for years, and after bumping our way down the bone-rattling dirt road that led to the Bechler Ranger station, we could hardly wait to get our permits and hit the trail.

The Bechler River Trail begins in the most southwesterly corner of the park, ending thirty miles later, at Lone Star Geyser, just two miles from Old Faithful. Knowing we had a long hike to our first camp and hoping to get in before dark, a sense of urgency took hold as we stood outside the ranger station, doing a last-minute check of our packs.

The bearded ranger manning the station looked to be in his early thirties. He seemed conflicted about our sudden appearance—almost irritated at first that his silence had been broken, but at the same time, eager for the company. After ten minutes sharing stories of ranger life in Yellowstone, we turned to leave.

Then I remembered to ask one last question.

"Has there been much bear activity along the trail?"

"Well," he replied, "you got forty miles of grizzly country ahead of you, but really nothing in particular."

Then, almost as an afterthought, he added, "But watch out for the elk carcass at the junction of the Bechler and Fall Rivers. It's about to pop, and there should be a griz on it sooner or later. And there have been sows with two cubs hanging out at 9B3 and 9B9."

Yellowstone's backcountry permit system is set up so hikers camp at designated campsites, most of which supply a sturdy bear pole, twelve to fifteen feet off the ground. 9B3 and 9B9 were our destinations for the next two nights.

"You should be fine," he called out as the screen door slammed shut behind us.

Crystal and I looked at each other. Was this guy crazy? Did he realize what he just said, or had he spent too much time down here in no-man's land?

Not to be deterred by this information, and no less enthusiastic about what lay ahead, we took off. After leaving the trailhead, we quickly reached the confluence of the Bechler and Fall Rivers. The huge grizzly I had envisioned tearing up the bloated elk had not materialized. But we still had nearly forty miles of trail to travel.

• • •

SHOULDERING A PACK AND HEADING into the depths of grizzly country spices up a trip the way crushed red pepper adds pop to your pizza. When hiking in places that are no longer home to the grizzly, I walk with a different presence; something is missing. I am not sure if it is my attention, instincts, fear, or some combination of all of these, but when venturing deep into Yellowstone Country, I instinctively sense—I feel—I've entered the world of the grizzly.

Yellowstone captures the imagination of people from all over the world. The geysers, mudpots, fumaroles, and hot springs undoubtedly play a major role; but there is more to this universal romance with the world's first national park. And for many, it is the grizzly.

My grandma grew up on a ranch in southern Wyoming. She heard stories of grizzlies but had little in the way of personal grizzly experiences; yet this did not stop her from giving her opinion and advice when I announced our upcoming journey through the Cascade Corner.

"Mikey, you just need to calm down. I don't want you getting eaten by grizzly bears."

Rounding a bend in the trail or breaking through alder thickets along a creek bottom awaken senses that have, for many, been long lost. Whether dulled by years spent in front of the television, surfing the web, or sitting in college philosophy classes, like a torn calf muscle atrophied from lack of use, our senses can only be strengthened by dedication and repetition—and walking the backcountry of Yellowstone serves as the perfect rehabilitation.

One can't afford to be careless in the presence of the grizzly. You make noise, hang your food, and if you are really serious about waking up in the morning without a piece of flesh missing from your ass, you hang the clothes you cook in too.

It's not courage speaking when someone says they don't fear the grizzly, or that they don't lose sleep in its presence. I find such talk foolish and disrespectful. In grizzly country, we are not in control. In Yellowstone, a canister of bear spray—the only rational choice for protection—may give me comfort but not unwavering confidence.

The numbers are in our favor; this I know. Perhaps we shouldn't fear the grizzly as much as we do. But in a place where ignorance or carelessness can help you become part of the food chain, I find a bit of fear healthy.

Each week, I proudly don the green and gray of the Park Service and give my bear talks, sharing with visitors my knowledge of bear ecology and explaining how to hike safely in grizzly country. After preaching the efficacy of bear spray and talking up the importance of making adequate noise (and hiking in a group whenever possible), I inevitably hear a nervous laugh or two when I say that the safest thing to do if a grizzly charges is freeze, slowly back away—without making direct eye contact—and create distance between yourself and the bear without turning your back, running, or making any alarming movements.

Nearly half of all charges are the bear's way of bluffing, but it seems my audience's favorite part of bear talks is when I tell them what to do if they aren't dealing with a false charge and the grizzly continues to advance. At this point, I always ask four or five youthful volunteers to "play dead" in order to demonstrate the difference between the old-school, fetal-position approach (where a bear can easily roll a person over, allowing access to his or her chest, stomach, and face) and the now widely accepted "flat on your stomach, legs spread with toes digging into the ground, hands clasped behind the neck, driving elbows into the ground" approach, which is more successful in resisting a bear's attempt to roll a person over.

I have a great deal of respect for the grizzly. I know that when hiking through the backcountry of Yellowstone, I am at the mercy of the muscled bear. Still, I tell visitors—with all honesty—that by day, I don't fear the grizzly. In fact, I rarely have a worrisome thought about the bear. I walk with great care, but the truth is, I often disregard the very advice I give to visitors and move in silence—so deep are my hopes of seeing the creature I revere. As the sun starts to fade, however, and darkness takes over the thickly covered lodgepole pine stands and sweeping open meadows, my mind works differently.

I may not fear the grizzly during the day, but at night, my fear of the grizzly bear becomes a reality. When the cold air starts to creep through my Capilene—around 9 P.M. at 7,900 feet on the Yellowstone Plateau—I retreat to the safety of my nylon tent. My blue nylon tent.

What is it about this thin-shelled piece of nylon that gives me comfort?

Male grizzlies in the park weigh between 300 and 700 pounds, and despite their size, these great bears can run up to thirty-five mph. Am I so naïve as to think my six-pound tent could possibly deter this creature if he became truly curious?

Since the establishment of the park in 1872, there have been a mere seven bear-caused human deaths. My chances of being killed by a grizzly roughly equal that of being struck by lightning. But as the darkness takes hold in my blue nylon tent, these logical thoughts are trumped by thoughts of a bear named Thumper.

Thumper was a troubled grizzly. Probably two or three years old at the time, this young bear earned his name from a bad habit he had acquired: pouncing tents. Blue tents. On the many nights each summer that I am camped in my blue tent (a gift from my parents) and on the brink of falling asleep, I find myself thinking of Thumper.

I think back to my first summer with the Park Service. It was the beginning of Thumper's tent-pouncing career—the summer Thumper became famous.

Backcountry rangers had set up mock camps (with blue tents) in hopes of catching Thumper in action so they could play target practice with rubber bullets on his ursine hindquarters. But time and time again, the young bear outwitted the men and women wearing the flat hats. And although thoughts of Thumper have contributed to many a restless night for yours truly, I always pulled for the bear, hoping he would elude my fellow rangers.

As long as the likes of Thumper and other grizzlies remain wild—roaming the depths of the park and the Ecosystem—when I lie in my tent, my heart rate will rise and my mind will become restless with every crack of brush, every sweeping footstep, every breath I manage to hear.

• • •

ON THIS OCTOBER YELLOWSTONE MORNING, I awoke early and lingered in the warmth of my sleeping bag, fighting the urge to rise. Away from the noise of civilization, immersed instead in the sounds of nature, I find morning to be the most sacred of times. I wish I had words to share this feeling—gifts to those dwelling in cities or hampered with physical limitations—because every man and woman should, for at least one morning a year (but preferably a week or, better yet, a month) experience the wonders of a new day in the wild.

Waking up to a bright new day, the fear now behind you, you breathe with ease again. The heart rate slows. Waking up to another day in grizzly country is like hearing the doctor say your chest X-ray is clear—you are fine, you are healthy! You should live a long life. And today, you will live a beautiful day in Yellowstone.

Crystal and I moved slowly on our final morning, savoring the rhythmic pulse of Yellowstone unfolding before us. I was thrilled to be along the Bechler, in the depths of the backcountry. And though I have always loved mornings, I especially loved this one. Everything was calm, just the way a morning should be. The clear sky and cool, crisp air made this a perfect beginning to another day in the wild.

I went for a walk, back on the trail we had traveled the night before, the sky a gentle blue. It would be a brilliant day—maybe the best of the trip. The sun was rising fast but not fast enough. It had been a cold night in wonderland. A cold night in grizzly country.

On this morning, things were silent; the cold bit deep into the skin. And the leaves of the willows were crackly—brown, red, and yellow—fading into winter, glistening with frost.

Every little sound turned my head.

I had grizzlies on my mind.

2

Medicine Warrior

Temperatures in the hot and arid desert of Gardiner, Montana, had reached record levels. I wrestled with the bedcovers in hopes of soothing the nausea that had consumed me for the better part of a month.

How could this be? After struggling to redefine myself—from urban basketball junkie to wilderness advocate / Yellowstone Park Ranger—my world seemed on the verge of being rocked again.

Four months earlier, I began complaining of fatigue, but it was only after my anti-pharmaceutical mother (who had worked as an attorney in the biotech industry) began doing research that we discovered the cause was a medication my doctor had prescribed—off-label—to treat the aches and pains associated with my recently diagnosed autoimmune disorder. We had never been warned that abruptly stopping the drug was not only ill-advised, it could be downright dangerous. I suspect my body's reaction to drugs of any sort was heightened by the fact that I rarely touch alcohol and have blood that must be as pure as spring-water from high on the Beartooth Plateau. I've always said I would be a great Mormon if I didn't have such a dirty mouth and such passion for unspoiled wilderness.

Prior to being hastily hired by the National Park Service on a 2002 visit to observe Yellowstone's newly introduced wolves, I had spent three years fighting my diagnosis, which had ended my days on the hardwood and shattered my dreams of the college basketball career that had consumed me since my youth. But all of that pain and heartache vanished the first time I donned the green-and-gray ranger uniform. I will always cherish that first summer I sported the straw flat hat, polyester shirt, and wool pants while roaming the Mammoth Hot Springs as a nameless ranger (I didn't get a nametag until the next season) during the dog days of August.

Now, a year later, I was entering my second summer season as a Yellowstone National Park Ranger, and a bad drug reaction was threatening to dismantle my dreams of spending my first entire summer representing the world's first national park. After several challenging months of dizziness, fatigue, and nausea, the fate of my summer—and my dream—teetered on a cliff.

• • •

TRUTH BE TOLD, MY EXPERIENCE wearing the uniform the previous summer never felt quite real. My vision of becoming a ranger first came to me a year earlier, in 2001, on a road trip to the desert southwest, as I camped with my high-school-sweetheart-now-wife in the cathedral known as Zion National Park. At the time, I was twenty-one and had spent the past two years worrying about what I would do with my life now that my ailing back had robbed me of basketball. Crystal and I had just finished up our first semester at North Idaho College, and we planned to become teachers.

During our fourteen-day tour of Red Rock Country, I asked every approachable ranger—from Arches to Canyonlands, Capitol Reef to Bryce—to share his or her story of getting hired by the Park Service. At the Springdale entrance to the legendary Zion (the Southern Utah gem we had saved for last), a charming ranger in his late thirties handed us a map of the park. He was in a wheelchair.

I couldn't sleep that night as we camped among the swaying cottonwoods in the Watchman Campground. With one fortuitous encounter, I had discovered a new vision. All my worries had dissolved into purpose. Rising from our tent at about 4 A.M., I scrambled to the pay phone to awaken my mom with my news.

"Mom. I've found what I want to do. I want to be a ranger!"

I went on to tell the story of the man in the wheelchair—a memory that had paced around my mind for hours. If he could be a ranger with his disability, then why couldn't I with my chronic back pain and arthritic condition? In less than two minutes, with the simple gesture of passing us a map with a smile on his face, one man had changed the direction of my life.

One year later, back in our beloved Yellowstone, camping out at Pebble Creek Campground—with my vision still in place but having taken no tangible steps toward accomplishing it—Crystal and I mustered the courage to walk into the Yellowstone National Park Administration Office to inquire about how to apply to wear the pinstripes. Yes, "pinstripes," because wearing the green and gray in Yellowstone (we were told on countless occasions by rangers in other national parks, who chuckled at our desire to start our Park Service careers in the park of all parks) was akin to suiting up for the Yankees. "Good luck with that" was the look we were always given. But the Yellowstone gods were with us that magic day in mid-July, perhaps conspiring to bring us hope and direction, which we desperately yearned for as we tried to find our place in the world.

I will never forget the name of the person we were directed to inside the Double Cavalry Barracks, which houses the park's administrative staff. Carrie Lang. She was in her midthirties, blonde, with fair skin and an athletic build. It was her welcoming smile that I remember most. While the intangibles that abound in a place as wild and sacred as Yellowstone are what resonate so deeply with Yellowstone's countless followers, that day it was the suddenly tangible possibility of becoming a ranger—something Carrie validated during our one-hour visit—that put a bounce in our step.

Minutes after leaving her office, my wife and I were startled when Carrie chased us down in the parking lot. A position had just opened in Mammoth! A family emergency had forced one of the ranger naturalists to resign, and Carrie wondered if we would like to meet with the North District Ranger, who oversaw the entire staff of North District interpretive rangers.

We had come to the park to spend a month watching wolves, chasing trout, and wearing down the rubber on our hiking boots. We reeked of campfire smoke, my hair hung to my shoulders, and the unkempt and rebellious beard covering my face screamed of a young man trying to remake himself. Still, without hesitation, we replied in unison, "Sure!" and followed Carrie to a dingy office on the second floor.

Within minutes of sitting down, it became clear that we had either developed really strong Yellowstone karma or the gods were, indeed, working their magic to deepen our bond to the iconic park we had visited each year since our courtship—the park where we spent the first nights of our honeymoon. The North District Ranger's name was Brian Suderman, and he was a gift.

Crystal had a better resume, but it was a Yellowstone Ranger position—my dream—so without hesitation, she volunteered for me to be the one interviewed. Though it was only the second formal job interview of my life, Brian seemed impressed with my passion. We left feeling optimistic about the chances. One week later, from a pay phone in Cooke City, I called Brian, who delivered the second best news I had ever received (Crystal accepting my marriage proposal being the first).

"Congratulations, you are a Yellowstone National Park Ranger."

I could hardly contain my excitement. August flew by. The shifts were long and the weather hot, but not a day of that first summer felt like work. Green and full of excitement, I relished answering the questions that the other rangers had grown tired of and beamed with pride each day I put on the uniform.

• • •

TEN MONTHS LATER, TOSSING AND turning in bed with gnawing nausea, I couldn't stop thinking about what this job meant to me. "Job"—the word did not begin to do it justice. Serving as a Yellowstone Ranger was my calling. I had spent the entire fall, winter, and spring attending North Idaho College along the shores of Lake Coeur d'Alene, yearning for my return to the park.

On the day we had arrived back in Mammoth, in May, snow flurries greeted us, whitening the landscape, and we couldn't wait to see our quarters. A replica of our housing accommodations from the summer before, during our brief stay at the YCC (or Youth Conservation Corps, known to locals as the YAK Camp), we found our second "transit"—as the Park Service called the ancient, trailer-like employee housing—humble and glorious all at once. It consisted of two postage-stamp-sized bedrooms (a twin mattress in one and a single in the other, and each with an ancient dresser bearing a government stamp dating back decades); a small bathroom with peeling linoleum; an archaic kitchen (equipped with a functioning stove and refrigerator); and a simple, carpeted living area with an uncomfortable wood-framed chair, matching couch, and temperamental furnace. While calling our dwelling modest constituted a gross understatement, it was home—our first real home of our own as a married couple—and we couldn't have been happier. Even when the lack of trees made the transit feel like a sardine can baking in the hot desert sun of Gardiner, especially during the hottest June in recent memory, the glory of its setting—behind the Xanterra employees' Bunkhouse, perched above the confluence of the Gardner and Yellowstone Rivers—left us overflowing with gratitude.

The crank windows opened to the watery songs of these raging rivers, filling our living space with wild delight. Sweltering temperatures had ravaged the snowpack throughout most of June, which kept the mighty Yellowstone off-color—not quite chocolate milk, as it was early on in a frenetic runoff, but not yet fishable. The enigmatic and underappreciated waters of the Gardner began to fish, however, and I couldn't help reliving the magical moments I had already experienced along its hurried waters.

Just weeks after arriving to the park for my first full summer season, I was struck with this, an episode that had left me bedridden, and now my mind raced with a mixture of hope and dread over the trip we had just scheduled to see a Coeur d'Alene doctor about the headache, nausea, and fatigue that had finally brought me to my knees. Had I caught my last fiery Gardner River rainbow? Had I spent my last evening rejoicing in my secrete rendezvous with a protective but tolerant great horned owl and her three owlets preparing to fledge? I didn't know the answers to these questions, but I knew I could not allow myself to lose this opportunity to live my dream as a Yellowstone Ranger. I also knew my "brother" Darrell was on his way to the transit with my mom, and that within hours, I would be in the presence of his wisdom and powerful medicine.

• • •

I FIRST MET DARRELL IN September of my first semester back home, in Coeur d'Alene, where I was born and lived for eight years before moving to Seattle. It was the year 2000, and Crystal and I were newlyweds, a month removed from that day of perfection in Moose, Wyoming, at the foot of the Tetons, where the Leach and Christofferson clans had gathered to celebrate our covenant of a life together. As a fourth generation Idaho/Montana/Wyoming boy, I take great pride in my Wyoming roots, which began in the latter part of the nineteenth century, when ancestors from my mother's side of the family pushed cattle up the Chisholm Trail, eventually laying down roots in what would become known as the Cowboy State. So when my maternal grandmother (whose father, my Great-Grandpa Doc, was a Wyoming state veterinarian and the youngest to ever win the world champion saddle-bronc competition at Cheyenne Frontier Days—the "Daddy of Them All") asked me to honor my Wyoming blood by tying the knot in the historic Chapel of the Transfiguration, it was a done deal.

Crystal and I were in the process of mounting a black-and-white photo of us, taken along Mormon Row in Grand Teton National Park on our wedding day, when Darrell's van pulled into our steep gravel driveway. The Christofferson clan had given us permission to stay in our family's summer cabin, nestled in the forest along the eastern shoreline of Beauty Bay, while we attended college. The summer Olympics were in progress, and we had purchased a newer and larger antenna in hopes of establishing a better connection with the four channels our rabbit ears failed to deliver. Darrell was there to install it.

I was also about to celebrate my twenty-first birthday, for which we had planned a two-day getaway to Yellowstone, and while we were looking forward to our first real time alone as a couple, we knew it would likely be a long winter in the cabin with just the two of us. Thus, we relished our time with my Grandpa Chris (born in Rock Springs, Wyoming) and my Grandma Isabel, who despised the fact that she was born in Casper, Wyoming, and preferred talking about her time in Hollywood, where Great-Grandpa Doc worked as a stunt double for the legendary Tom Mix. Stories of days gone by occupied our evenings, and we cherished yet another summer together in the family cabin, which was purchased the year I was born.

Darrell lumbered up the steps, the rickety deck shaking under his weight, and with a booming voice and thunderous fist, announced his arrival as he knocked on the screen door. When my grandma greeted him at the door, this hulk of a man immediately transformed from what might have seemed an intimidating figure to a gentle giant. It quickly became apparent that Darrell felt reverence toward his elders. After exchanging handshakes, she offered him a cup of coffee, which he graciously accepted.

To the delight of my grandma, Darrell was a handsome man—six foot three, 240 pounds, with dark skin; a black, graying mustache; glasses that gave him an air of distinction; and long, black hair tightly bound into a ponytail.

Within five minutes of standing in our living room, surrounded by Crystal, Grandma, and me, Darrell's gaze landed on another picture from our wedding day—that of a bull bison grazing beneath the seriated Tetons. He began asking questions; the bison hypnotized him. Once again, it was clear that this was a man with a deep respect for symbols of the "old way"—a man after my own heart. (Since I was a kid, I had always felt a strong connection to the natural world. And when the struggles began with my back, I started to seek meaning through various traditions and spiritual beliefs.)

A good twenty minutes went by, with Darrell holding center stage, telling stories about his work, his youth, and his life. He wore a tightly woven necklace of Plains Indian origins, and while he seemed to have some Caucasian in him, it was obvious the man was Native American. But this didn't stop my grandma from asking if he was Indian. And while her boldness unnerved Crystal and me, it didn't faze Darrell. Quite the opposite. He took a seat and continued sharing details of his life and struggles.

Grandpa Chris had appeared from his bedroom downstairs. While the three of us—Grandma, Crystal, and I—remained mesmerized by Darrell's charismatic storytelling, the dutiful civil engineer in my grandfather couldn't understand why this man, on the company clock, wasn't outside doing the work we had paid Radio Shack for him to do. To our horror, Grandpa interrupted our new friend to ask when he was going to get to work. Darrell smiled, handed his cup of coffee to my grandma, and with a humble grace—the likes of which I had rarely witnessed—replied, "Right now, sir." Then he stood up and said warmly, "Thank you, Isabel, for the delicious coffee. It has been a pleasure visiting with you."

Once Darrell was outside, I lovingly chastised my grandpa for the interruption, giving him a big hug and a kiss on the cheek before venturing out to reconnect with the mystery man. And though I felt the need to apologize to Darrell, I'm not sure what else led me to seek him out on that beautiful autumn morning—perhaps my fascination with Indian culture. But I believe it was more than that; I think I knew I was in trouble. I struggled those first four weeks at North Idaho College, a lone man walking around campus and missing the membership of a basketball squad. I was lost and I needed guidance. And I sensed this stranger might have some of the answers I'd been seeking.

I found Darrell at the backside of the house, gazing out over the family's pet burial grounds where Zappa, Mikey Cat, and our beloved Samoyed, Kip, now rested. As a young boy, I didn't always understand the significance of watching my father dig so deep—or so I thought—into the hardened ground, with the lifeless body of one of our pets wrapped like a Christmas present in one of our blankets nearby. But in later years, I had come to see this home cemetery, with its altars of rocks, as a place of substance. It was, in fact, during one of these moments, staring at the rocks of our four-leggeds' graves, that I bumped into my Uncle Wayne, who lived just below us and had his own official sanctuary for his deceased critters. We spoke about dogs and cats of the past, and he shared a story unknown by any in my immediate clan. As I stood there next to Darrell, I found myself surrounded by these sacred memories—memories enhanced by Darrell's spiritual aura.

To call the ground "hard" in Beauty Bay is an understatement, as I would learn firsthand years later, when digging a grave so deep and wide that our beloved yellow lab, Archie, would be able to stretch his tired legs. Uncle Wayne's story about a coyote unearthing one of the cats (my father clearly hadn't dug deep enough) motivated me to battle the clay and rock that much longer when it came time to put Archie to rest.

In an attempt to help Darrell better understand my clan and our deep reverence for all four-legged members of our family, I shared these stories with him that day. Darrell had an infectious personality accompanied by a deep, bellowing laugh—that of a sage or philosophical guru. Though it was clear that Darrell had no shortage of words or stories to share himself, he also had a rare gift for a storyteller: an incredible ability to listen.

For the next three hours, Darrell asked me questions and I spilled my guts. I told him my story of being a struggling student, a standout basketball player, and the car accident that injured my back three weeks before my freshman season at Edmonds Community College, triggering the subsequent diagnosis with a nasty autoimmune disorder that changed the direction of my life. He listened with such compassion, such genuine concern, and with what seemed to me a profound sense of understanding. There was wisdom in Darrell that I didn't entirely understand but couldn't help but gravitate toward. I didn't want our time to end. I could have sat on those steps and talked with him until the sun set—until the wild turkeys lined up in preparation for their nightly takeoff to their roost in the ponderosa pines and the stars emerged from a black hole, swallowing up the sky and lighting it up with a uniquely North Idaho glow.

A job that should have taken him just over an hour landed Darrell at our house for half the workday. He said his good-byes to Crystal and Grandma Isabel, but what I remember most about that morning was his good-bye to Grandpa Chris. Darrell went out of his way to walk over to my grandfather's chair and thank him for welcoming him into his home and sharing his beautiful family. It was not an act of vengeful payback for being asked when he was going to get to work, but instead represented his genuine and thoughtful effort to show his respect for the patriarch of our clan.

As I followed him to his van, I asked if he was going to get in trouble for spending so much time on our job. But Darrell showed no concern; he seemed at peace.

"The world works in mysterious ways, Brother Mike," he said. "My people call this the Indian telegram. I don't question it. I trust that this was meant to be."

I hated seeing him drive off. So when his van reappeared fifteen minutes later, my heart leapt. I ran outside and met him in the driveway. Darrell said he had a gift for me. He reached for his visor and detached a silver-dollar-sized drum with a bison hand-drawn on its leather covering. Handing it to me gently, he told me his grandmother from Fort Belknap had made it and placed it in his crib when he was a baby. He had carried it with him ever since—and now he was giving it to me.

"I don't know what to say, Darrell," I replied. "I can't take this."

"You can and you will, Mike. My people find it offensive if we offer a gift and it is refused. I've had my time with this little drum, over forty years," he said with a smile. "But now you need this medicine more than I do. In this way, blessings will come to us both. For nothing is truly ours, Mike; we share this journey. Our time is only temporary on this earth, and materials are just that. Some represent more powerful symbols than others, but we must not become attached, my friend.

"The drum represents the heartbeat of the earth to my people, Mike. I believe that this will give you strength in your time of suffering and struggle."

And with that, Darrell embraced me with his barrel of a chest and massive paws and held me tight, as if we were kin. We exchanged numbers, and before driving off, he left me with the simple words, "We will meet again, Brother Mike."

• • •

BACK IN OUR ROASTING, SARDINE can of a transit, I continued to toss and turn, grappling with the covers that I no longer needed to protect me from the early morning chill. There is something comforting about being wrapped in a blanket a mile above sea level when you are sick, even when the temperatures soar into the nineties. I'm not sure if I had a fever or if the combination of a comforter and hot air radiating through the windows were the culprits, but I spent most of the day beading with sweat.

I had spent the entire morning almost in a state of reverie, reflecting upon how Darrell had come into my life. I was scared that I wasn't going to be able to keep battling whatever it was about the medication that was making me feel so sick. Whenever my eyes wandered to the closet, the sight of the hangers full of green-and-gray polyester and wool made my heart sink. I had come to believe rangering was my destiny; I had to find the strength and fortitude to rise above the nausea and headaches that had plagued me and now threatened my Yellowstone future. I knew Darrel would find a spiritual way to shed light on my current predicament.

Just then, the phone rang. In no mood to talk, I checked the caller ID: my mom's number. I answered.

"Brother Mike, how are you?"

Music—actually, medicine; vital, critical medicine—to my ears.

"I'm scared I'm not going to get better in time to go back to work here at Mammoth."

Just as I'd hoped, Darrell's calm voice immediately comforted me.

"One thing at a time, brother. One thing at a time. We are in Deer Lodge and will be to you soon. Hang tight. I'm bringing powerful medicine. We are going to get you feeling better."

Head throbbing with a migraine that had ravaged my skull for over a week, I placed the phone back on Crystal's pillow and nestled my head into the covers. As I slipped in and out of sleep for the remainder of the afternoon, my mind ventured back to earlier times with Darrell.

After our initial meeting at the house in Beauty Bay, we lost touch for a couple of months. A few days before Christmas, I decided to give him a call. I remember it so well—as with everything with Darrell, our conversation had a mystical quality to it. He had been out wrestling with an engine in an old beater truck he was preparing to sell. It must have taken five minutes for him to get to the phone after one of his kids answered and said she would get him.

I apologized for interrupting him in the middle of his mechanical battle. He chuckled, and with his booming laugh, said, "Mike, this is what we like to call the Indian telegram—I think your call saved me tonight. I've never had any trouble starting this truck. I was supposed to meet this guy who was going to buy it thirty minutes ago, but I couldn't get the damn thing to start. When I heard you were on the line, all of my anger and frustration vanished, because I realized that I was meant to be here to take your call. That is how the universe works, you know."

He went on to tell me how the truck had just fired up as his daughter yelled to him that he had a telephone call. "Had I not received your call, Mike, I was going to hustle down to meet up with the guy in town, and I believe your call saved me from getting into an accident. That is the power of the Indian telegram, Brother Mike."

It would be the last week of June the following year before I would hear from Darrell again. Crystal and I returned from class to a voicemail on our answering machine inviting us to attend his brother in-law's concert at the Met, forty-five minutes away in Spokane, Washington. Being young, broke college students, the idea of live music (and what sounded like free passes) was appealing enough for us to make the drive. I spoke to Darrell en route, and he explained the power of his brother in-law's music. Jim Boyd had just been nominated for the Native American Music Awards for "Songwriter of the Year," "Album of the Year," and "Artist of the Year" after the release of his hit record alterNATIVES.

Like every experience I would go on to share with Darrell, the night was filled with incredible energy and power as we sat with Jim's family—front and center—on the bottom level of the Met's two-tiered theater. The sold-out venue in the heart of Spokane pulsed with an electricity, a spirit that I had never before experienced—one that would go on to shape the next several years of our music-listening lives.

After raiding the cash machine and purchasing every Jim Boyd CD ever released, we journeyed to Dick's Hamburgers with Darrell and his partner, Ladonna, for a late-night burger and shake. Ladonna was a beautiful woman, with long, flowing black hair, strong features, and eyes blue as the ocean. Like Jim, she grew up on the Colville Indian Reservation in Washington—a place we would become familiar with in the coming months.

Still riding high from the raucous vibe pulsating through the theater that night, I was buzzing in a way I hadn't for quite some time. Darrell began peppering me with questions. When the topic of our conversation turned to Yellowstone, Darrell's eyes lit up as the fire already burning in my belly unleashed with a rapid torrent of passionate speak. Ever since I was a child visiting the park from our home in North Idaho, I had a deep fascination with Yellowstone, and now, at twenty-one years old, my interest had turned into veneration.

Before the night was over, Darrell had made plans to accompany us on our upcoming trip to Yellowstone. Having never been to the park, he wanted to experience firsthand what his ancestors—the Assiniboine–Gros Ventre, one of twenty-six tribes associated with Yellowstone National Park—had experienced on their journeys through the enchanted land.

During the week after the concert, as Crystal and I studied for an important exam, we never heard from Darrell, so we assumed he had lost his primal urge to join us on our sojourn to Yellowstone over that Fourth of July weekend in 2001. The day of the test, delighted at having it behind us, we drove back to the cabin to prepare for the seven-hour drive to the park, just the two of us.

It was only after we had locked the door of the cabin that a black sedan, feathers dangling from the rearview mirror, pulled into our drive. Shocked when we recognized its driver, Crystal and I looked at each other, shook our heads, and proceeded toward Darrell's rig. The mountain of a man sprung out of the car and greeted us with bear hugs.

Though I've never liked giving up control of the itinerary of a trip, it was clear from that moment that Darrell was taking charge. After throwing his gear into the back of our SUV, he ushered us to the deck, where he unearthed a shell, an eagle feather, some dried sage, and a lighter from his pack.

"Brother Mike," he spoke in a calm and reassuring way, "I knew when we met on this porch last autumn that you were a young man of passion, conviction, and fire. I've prayed for you over the winter and spring, but it is clear your struggles continue. During these times, my people believe we must pray to the Creator and ask for strength and direction.

"For the next six days, Brother Mike, we are going to be journeying through a land that is sacred to you and your family. The place where you and Crystal began your life anew together, as husband and wife. It is a place of spiritual significance to my family as well. My family means everything to me, Brother Mike, and I struggled at the thought of being away from them this week. But you need me more right now, my brother, and I, too, need this spiritual awakening.

"There are two reasons I'm here, Brother Mike; I knew I had to come. I knew I needed a spiritual journey of my own and that I was meant to grow close to you and Crystal. But I also want to help awaken your spirit. I see so much in your soul—so much power, so much passion and fire—but your spirit is dying, Brother Mike. Your fire is burning out, and the Creator has sent me to awaken your spirit and to change your way of thinking."

No matter how open to absorbing the religious or cultural beliefs of someone else, hearing the words "your fire is burning out" is bound to make anyone uncomfortable, and Darrell could sense my worry.

"For these next six days, I ask you to trust me, Mike. We are going on a vision quest of sorts. Not in the traditional way, but in a way that will rekindle your fire. But you need to do what I ask of you, and you need to open your heart and mind so I can awaken your spirit for good."

Thirty minutes later, we had smudged our bodies from head to toe with the smoke of the burning sage and the fan of the eagle feather. We prayed to all four directions: to the east, where the Great Eagle Spirit soars; to the south and the little mice representing the children; to the west and the Spirit Bear, the adults; and to the north and the White Buffalo, the elders, and those no longer with us.

I wasn't prepared for the raw power and emotions of the experience. Darrell paid special attention to my ailing back as he brushed it over and over with the eagle feather. And for the first time since my car accident, I felt a sense of hope that there was a real possibility I could regain my strength and vitality. Before leaving, Darrell blessed our pony—our aging Ford Explorer—with a smudge and four strokes of his eagle feather, and we were off on an adventure that would change all of our lives.

The five-hour drive to the I-90 cutoff in Cardwell, Montana, flew by as Darrell shared his stories. In Whitehall, Montana, where we stopped for gas, we ended up spending an hour trying to find the home of a bobby-socked stray wandering the streets. After a successful reunion with the pup's owner, we watched with tired eyes as the digital clock in the truck struck midnight. I had planned to honor my family's tradition of spending the first night of every Yellowstone trip in Ennis, followed by breakfast at the Silver Spur Cafe in West Yellowstone, but the forty-five minutes of winding pavement that would entail made us call it a night.

Eager to find a place to throw down our pads and a tent, we settled on a small campground behind the lone gas station that has always appeared to be the sole representation of the Cardwell constituency.

Darrell's eyes fired up as our headlights flashed across the surface of a painted tepee at the campground's center. (The following morning, Darrell would learn from the gas station's owner that the artwork decorating the tightly wound canvas was Blackfoot, but when we arrived just before 1 A.M., the lodging's tribal origins didn't matter to any of us.) Elated, Darrell slowly and softly walked around the shelter, not knowing if it was occupied by sleeping road warriors. Before we knew it, we saw him sticking his hand into its opening. I couldn't help but imagine a Midwest family inside, still unnerved by their restless nights in Yellowstone's grizzly country, ready to unleash a can of bear spray on intruders of any kind. But Darrell wasn't worried about it. He had an innate sureness about him unlike anything I'd ever seen. His people called him Medicine Warrior, and I couldn't understand how this man, shaped like an NFL linebacker, moved with the fluid grace of a ninja. Unflappable in his confidence that the structure was unoccupied, Darrell simply knew it represented a profound beginning to our spiritual odyssey.

Our peaceful warrior entered the tepee, then erupted back through its opening with a booming laugh that had to have awakened the handful of campers.

"This is our home for the night, Brother Mike," he proclaimed. "And it is a good home indeed. You see, the number seven is sacred to my people, and the Raven is my spirit animal, who will guide us and give us clarity on this journey."

For much of the drive, I had been learning about the spiritual significance of the number four. Confused by his reference to the number seven, I followed Darrell in a lap around the shelter. We counted seven ravens and four buffalo.

"This tepee was empty for a reason, Brother Mike. The Creator knew we were coming. This will indeed be a sacred journey."

For the next five nights and six days, we shared moments of unmatched inspiration and beauty. We awoke every morning, facing the east, greeting each new day with a smudge and a prayer. We watched Darrell's eyes well up with tears as he witnessed his first wild Yellowstone bison—behemoths the size of his sedan. We submerged ourselves in the cold and swift-moving waters of the Lamar Canyon, where Darrell discovered something that he quickly hid from us by wrapping it in a towel. He stayed up most of that night, and I knew he was up to something significant. After that, we embraced prolonged periods of silence, ordered by Darrell during his daily fasts, which began following his discovery on the banks of the Lamar.

We bathed in the tranquil waters of a hot spring emerging from the Wind River Range and shared late-night conversations as deep and exploratory as the black canvas above us, and just as infused with constellations and stars. We endured a thunderous mountain onslaught, with vicious winds threatening to tear apart the fabric of our tents and brilliant streaks of lightning igniting the sky.

We wandered into the wild meadows of the Hayden Valley, gathering tufts of bison hair, but we had no tobacco to leave in its place.

I discovered a pair of dirty underwear and decided that removing them from the environment would represent my offering, leading Darrell to jokingly brand our trip as "The Journey of Dirty Chonies."

On the final night, we camped under the sharply serrated peaks of the Tetons thrusting up from the valley floor. Darrell presided over a ceremony. After presenting us with a beaded medicine wheel he had been working on for the bulk of our trip, he shared a prayer that reached into the deepest recesses of my soul.

When Darrell spoke in his deliberate and thoughtful tone, straight from what I sensed to be a place of both suffering and wisdom, he commanded our full attention. And while I typically shrugged off most suggestions that my back would become strong, having grown leery of such grandiose pronouncements after three years of trying every form of traditional and nontraditional treatment that promised relief, there was a sage-like sincerity to Darrell's words. It made me believe them.

But when Darrell unveiled his secret reason for fasting—a bison spine he had unearthed during his wanderings along the banks of the Lamar—and shared with heartfelt conviction his confidence that the fully intact spine of an animal representing strength and perseverance meant my back would heal, for the first time in two years, I felt genuine hope that I would again shoulder a pack into the backcountry and return to a life of adventure.

The next day, Darrell took the sage he had picked, the hair he had plucked, and the spine he had discovered and ventured to the edge of the forest alone. I could see him gently placing the items back on the earth, giving thanks to the Creator for all of the blessings on our journey.

Darrell taught me to recognize that when we live in awareness and pay attention as we look for meaning and answers, we can uncover the spiritual in the most simple of events and occurrences. He had become a master of this art. But our journey had been more than practicing the art of living in the moment or an exaggeration of the happenings that unfolded in the dramatic and spiritual temple that is Yellowstone. I've never been able to adequately express Darrell's ability to harness Yellowstone's magic—to turn it into spiritual fuel to stoke my fire—but that's what he did.

Lying in bed back in the transit, two years later, with sweat lodge ceremonies on the Colville Indian Reservation and the VA hospital in

Spokane, Washington, under my belt, Darrell's teachings are what brought me comfort and gave me hope. Darrell was making his second journey to Yellowstone, once again to support and heal his brother.

As I awaited his arrival, I pulled my journal from that memorable summer out of a box stored under the bed. I always had the desire to write about what he called our "Bundle Trip"—in reference to a medicine bundle—but I had concluded it to be fruitless to attempt putting on paper something so deeply personal, unfamiliar, and spiritual. I remember expressing this concern to Darrell, and with his best Socrates impression, he replied, "It's all about you and your spirituality, Brother Mike. It's mine and it's yours, and you can't let anyone take that from you. Remember Mike: when one drinks alcohol, one's spirit is gone. You may not drink, but the same thing is happening when you give in to society and dress like a mannequin, or do all that bullshit body crap in the gym. It's all BS, and your spirit will die. You must awaken your spirit and listen to it, Mike. That is what this journey was all about. Don't let anyone or anything stop you. Persevere. Believe, and do it."

Here's what I ended up writing in my journal: "I fear any attempt to replicate our journey on paper would diminish what I feel about a time the three of us shared. I can by no means articulate with words this spiritual awakening of the heart."

By midafternoon, I had fallen back asleep, my only defense for the raging migraine. Tossing and turning in the furnace that was our trailer, I resisted the urge to rise. It wasn't until the early evening that I awoke to the gentle kiss and soft words of my tanned bride whispering, "How you hanging, Sweetie?"

I'm not sure there is a more attractive sight than a beautiful woman sporting the iconic National Park Service uniform. I asked Crystal how her day had been, and she reported a constant throng of long lines at the entry gate, where she greeted park visitors. I longed to have been at work, walking the boardwalk, answering those visitors' questions.

I decided to step outside to get a breath of fresh air, despite the fact that a fiery breeze had been flowing through the opened windows all day long. Walking out into the bright sun, still high above the shoulder of Sepulcher Mountain, proved far too much for my eyes, made sensitive by a day in bed and the surging headache that seemed to pulse with the beats of the Gardner River's churning.

Before turning back inside, I closed my eyes and listened to the river that had been my only source of company throughout the day. I marveled at its clarity and cadence, which soared to new heights without the tin walls of the transit muffling its joyful song. Just as I reentered our quarters and sat down on the stiff couch, I heard Mom's car pull onto the gravel.

Any mother would have reason to be scared when her twenty-two-year-old son has battled nausea and migraines for months. But my mom had witnessed my struggle to re-create my life after being forced to give up my hoops dream. She had seen my fears about the future and my transformation, and a new love that exceeded anything I'd felt for basketball—my burning passion for the park and life as a ranger. The thought of me losing my Yellowstone dream too was almost more than she could bear.

Entering the transit, she hurried to hug Crystal, then, arms extended, she gave me the most comforting of hugs—a hug that can only come from a mom.

Feeling my chest heave, she cupped my face in her hands, and calmly and sternly said, "Mike, we are going to get you feeling better. I promise you that. We won't stop until you feel better. And this Yellowstone love of yours isn't going anywhere."

Her words provided a soothing degree of confidence that the eye of the storm would indeed pass. And then, in walked Darrell.

Without a word, Darrell, too, embraced Crystal with his customary bear hug, and then moved toward me as Mom stepped away. Always an optimist, my mom cherishes my relationship with Darrell as if it were her own. She is deeply spiritual, hates our culture of pharmaceuticals, and believes in Darrell's medicine and its ability to positively impact the mind and therefore the body.

With tears in my eyes, I opened my arms in anticipation of Darrell's back-cracking squeeze, but he met me with more tenderness than any other time in the past.

"I've brought strong medicine, and we are going to get you better, Brother Mike. You keep resting now. I've got a lot of work to do. It's going to be a long night, but I need you to trust me. We are going to get you well."

After my nod of approval, Darrell gave my mom a big hug and touched Crystal's hand as he walked out the door. As suddenly as he had arrived, he was off, a man on a mission.

I spent the next several hours, as my headache allowed, enjoying the company of my mom. She explained that the night before, just after Crystal had called to tell her how sick I had become, she received a phone call. I had not talked to Darrell in months. His first words to Mom were, "What's wrong with Mike?" He told her that, sensing I was in trouble, he had taken out all his sacred objects, placed them on his bed the night before, and slept on the floor.

Mom proceeded to tell him what was going on and that she planned to drive over to Yellowstone first thing in the morning. Darrell replied, "I'm coming with."

Mom described how he had arrived early the next morning dressed like a warrior going to battle, wearing a beautiful vest with buffalo painted on it, with his often loose, disheveled hair braided tightly. They had done a smudge—of Mom, Darrell, and her new car—and then taken off with a box Darrell transferred from his old van to her vehicle.

I found myself wondering if I would be up for whatever Darrell had planned. My previous "ceremonies" with Darrell had been profoundly impactful but were physically exhausting. Following my first trip to the Colville Indian Reservation with Darrell and his family, I slept for two days, just trying to recover from his family's habit of eating dinner after 9 P.M. and crashing well after midnight each night. But on that trip, it was my first sweat lodge ceremony, on the shores of the Franklin D. Roosevelt Lake, that kicked my ass. As an early-to-bed, early-to-rise kind of guy, making it to midnight two back-to-back nights proved challenging to my internal clock.

The placid waters of the Columbia River lapped against the lake's shore as we arrived at the site of the sweat that first night. I almost felt I could hear sadness in the molecules of the once mighty river water, stagnant now after the construction of the Grand Coulee Dam.

Darrell's son, Nathan, and stepson, David, had been tending to the fire since late in the afternoon, heating the rocks that, when doused with Columbia River water, created the steam inside the lodge that would cook our skin. I had been nervous to meet Darrell's sons, as I wasn't sure how they would welcome their new, white uncle into the clan; but their respect for Darrell clearly held precedence over any racial prejudice. Neither their own struggles nor those of their Lummi and Assiniboine ancestors existed between us.

After cleansing my body and spirit with a smudge led by Darrell, I entered the sweat lodge clockwise, as instructed, and took my position. I don't know why, but I was surprised by the depth of the darkness as Darrell's son climbed into the lodge and we prepared for round one. When the flap of the door shut, the blackness engulfed my senses.

Not wanting to be the first to exit (and being thoroughly hidden in the blackness), in between guided prayers, I laid my chest on the bare earth and pressed my cheek into the dirt, seeking any relief from the blistering steam scorching my skin and consuming my lungs. When, after the first round, I emerged from the lodge to a glorious starry night, I felt a gratitude for the enormity of the Western landscape that I had never felt before. It wasn't until later rounds, after making it through the first two without dying, that I began to appreciate the spiritual blessing of this experience Darrell had worked so hard to create.

I will never forget those last three rounds when, following the prayers, Darrell sang with such passion, zeal, and intensity as he rhythmically—instinctually—beat away at his drum. Meanwhile, temperatures in the lodge continued to rise, far exceeding anything I had ever experienced. With each round lasting upwards of forty minutes, and the time spent jumping into the lake and talking story, the ceremony went on into the early morning hours. It was only in those final rounds that I was able to reach for the cottonwood branches crisscrossing the dome of the lodge and recognize why Darrell described them as "the ribs of Mother Earth."

"You see, Brother Mike," he'd said, "when we enter the sweat lodge, we are entering the womb of all that is sacred."

Having survived my initiation to this sacred practice, I accepted Darrell's invitation to a sweat ceremony a couple months later at the VA hospital in Spokane with the confidence of a sweat vet. Surrounded by brave warriors whose battles—both in the field and with addiction—surpassed anything I had endured, it was clear from the start that I'd be the first to leave this lodge. Still, I was proud when I made it through the first four rounds. It was the fifth and final round—known as the Warrior Round (and a surefire way to inspire a mischievous grin on Darrell's mustached, handsome face)—that proved more than I could take.

At both sweats, I envied the doorman—the last to enter and the keeper of the flap that officially cuts ties with the outside world. In preparation for the Warrior Round, with religious gusto, the man in charge of the water poured ladle after ladle on the five new rocks that had been brought in on a shovel. Though no one said as much, it was clear nobody wanted to be the first to disturb the participants' Zen-like meditation by fleeing the confines of the lodge. Even in a group of men wearing nothing but basketball shorts soaked with sweat, a competitive pride made the idea of being the first to request respite embarrassing. So I tried to reason with myself that allowing some of the heat out would surely reduce the misery of the others. Feeling as if my lungs were weighted by bricks and the hairs on my arms and legs were ready to ignite, I had to disturb the two men to my right in order to flee for my survival. I will never forget bursting through the flap—how the winter chill beyond the lodge made for a glorious reemergence to the outside world.

These earlier experiences in mind, I asked Crystal to remind Darrell that I was in a weakened state. And it wasn't that I didn't trust my adopted Assiniboine–Gros Ventre brother; it was simply that I didn't believe as fervently as he in the power of his medicine. I wasn't up for much additional suffering—or an all-nighter.

Sometime after the sun set behind the massive igneous outcropping that is Electric Peak, Darrell lumbered back onto our rickety deck. With the only door to the transit open, in hopes of cooling the steamy quarters, I could see he had his hands full.

While it had never crossed my mind the summer before—when we shared our spiritual journey through the Ecosystem—I now knew that he had broken park regulations by removing the bison spine from Yellowstone and later placing it in Grand Teton National Park. As a dutiful and proud ranger with a passion for protecting the park's resources, I watched apprehensively as Darrell entered the trailer with an armful of "medicine" he had gathered the last two hours in his wander along the banks of the Gardner River. As he disappeared into our bedroom with a box full of supplies, my ranger brain kicked into high gear. He had come a long way to help me continue this new life and new mission of mine—inspiring others to become Yellowstone stewards—so I rationalized that it would be okay to let any transgressions slide this night.

Crystal decided she would crash on the couch, while my mom retired early to the guest room, roughly the size of a large closet, its window overlooking McMinn Bench.

Darrell operated on what he described as "Indian time," and with the exception of his 9 to 5, he seemed to have no comprehension or concern about the clock. Things happened when they were meant to happen. When Darrell finally emerged from our bedroom, it was almost 10:30, and I was already exhausted.

Darrell entered the kitchen, a narrow corridor separating the bedrooms and bathroom from the main living space, and said it was time to begin. I felt a sense of dread. He had decorated his two long braids; adorned each wrist with a beautiful silver-and-turquoise, cuff-style bracelet; and added a regal choker necklace around his neck. He had also changed from jeans into a pair of black Nike basketball shorts, white Converse shoes, and a faded blue T-shirt with the words "The Healing Lodge," a residential program for teenagers fighting chemical dependency, on the back.

Having fought alcohol dependency himself, Darrell's immersion in his people's traditional beliefs and spirituality has helped him become a more engaged and present father. And while the ceremonies we have shared have focused on my health, both physically and spiritually, I recognize the profound impact these rituals have on Darrell's psyche and spirit as well.

Entering the bedroom, I was astonished by its transformation. The room previously had the feel of a colorless infirmary, with white walls and white, roll-up style blinds. Darrell had turned it into a temple. The first thing that drew my eyes were the objects deliberately placed on a Pendleton-style blanket atop the dresser.

While I had come to expect the shell, sage, bundle of sweetgrass, eagle feathers, rocks, jewelry, and other items sacred to his people, I have to admit, the numerous Elvis collector plates flickering in the candlelight caught me off guard. Mom had already told me that they had played the same Elvis CD over and over again on the seven-hour drive, so perhaps I shouldn't have been surprised.

Darrell had tacked an American flag with a Native American warrior in its center, to the wall above the bed. The entire, outstretched wings of what appeared to be an eagle were attached to each of the top corners, which, in the candlelight, gave the sense that the wings suspended the flag in the air. At both bottom corners of the flag hung the clenched talons of some kind of hawk—a red-tail, I imagined.

Never before had I met a man, or learned of a people, who held so many symbols in such high esteem. The only comparison I could draw was that of the Christian cross, but for me, the veneration for that which is bound to the earth—so pure, so real, and so full of meaning—is what resonates with my love for our wild places and wild animals.

The ceremony itself differed little from the structure of the sweats I had participated in with Darrell in the past. We prayed for hours. Darrell started by asking the Creator to guide him in our ceremony. It was the first time I sensed Darrell to be uneasy or concerned about a ceremony. He had put so much thought and effort into its execution and wanted all to go well.

Darrell spoke directly to the matter of my nausea, fatigue, and the constant throbbing of my migraine, but his focus extended beyond the ailments to healing my whole person—healing me by making me whole. He was of the belief that my health problems arose from a spiritual disconnection, and he clearly intended the ceremony to help restore that relationship.

Darrell sang, he chanted, he drummed, and oh, how he prayed. As he hit the leather hide of the drum with the heel of his hand, I was reminded of his teaching that the beat of the drum represents the heartbeat of the earth. I often found myself sneaking a peek during a prayer, looking around the room, humbled and inspired. Time and time again, I had to bring myself back to the moment—back to the spiritual—as my analytical mind wandered and wondered about how I would ever remember the power of his words and the strength of his conviction. It was only after I caught myself drifting into the "What if I lose this job that I love?" mind-set that I realized I was failing to fully embrace Darrell's gift. From then on, my focus and elementary meditative abilities became stronger, more graceful, even seemingly effortless in the presence of Darrell's supreme focus, energy, and confidence. It reminded me of how the really special ballplayers like Magic, Lebron, or Michael made those playing around them better and more complete.

With the bitter celery taste of Kinnikinnick—which Darrell calls "Ghost Chaser"—in my mouth, I soaked in the rich incense of the burning grasses. He spoke of sweetgrass with such respect that I could not help but embrace his words: "Sweetgrass brings out very powerful emotions, Mike. Maybe this is because it is from the Plains, where all the killing and fighting took place. I don't know. But tonight, it is important to burn sage afterwards to make sure we calm it down."

I didn't know where all of Darrell's beliefs came from or by whom they'd been taught, but I did know that his conviction inspired me to discover a similar faith in something of my own—something I could stand behind and believe in.

Nearing the end of the ceremony, Darrell pulled a black rock, volcanic in origin, from one of the burning candles and placed it in my palm. Wrapping my fingers into a ball, I felt the smoothed stone burn into my skin.

Darrell spoke his final words of the evening.

"The rocks are our grandfathers, Mike. They hold untold wisdom. This rock is powerful, Brother Mike, as it was born of fire, here in your beloved Yellowstone. I found this simple black rock one year ago, on our Bundle Trip, and it has been in my medicine bundle ever since. My people's language is straight up, Brother Mike; no bullshitting like the white man. There is meaning to every word, spoken or thought."

Though clearly Native, like so many American Indians, Darrell had white blood as well, and I always smiled when he began spitting his passionate, Leonard Peltier–style speech. I nodded, as I always had when he was teaching or talking story.

"Your spirit is strong, Brother Mike. You've come a long way since our journey last year, but you are still living in too much fear. If you have to go home to heal, well then, you have to go home to heal. Nothing more. Nothing less."

He continued in a firm but loving tone, "There is nothing wrong with your spirit, Mike. It is simply out of balance, and this will be a constant challenge and source of your spiritual practice. You need to cleanse your body of the medication that is making you sick, and you must believe in your body's ability to regain its strength, energy, and vitality."

The rock had slowly cooled in my hand, providing a quiet sense of peace as I ran my thumb over its smooth surface.

"You are going to get better, Brother Mike. I want you to trust me when I say that you will be back here next week—back doing what you love."

I closed my eyes and nodded again, in hopeful agreement.

"You have to believe, Brother Mike. Your headache will soon be gone. You may have reminders of your pain from time to time, but you are on your path to healing. When you doubt, I want you to pull out this rock," he opened my hand and rested his gently atop mine, sandwiching the rock between our palms, "and I want you to return to this moment, this confidence, and this belief.

"I pray to the Great Spirit that you can begin to accept your mistakes and shortcomings rather than beating yourself up so harshly. Be kind to yourself, Brother Mike. You are a good soul; you are a strong soul. And you deserve goodness. But you must first learn to be good to yourself. You, Brother Mike, must learn to love yourself as we all love you."

Like a child being scolded, I bowed my head and prayed he was right—that I was going to get better in the seven-day window my supervisor had given me to go home to see my doctors.

"Believe, Brother Mike. Believe."

• • •

IT WAS AFTER 2 A.M. when I left the cathedral that our bedroom had become to wake Crystal. But before doing so, I leaned against the glass window overlooking the Gardner River and marveled at the glow radiating off the northern slopes of Mount Everts in the brilliance of the moonlit sky. Despite the streetlights from the warehouse and Bunkhouse, the stars shone bright, and I scanned the flat plain for a lumbering grizzly or bison. Such is the hopeful power and magic of Yellowstone. Whether or not you actually see one of the iconic species that dwell in the park is a moot point; simply knowing they are there fills one's cup.

When I awoke, late the following morning, I caught a glimpse of a western tanager undulating toward the willow-lined banks of the Gardner. Crystal had opened the blinds to get me to stir, so we could get started on our drive back home to Coeur d' Alene.

It took me several minutes to recognize the difference. I no longer felt the constant pressure and pulse that had occupied my temples and ravaged my eyes. For the first time in weeks, I was clear of a migraine.

With my bag already packed and a box full of Yellowstone books that I planned to utilize to create my Fort Yellowstone history walk and evening campfire program, I felt eager to hit the road. The sooner we left, the sooner I would be back in uniform by day, hiking the trails and chasing trout by night.

I would ride with Darrell in my mom's rig and she would jump in our red Toyota pickup with Crystal. As I approached Mom's Volvo, Darrell stood leaning against the driver's side door. He looked exhausted and lacking his usual vitality.

"How are you feeling today, Brother Mike?" he asked me first thing. "Is your headache gone?"

Later, my mom would tell me what Darrell shared with her before I awoke that beautiful summer morning: "April," he spoke gently and in obvious discomfort, "Mike's headache is gone. I have it now."

As we pulled away from the transit, I could see that the line at the North Entrance gate had already backed up. I said a quick prayer that I'd be back in a week and ready to roll—ready to pursue the dream born the previous summer.

I noticed Darrell had borrowed my mom's sunglasses, which he acknowledged by grunting, "Eyes are sensitive to the light today."

Just as we drove across the Yellowstone River Bridge on the main drag through Gardiner, Darrell pressed the power button on the stereo and looked over at me with his big magnificent grin as he placed his hand atop mine. With Elvis's "In the Ghetto" blasting, I peered into the waters of the Upper Yellowstone River as we passed through the enigmatic town that I was just getting to know and hoped to be a part of one day.

Under a cloudless sky, the pockets of snow in the bowl of Electric Peak glistened. The monarch mountain overlooking the Gardiner Basin stood stoically, inspiring an aura of assurance.

This was my place. This was my purpose. Though fear was present, for the first time since the start of this latest physical blow, with the Medicine Warrior I called brother beside me, I embraced the uncertainty of my situation, confident in the knowledge that my Yellowstone saga had only just begun.

3

The Journeyman, 253M

October 21, 2013

His was a story of disability, perseverance, and discovery. Over the course of his eight years spent wandering the wildlands of Yellowstone Country, he unknowingly lifted the spirits of thousands of Yellowstone National Park visitors who had the privilege of witnessing his beauty, or perhaps had simply heard of his remarkable journey.

I wrote the following essay about this extraordinary wolf in the spring of 2005 while attending the University of Montana. I was a senior in the Environmental Studies program, but unlike most students in their twenties, who are healthy and full of vigor, I was in the midst of a personal health struggle that would profoundly affect my life.

As the cottonwoods blossomed, beckoning a return of spring, I typed on my computer in an ancient Tamarack Trail trailer that sat 100 yards from the meandering Bitterroot River in Lolo, Montana. In six weeks, I would return to the wilds of Yellowstone National Park, where I would begin my fourth summer as a seasonal park ranger. The thought of standing along the roadway that courses through Yellowstone's Lamar Valley, hovered over a spotting scope in search of a black wolf known to park biologists as 253M—but better known to his disciples (wolf watchers) as Limpy—gave me the strength to endure the hardships standing in my path.

The story of wolf number 253M will surely go down in Yellowstone folklore, for it is a story unlike any other. Over the years, he developed a following that looked more like the paparazzi than your typical national park tourist sect. They followed his every move with spotting scopes and cameras in hopes of gaining a better understanding of his life.

His dramatic story, which began in the spring of 2000, came to an abrupt and brutal end as the cold winds blew in the spring of his eighth year. On March 28, 2008, the Northern Rockies gray wolf population lost the federal protection they had been afforded for over a decade under the Endangered Species Act. On the same day wolves were delisted, bullets coursed through the body of the wolf that had captured the hearts and minds of visitors to our world's first national park for nearly a decade. Two fifty-three M died near an elk feeding ground outside of Daniel, Wyoming.

Since his untimely death, we've witnessed protection for Yellowstone's wolves restored, following the 2009 hunting season—which saw nine Yellowstone wolves shot beyond the park's boundary within a few short weeks—then stripped again for the wolves of Idaho and Montana in 2011. With the delisting of Wyoming's wolf population in 2012, wolves are once again in the crosshairs throughout the Greater Yellowstone Ecosystem. As of this writing, we are entering the fourth wolf-hunting season in Montana and Idaho and the second in Wyoming. Incredibly, in 2012, the state of Idaho legalized trapping—one of the most barbaric, indiscriminate, and inhumane means of wolf "management" imaginable. Montana followed suit in 2013. While hunting and trapping aren't allowed within the confines of the park, when wolves leave its invisible boundaries, they are fair game.

The impact of state-sponsored wolf hunts has changed the dynamics and family structure of many of Yellowstone's most observable packs. It's estimated that over one million people have observed wolves in the park since their reintroduction, but these sightings have become less reliable as hunting impacts their numbers. When I received the news in December of 2012 that wolf number 754M of the Lamar Canyon Pack had been shot by a Wyoming hunter, my heart sank. Then, weeks later, on a fellow guide's Facebook page, I read that the spirited wolf 832F, better known as the 06 female and beloved alpha of the Lamar Canyon Pack, had been shot during the same mismanaged and morally repugnant hunt. I had spent many powerful mornings with friends, clients, and students observing 06F and 754M in the hallowed grounds of the Lamar. But with two rifle shots that shattered the silence of winter in Yellowstone Country, the park's most famous wolf and her pack's loyal beta male were gone. The wild pulse of Yellowstone beats with a little less vigor with the loss of these iconic members of the Yellowstone landscape.

Learning that 06F had been shot brought me back to that sickening morning in 2008, when I read that 253M had been killed. I felt a deep sense of loss; his death marked the end of an era. The essay that follows is a celebration of the life of this modern-day journeyman.

THE ALARM ON MY WATCH rings at 5:45 A.M. on July 4th each summer. Within five minutes, the pickup will be humming, awaking a few edgy campers who wonder why I am dragging myself out of the warmth of my sleeping bag before the sun has even begun to rise. The answer is simple: I have come to observe the Druids, and according to my journal, the first week of July coincides with the first time we see the year's new pups.

Three years ago, while passing through the Lamar on a morning fishing quest with my dad, I saw my first wolf. Tears fell from my eyes when I saw the black dog stretched out on a dirt mound a half mile in the distance. I had seen a PBS special a few years earlier about the Yellowstone wolf reintroduction, and from that day on, wolves had become my passion.

Now, five years later, I have observed many wolves and have come to know individuals from the world's most famous pack. Everyone has his or her favorite; just drive through the Lamar Valley and look at the personalized plates: "Wolf 21M," "Alpha 42," "Druid 38," and on it goes. I also have my favorite—but no special license plates. Just a wolf who has captured my heart and imagination.

If you love an underdog, you, too, would love 253M.

• • •

I NEVER LIKE DRIVING THE roads in Yellowstone National Park in the dark, especially the road dissecting the Lamar Valley, affectionately referred to as North America's "Little Serengeti." But reaching the knoll overlooking the Druid rendezvous site in time to see the sun crest the jagged edges of the Absaroka Mountains makes it worth the additional care I take on these mornings. The best word I can find to describe the experience is "sacred." Yellowstone is a holy place for those whose temples are the mountains and the wilderness. The Lamar is my church; the wolves my teachers. As the shadows of light spread like giant fingers across the expansive valley, I can't help but think there is no better place on earth.

There are eleven of us hunched over our spotting scopes, scanning the valley floor. Although the morning crowd of wolf watchers pales in comparison to the evening's, there will be another fifty arrivals within the next two hours. Some will be coming out for the first time, in hopes of catching a glimpse of their first wild wolves; while others have purchased homes in nearby Silver Gate or Cooke City to maximize their exposure to the wolves and the mystique they've created with their return.

The Lamar Valley is located in the park's northeast corner. It has none of the grand attractions of other parts of the park, such as the Mammoth Hot Springs, Old Faithful, or the Grand Canyon of the Yellowstone, but it boasts an abundance of wildlife and scenery that is unmatched anywhere else in the park. While the dedicated fly fishermen always visited this valley, the Lamar remained the "quiet" corner of the park, the last piece of wild roadway in Yellowstone. But in 1995, fourteen wolves were brought here from Alberta, Canada, and that—combined with the publicity that followed—quickly changed this.

To call the reintroduction of *Canis lupus* a success would be a gross understatement. It may be the greatest—and most controversial—wildlife conservation success story in the history of the Northern Rockies.

Over 100,000 people have now seen a wolf in the park; no pack is as famous as the Druid Peak Pack. Standing under the pack's namesake mountain, hundreds of people gather each day. While the alpha pair always receives the most attention, on this morning, I scan the valley in hopes of seeing a steel-black wolf with a limp. Wolf number 253M.

Wolves collared in the Greater Yellowstone area get numbers. Those without numbers are identified by unique characteristics: color, markings, or often, physical traits, such as size. But even without the aid of telemetry, it is hard to miss 253M. His damaged back leg sets him apart from the others, giving him a distinct limp.

Number 253M was just a few weeks old in the spring of 2000 when the Cinderella wolf, number 42F, became the alpha. Forty-two's sister, 40F, was a rigid alpha who would not stand for a second litter in the pack. She traveled to what has become the Druid's second den site for reasons that are still speculated but unknown. While wolves are generally subservient to the alpha, there is one thing they value even more than pecking order, and that's wolf pups. Forty F died a slow death from the trauma associated with the bruising of bites that occurred that day, most likely courtesy of her sister and the other wolves protecting the pups. Thus began 253M's tumultuous journey into the world.

In October of 2001, eight members of the Nez Perce Pack (the second largest pack in the park at the time) wandered into Druid territory. Although the Druids had fallen from a high of thirty-seven wolves—the most ever documented in a single pack—they remained a daunting force in the Northern Range. Known by some as "the bad boys of the Lamar," the Druids had a reputation for killing stragglers; but the Nez Perce Pack—notorious for its wanderings—had become a force in its own right.

On that October day, wolves from the park's two most powerful packs would square off; and it was during this battle that 253M earned his badge of courage. Young and full of fight, the black wolf fought off several Nez Perce wolves. His rear right leg was torn up in the process, leaving him with a distinctive limp and the nickname "Limpy."

But it was not the limp or his courage in taking on intruding wolves that made 253M famous. Nearly a year after the battle with the Nez Perce, 253M was two years old and ready to mate, but he was not the alpha. And although alpha male 21M was forgiving, there would be no mating on his watch. So 253M did what any excited young man would do: he struck out on his own. To do so is the toughest decision a wolf can make, however. A wolf may want to mate, but his life revolves around the pack, the family structure. A lone wolf is usually, quite simply, a dead wolf. If caught in another pack's territory, the chances of 253M being welcomed would be slim. But 253M is not your ordinary wolf. He is a loner and a survivor. A journeyman.

Nearly one year after the fight that injured 253M, he disappeared. It had been over a month since he was last spotted. A favorite of the wolf watchers, people were becoming worried. Then, on November 30, 2002, word came that a young male wolf had been discovered in a coyote trap northeast of Salt Lake City, just twenty-five miles southeast of Ogden, Utah. This was the first documented wolf in Utah in more than seventy years. Wolf supporters were ecstatic. Although no wolves had been reintroduced in Utah, the state falls within the recovery zone, which dictates that a naturally migrating wolf into the state receives a higher level of protection than the experimental, nonessential populations in Idaho, Montana, and Wyoming. Remarkably, the wolf turned out to be 253M. He had traveled over 300 miles as the crow flies, on three legs, to find a mate and establish his own territory. As exciting as this news was to some, 253M's stay in Utah would be short-lived.

The three-legged black wolf created a political and media frenzy. Biologists discovered a second pair of what they believed to be wolf tracks near where 253M was trapped, indicating he had a partner, a mate—the beginning of a possible pack of wolves in Utah. After two days in a cage, 253M was brought back to Wyoming by lead Wyoming wolf biologist Mike Jimenez. Wolf advocates were outraged by this decision and its implications for wolf recovery in Utah. I, too, was sickened by the move, but then my sadness became disgust when I learned that 253M was not brought back to the Lamar; he was instead dropped off near Flagg Ranch Resort, outside Yellowstone's southern boundary.

What would he do now? Having sustained injuries in the coyote trap, he now found himself gimping on two legs. What a sad sight he must have presented, limping his way through the park, trying to find where he belonged. It seemed impossible that he could make it on his own. His pack was over fifty miles away, and he would need to travel through numerous other packs' territories to get there.

Biologists predicted that 253M would hightail it back to Utah. But miraculously, within two days, he was back in the Lamar, rejoining his natal pack, the Druids.

By now, 253M had gained celebrity status. Reporters and wolf lovers from all over the world descended upon the Lamar to catch a glimpse of him, the journeyman. How had this sleek black wolf with a limp worked his way through wolf-dense Yellowstone Park, and then the rancher- and cattle-abundant Wyoming range to Durst Mountain in Utah, only to return to the Lamar when dropped off south of the park?

For a while, 253M seemed content to stay put with the Druids. And his second gimpy leg made him even more beloved by the wolf watchers. Whether he wanted it or not, 253M had a following and a fan club.

With his return, 253M became a devoted beta (the second in command, navigating the slippery slope of enforcing the pack structure while remaining loyal to the alpha) to the longtime Druid alpha 21M, who had gained legendary status after *National Geographic* captured his story on film. Although he was relegated to the use of three legs most of the time, when it came time for the hunt, 253M still had great speed and contributed hugely to the success of the Druids. And as his front leg healed, his prowess in the hunt returned. The Druids may have decreased in size, no longer the force they had been when they numbered over thirty, but they remained the most observed wolf pack in the world.

By the summer of 2004, after mourning the loss of his longtime partner 42F, 21M appeared to have things back on track for the Druids. At the ripe old age of nine, 21M still looked strong and had far surpassed the average wolf age in the park (a mere four and a half years). But in early June, 21M went missing. Within two weeks, his carcass was found.

Several Yellowstone wolf biologists predicted that 253M would become the next alpha of the Druids, and everyone was rooting for him to take over the role. But first, 253M had to deal with 302M from the Leopold Pack, who had mated with three of the Druid females the year before and fathered several of the pack's yearlings.

At first, 253M seemed to be dealing well with the challenge of the Don Juan Leopold and looked to be the choice of the new alpha female; but then a second contender came on the scene—a big black male known as New Black. Two fifty-three M's hopes of gaining the role of alpha male soon dwindled. By late summer, 253M left the Lamar, striking out once more for his own territory.

The loner with the limp was again on the move.

The Yellowstone wolf-study team spent the next few months searching for 253M in their weekly flyovers, but the limping black journeyman was nowhere to be found. Speculation spread like wildfire up on the wolf-watching hill. Where had he gone, and was he still alive? In early January 2005, wolf watchers rejoiced when Mike Jimenez found 253M looking strong and healthy in a remote region of the National Elk Refuge, outside Jackson Hole.

The goal of a lone wolf is to one day have its own mate and territory, the beginning of a pack. If 253M lives as long as 21M, the wolf he so devotedly followed, he will have another four years to pursue this goal.

My hope is that this is just the beginning of another journey for 253M. Calls have flooded the Wyoming wolf office. Druid devotees desperately want to see for themselves this last legend of the famous Druids, and they will travel any distance to do so.

I think it is best to let 253M be—let him have his peace and just be grateful for the perseverance he has taught us. These wolves we follow and observe are the greatest teachers we can find. They are devoted to the needs of their young and the survival of the pack; and they always stay in the moment.

The last time I passed through the Lamar—before 253M turned up on the Elk Refuge—I found myself searching, stopping in familiar spots and places where I had watched him before, in hopes of seeing a black wolf with a limp. I saw no wolves that day, but I stopped at the rendezvous site where I first heard the story of the three-legged wolf. And I said a prayer that he will find what he is searching for.

When I return to the Lamar soon, to watch the Druids, who are now on the verge of losing the premier wolf territory in the park to a neighboring pack, I know I will feel something missing. I suspect it will feel something like the first Thanksgiving without a close friend who has always been there.

Two fifty-three has become a part of the surrounding areas. But wherever he may be, his spirit will always remain in the great valley.

If 253M ever comes back to the Lamar, I will be there to see him. Whenever I head out to look for wolves or hit the river for an evening of fishing, I will glass across the valley and its surroundings in hopes of catching a glimpse of the wolf I have grown to love. But if he has found his home—his sense of place and family—elsewhere, I will be content with simply knowing he is out there. This black wolf with a limp has taught me about courage and perseverance in the face of struggle.

A friend recently shared a quote from the explorer Ernest Shackleton that has guided me through many difficult days. I think it sums up the life of 253M: "Through endurance, we conquer."

The black wolf with the limp in his gait is a warrior who has endured more than any wolf I know. Two fifty-three and I have shared a similar journey of endurance. I have spent the last two years fighting to regain my health. Until one has truly struggled and been forced to endure each day, they cannot understand the kinship I share with this wolf.

At times, when the aches, pains, and fatigue of my medical journey are at their peak, I often wonder how I can face another day. My well of hope begins to run dry. But then I look to a fellow survivor who has not fallen victim to the labels of "injured" or "ill"; 253M is my beacon of hope. His courage inspires me to face my struggles with the confidence that I can overcome. According to Jimenez, "Usually when we see him, he's sleeping with a full belly and a dead elk."

• • •

THIS COMING JULY, I WILL continue my annual tradition, skipping the fireworks displays in the small towns neighboring the park in hopes of catching a glimpse of a wild wolf. I will rise early, before the sun, and claim my loner spot upon the hill, away from the crowds. And as the light bathes the most gorgeous valley on earth, I will thank the Creator for this day, scanning my scope over the valley with an eager eye, looking for an old friend.

4

Winter Adventures

As someone who grew up in the panhandle of North Idaho—
a haven for rednecks and their preferred form of recreating—one
might assume that I have spent at least a little time on a snowmobile.
And while I am sure my family's decision to move our household to the
bustling suburbs of Seattle, Washington, when I was just nine helped to
derail my opportunities at two-stroke-powered adventures across snow,
the truth of the matter is that I come from two parents who placed great
emphasis and value on self-propelled endeavors. Maybe that explains
why I have long had a strong dislike for the loud, cloud-puffing machines
that are held in such high esteem around much of Idaho, Montana, and
Wyoming. Their raucous engines rumbling through the winter wonderland of Yellowstone National Park has never made sense to me. By the
winter of 2006, I had worked five summer seasons in Yellowstone as a
ranger naturalist, and contrary to the apolitical teachings of my division,
there are two issues about which I never hesitate to make my opinion
fully known: bison and snowmobiles.

While the use of snowmobiles in the world's first national park
has been a contentious issue for most of the last decade—and perhaps
much of the last quarter century—I think it is safe to say that this court-
suffocating issue pales in comparison to that of bison management in
and around the park. Still, having written many letters on behalf of a
quieter, cleaner Yellowstone, I was faced with somewhat of a moral conflict in February 2006 (while working on intermittent status for the divi-

sion of interpretation) when the Public Affairs Office came knocking on my door.

The winter of 2005 was our first full winter living in Gardiner, Montana, on the northern outskirts of the park. And while I enjoyed the opportunity to romp around the park on skinny skis and embraced a somewhat prolific time with my writing, by the end of January, the winter doldrums began to sink in and with them, my mood and imagination ventured south to the enigmatic red rocks of the desert Southwest.

Only one month of the winter season remained when the representative of the Public Affairs Office walked through the door of the Albright Visitor Center, where I worked the front desk—a mind-numbingly boring job in the winter, when seventy-five visitors walking through the door is celebrated (compared to the head-spinning three thousand who plunge into the building on a typical summer day—more often than not to ask where the bathroom is). Seeing that I like to talk, it didn't matter that the pretty blonde rep, born and raised in Gardiner, was wearing a uniform and had little need for me to give my typical typhoon of a mini-presentation; it seemed we had plenty of catching up to do. Finally, Stacy asked if I was interested in filling in for their film monitor for the remainder of the winter season. It would entail, she mentioned casually, several snowmobile-aided forays into the park's interior.

While a part of me felt conflicted, it took no more than a few seconds for me to blurt out, "For sure!" I had never been into the park's interior in winter, and this seemed like the opportunity of a lifetime. Plus, I needed to make a little extra money, and the film monitor work paid better than the Visitor Center, simply because the hours were so long.

Aware of the fact that I hailed from North Idaho, the first question Public Affairs asked me—had I ever ridden a sled?—seemed a mere formality. "Of course," I lied. And that was it. They quickly signed me up for one of the many snowmobile training courses held throughout the winter.

After a two-hour seminar on what to do if your sled breaks down ("don't die of hypothermia; that is a pain in the ass for the park" was what I walked away with), we ventured over to the garage where a six foot one, three-hundred-plus pound man taught us how to change a belt. It quickly became clear that I was fucked if I busted one.

One thirty-minute session (in which I don't think I was even taught how to start the damn sled) and I was certified. I was actually a little shocked—and pleasantly surprised—by the ease of the process because everything with the Park Service seemed to be such an ordeal. For example, though I am fairly competent with a chain-saw, that was of no value one day the previous June when they were looking for someone to clear downed lodgepole pines at my beloved Indian Creek Campground. It wasn't that I desperately wanted to wield a saw; far from it, as it takes several days to get my lower back muscles reorganized after being stretched away from my core by the load of slicing through trees with a fifteen-pound weight in hand. It had instead been more about wanting to spend a day smelling the sweet scent of dew-covered grasses while being hypnotized by the tranquil waters of the upper Gardner River. But it wasn't to be. My rapture-like vision was quickly shot down when I wasn't able to present paperwork stating that I had been through the NPS chain-saw training course.

This time, I did have a NPS certificate in hand and still didn't have a clue about how to operate the sled that was going to be my lifeblood the following day, for my journey far south, into the depths of Yellowstone's interior. But hey, it didn't matter—to me, anyway. I was young—twenty-six years old—and yearning for adventure. Plus, I was geared out with what felt like a five-pound helmet and a green Park Service snowsuit that made me look as if I were heading to Jupiter.

I hardly slept a wink the night before my pioneer journey as a film monitor. And while I wasn't supposed to leave until later in the evening, my excitement and nervousness about the odds I'd wrap this $12,000 snow toy around a tree trunk prompted me to start out while there was still a hint of light.

The objective was to make it to the Old Faithful Snow Lodge that night, wake up three hours before sunrise the following morning, and meet with the *Good Morning America* film crew south of the park at 7 A.M.—still under a blanket of darkness—on the John D. Rockefeller Jr. Memorial Parkway. Since this was the first of many proposed jobs, I really didn't want to screw it up.

Fully equipped with bungee cords, avalanche shovel, headlamps, extra batteries, tarp, sleeping bag, clothes, radio, and snacks, I pulled into the garage up at the YCC camp above Mammoth, ready to roll. Perhaps more than any other park, Yellowstone has some odd dynamics when it comes to divisional rivalries. My understanding of the park system as a whole is that there is much more teamwork at the smaller parks; but in the competitive culture that is Yellowstone, there often seems to be a bit of distrust among members of differing divisions, especially when meeting for the first time. So you can imagine the look of concern I received when I arrived at the garage office to pick up keys to my trusted steed for the next forty-eight hours. Though barely a word was spoken, the eyes of the gentleman behind the desk clearly said, "Hey, knucklehead, if you mess this machine up, it's my guys who'll have to fix it."

Enough said, I had my keys, and thirty minutes of daylight remained; it was time to get the show on the road. My anxiety level peaked as I was packing my gear onto the snowmobile and two other NPS employees came grinding in on the ice-covered asphalt that was home to the resting sleds. I really didn't want to start this journey with any fanfare. Having never ridden a snowmobile, I wasn't sure if there was a choke. Hell, I didn't even know if I would figure out how to start the damn thing. It was almost as if the two biologists, who were returning with telemetry from a day in the field, knew the angst I was feeling, because they took their time and leaned up against their machines, as if waiting for me to screw up.

Thankfully, my concerns about finding the actual ignition were short lived, as I quickly found the slot and slid the short, stocky key in. No sign of a clutch, so I held my breath and turned the key. The soft rumble of the four-stroke engine—nothing like the obnoxious sound of the two-strokes ripping through the forests of my youth—felt like music to my ears.

I squeezed my head into the helmet, flipped the visor down, and glided onto my sled's saddle. After I switched into reverse, steady beeps rang through the air. Then, with mostly bare concrete as my launch pad, I moved into forward and the real adventure began.

For the next two hours, I experienced Yellowstone in a way I never had before. The first mile from the garage was a beautiful and thrilling ride on an old service road winding through forests and overlooking frozen lakes.

Literally bursting through Golden Gate, I soon arrived on the windswept flats of Swan Lake, where thirty mph side winds blasted me from the west, crashing off the Gallatin Mountains and creating white-out conditions. By the time I reached Gibbon Falls, darkness was taking hold. Here I was, riding a snowmobile for the first time ever, in the wilds of Yellowstone, under the cover of night, on empty roads, en route to the most famous geyser in the world.

Awestruck by the beauty and solitude while driving through the thermal basins dotting the Firehole River corridor, I came across a band of more than twenty-five bison in the middle of the road. I had already passed three or four bison along the way, but this was an entire herd, and it left no room to snake through. I shut off the engine and sat with my sled for twenty minutes, until the wind and cold biting through my suit became too much. Slowly, I began to inch forward, literally passing through the herd; it was a moment I will never forget. As a youngster traveling through the park, I came close enough to reach out and touch a bison wandering down the side of the road on many occasions, but this was always from the cover of a vehicle. Now I found myself face to face with young bull bison on each side of me, with nothing but my helmet and windshield to protect me.

My reverence for the bison knows no boundaries. I find them to be a deeply spiritual animal—the elephant of North America. And while I know my presence had to have disturbed them (elevating their heart rate, and adding stress that only compounds the lack of available food and cold temperatures draining their fat reserves), they made just enough room for me to squeeze through. It wasn't until I reached the end of the herd that I took a deep gulp of air and realized that I had been holding my breath for much of the encounter. I turned to give thanks. Many had bedded down along the road while others still stood, avoiding the knee-deep snow just off the groomed travel passage.

I reached the Old Faithful Snow Lodge exhilarated and empowered by my journey through the winter darkness of a primitive landscape. And after another restless sleep—this time more out of fear of oversleeping my early alarm than out of anxiety about what lay ahead—I was up, quickly outfitted in my Park Service uniform under my borrowed snowsuit, and readying myself for a long and wild journey through the same darkness that had engulfed me the night before. As I stepped out the front doors of the snow lodge, the bitter cold hit me, and I knew it was going to be a chilly ride to my rendezvous site.

Temperatures hovered just above 0 degrees Fahrenheit, with a dusting of new snow overlying freshly groomed roads. My confidence soaring after my first fifty-five-mile day of sledding, I practically flew over Craig Pass, pushing the limits of my machine, reaching speeds exceeding fifty mph. Each night, road crews groom the roads bent out of shape by the bombardment of snowmobiles and road-churning snow-coaches throughout the day. On this morning, I was the first and only vehicle on the road from Old Faithful to the South Entrance. After I crossed the continental divide for the second time at approximately 5:30 A.M., I stopped my sled in the middle of the road, shut down the engine, and took off my helmet.

I'd had a little difficulty starting my sled that morning, so the contemplation of the long walk back to Old Faithful caused heightened nervousness about turning off the machine. Still, I could not resist. Having grown up exploring the wildlands of the Northern Rockies and Pacific Northwest, I had been blessed to experience the silence of wilderness on many occasions. But the stillness I felt on this morning—a peace seeping deep to my core—in a landscape blanketed by snow, was beyond anything I had ever experienced. At almost 9,000 feet in elevation, the stars were so intense and vibrant that I thought I heard them shimmer as they sparkled in the deep black sky.

After passing the shores of Yellowstone and Lewis Lakes, I slowed through the empty South Entrance gate, still bathed in darkness, and journeyed four miles south of the park to my meeting point with the Manhattan film crew at Flagg Ranch. Surprisingly, they were five minutes early, so before we were even scheduled to connect, I'd loaded onto the snowcoach and we were on our way.

For the next ten hours, we toured the entire lower portion of the Grand Loop in a loud, bone-jarring Bombardier built in the 1950s. I later repeated this journey three more times with other film crews, but this was the first time I ever observed the vast and expansive sites of Yellowstone Lake, the Hayden Valley, and the awe-inspiring Grand Canyon of the Yellowstone in winter. It was something I had always dreamed of, and now I was living it—and living it, no less, while leading a film crew on a naturalist expedition fit for the popular morning show.

After a long and memorable day touring Yellowstone's scenic wonders, our trip ended as every winter Yellowstone adventure should:

watching the steam bellow and the water shoot up from Yellowstone's depths alongside a handful of curious onlookers. Though I rarely witness Old Faithful geyser during the craziness of summer, observing this geologic anomaly on a cold, winter afternoon in February transported me back to a time of discovery and purity. This is the wonder of Yellowstone in winter. An oft-made journey to the most well-known geyser in the world is no longer ordinary but once again mysterious and remarkable.

Hoarse from a day of interpreting over the loud rumble of the snowcoach, I rode back from Old Faithful to Flagg Ranch, where our day began, in a quiet and tired daze. I had left the Snow Lodge at 5 A.M. and now it was 6:30 P.M., and I was just returning to the sled waiting for me in the abandoned parking lot at the boarded-up resort. We parted ways with big hugs rather than handshakes—a warm conclusion that seems to happen after any day I spend with visitors to Yellowstone—and exhausted, I remounted my sled for one last push.

Little did I know that the ride that had taken just over an hour and a half on the smooth roads thirteen hours earlier would nearly double in time, as I didn't even approach that morning's average speed of over forty mph on my return trip. I will never forget the ride from the park's South Entrance to West Thumb Geyser Basin and the junction to Old Faithful. The soft, silky surface that I traveled en route to Flagg Ranch had become a rutted battlefield. And while I am lean and wiry, spending several days a week in the gym and pushing my cardiovascular limit in various ways in the field, I was not prepared for the head-thrusting, bobbing ride north—a grueling endeavor that felt more like I was riding a rodeo bull than a Yamaha 3000.

I may have been frozen to the bone, but it was the pain in my shoulders and neck that, at the bottom of Craig Pass, forced me to stop my sled twice, take off my helmet—the weight of which shook my cranium from side to side like a bobblehead—and simply commune with the stars. When I finally reached the hotel at 8:45 P.M., though hunger tormented my belly, all I could think about was the pain pinching my shoulder blades. Forgetting about my stomach, I lumbered up the stairs to the comfort of my bed, where I finally slept like a meat-drunken wolf.

Looking back now on my month spent traversing the snow-covered roadways of Yellowstone on a snowmobile, I cannot help but remember my last journey, a repeat of the Old Faithful to South Entrance route, this time to meet up with the BBC. Temperatures had plummeted and were hovering around minus sixteen degrees. The typical cutoff for government snowmobile travel in the park is a barbaric minus twenty. Once again, I set an early wake-up call, but this time, after a night entombed in freezing temperatures, my sled failed to start.

Miraculously, at 5:30 A.M., I found someone walking near the garage who happened to be an employee. After telling him my assignment for the day, he helped me acquire a sled that had spent the night in the relatively warm confines of the garage. Armored with a balaclava and three layers of clothing under my massive shell of a suit, I expected to hold up against the elements.

I hadn't traveled ten miles when my sled began to struggle up the pass, smoking and eventually coming to a stop. With snow so cold and frozen that it wasn't being recycled by the treads, the effort of speeding up the pass had become too much for the machine. I popped the hood and began shoveling snow on the engine in hopes of cooling it—and warming myself. I was able to get the engine started and souped up with enough power to slowly limp down the hill to the Grant Ranger station, where, after stumbling around yet another garage (I don't have a mechanical bone in my body and haven't spent much time in the presence of grease-coated, wrench-toting gurus), I once again found someone willing to help.

By 8 A.M., I was already on my third sled of the morning. Needing to make up for lost time, I began hauling ass through the flats alongside Lewis Lake, hunched over behind my windshield, doing anything to hide from the brutal wind biting through all my carefully chosen layers and deep into my skin. It was the closest I had ever come to frostbite, my cheeks burning a bright red. I began wondering if it was crazy to risk life and limb for a film crew who no doubt believed that having a monitor present afforded them a heightened level of freedom

Much like that spiritual moment on my first assignment, when I shut off my sled's engine on the summit of Craig Pass, I paused again on the divide, where waters flow from the great spine to one side of the continent or the other. Watching the sun finally crest the lodgepole pine forest as it gently caressed my path of travel became a moment I will always treasure. Though brutally cold, I knew then that, with the support of the sun, I would make it to the warming hut at the South Entrance.

And arrive I did, on time—even early—for my rendezvous with the film crew. The ranger on duty could see that I had been through an epic morning. He quickly poured me a warm cup of tea while I sat in front of the crackling, sap-spitting fire to thaw my tired limbs and wind-burnt cheeks.

• • •

FIVE YEARS HAVE PASSED SINCE these adventures took place, yet they seem as vivid today as when they occurred. I think the depth of an adventure can, in many respects, be measured by how long the agony and the "in-that-moment-ness" remain. Though no reflection of a journey can ever be as rich as the moment in which it actually occurred, with thoughtful meditation, these once-in-a-lifetime experiences can be recaptured—and perhaps, to some extent—even relived.

I recently read the back of a T-shirt that proclaimed: "The journey is the destination." My one-thousand-plus miles of snowmobile travel in February of 2006 led me on a twisted and transformational journey that I am just beginning to understand.

To know Yellowstone in winter is to unveil the enigmatic beauty of America's sacred wilderness in her most savage—yet vulnerable—time. I firmly believe that a worn pair of hiking boots or a battered pair of skis contain the soul of the trails they have traversed with you. Though propelled that winter by a motorized machine with absolutely no soul, I will always be thankful for these journeys that facilitated a deepening connection to my beloved Yellowstone.

5

Life Returns to Yellowstone

Witnessing the return of spring to Yellowstone Country is like catching a fleeting glimpse of a person with whom you shared a short-lived love. It may not last long, but that brief taste of spring's sweetness is a taunting reminder that summer—Yellowstone's season of glory—is just around the bend.

Spring in Yellowstone is an ephemeral affair. It is said by many residents of the Yellowstone Ecosystem that we only have two true seasons—summer and winter—yet there is something enigmatic and romantic about those border months that act as placeholders between the two. There is really no such thing as a typical spring day in our little corner of the world, since temperatures range wildly from the low thirties (with snow flurries) to the high sixties (with a lack of wind and swollen rivers). But if one were forced to pick a specific day to represent spring in Yellowstone Country, yesterday would have been a good choice.

The day started with temperatures in the low forties; partly cloudy skies, with breaks of sunshine reflecting off the east bowl of Electric Peak; and light winds waving the welcoming flag at the North Entrance gate. By afternoon, things had changed, with temperatures approaching the upper fifties and winds threatening to rip the flag to shreds. Unlike the previous evening, when a deep bank of snow-filled clouds shrouded Mammoth Hot Springs, the waning hours brought our first major electrical storm of the season, which lasted for over an hour and provided anyone willing to watch a mesmerizing look into a deeply charged Yellowstone sky.

All of the signs signaling spring's return to Yellowstone had been witnessed: the appearance of bluebirds, meadowlarks, sandhill cranes, ospreys, American white pelicans, bison calves, velvety elk antlers, Mother's Day caddis hatches, and electrical storms. But one last, long-awaited reunion in the Yellowstone River Valley had not yet occurred: the budding of the cottonwoods.

Over the past few weeks, life had steadily returned to a landscape that, for roughly five and a half months, remained brutally dormant. But it is not until the thick-trunked cottonwoods lining the banks of the Yellowstone begin showing signs of vibrancy that life truly and fully returns to the longest free-flowing river in the lower forty-eight. The Gardiner Basin itself is a banana belt where prickly pear cacti are more common than the deciduous trees most often associated with the Northern Rockies. And though Gardiner may be an extreme example of the climate in Yellowstone Country, one must remember that the Greater Yellowstone Ecosystem is nothing like the most succulent ecosystem in the Northern Rockies—in and around Glacier National Park, six hours up the road. It instead represents an arid habitat with high-desert, sweeping valleys; alpine and subalpine; and a landscape dominated by the thick stands of lodgepole forest.

So for those of us who call Yellowstone Country home—and in particular, the Gardiner Basin—the budding of Populus angustifolia, otherwise known as the narrowleaf cottonwood, is a long-awaited event and celebration signaling that we have indeed made it through another winter season. Though short-lived, it is the final announcement of spring's arrival.

Before the buds give way to the cottonwood's thick, egg-shaped leaves (each leading to a sharply pointed tip), the resinous and overwhelmingly fragrant buds are a treasure to those who cherish the medicines of the earth. In the past, many tribes across the region utilized the countless resources that the cottonwood medicine provided—such as the sweet inner bark (when the sap is still running) or the powerful leaves themselves, which can be applied to bruises, sores—even the aching muscles of horses. A well-known treatment for the common cold was to chew the cottonwood's bark, and though it was believed to be slightly poisonous, bark tea was used in conjunction with cups of warm water to relieve whooping cough and tuberculosis.

For the hippie residents of the narrowleaf cottonwood community, the collection of sticky, deep-red, fragrantly rich resin that can be squeezed out of the buds just prior to the emergence of their leaves is nature's gift to aromatherapy. Or for the more adventurous among us (one of my best friends falls into this category), the richness of the coagulated, blood-like resin can be added to a tincture to create a highly fragrant perfume.

The narrowleaf cottonwood provides endless resources to all residents of its community (two-legged, four-legged, winged, and finned), but the simple observation of a budding cottonwood is also a gift—one that is all-too-often overlooked by the casual observer of natural things. Though deserving of a circus, fireworks, music, and overflowing beer, this subtle transformation of the Yellowstone Ecosystem does not seek such attention.

Perhaps a major gala would not be fitting anyway; perhaps the crowning glory of the announcement is in its tenderness and humility—its fleeting stay. Still, it would be appropriate for all of us who recognize the symbolic return of life to Yellowstone to take the time to tip our hat, give thanks, and appreciate for a moment the fact that another milestone of spring has passed; and with it, we have taken one more step in our own journeys—a journey that will undoubtedly end one day, placing us back into the Ecosystem to provide the nutrients the cottonwoods require to continue their work of returning life to Yellowstone Country.

For now and always, let us enjoy the fecundity of another season—another rebirth—in that fertile ground we call Yellowstone.

6

Mammoth Madness

Who can forget a moment that changes their life forever? I certainly couldn't. I was twenty-two years old and had already gone through several difficult years of struggle, transformation, and self-discovery—a severely premature midlife crisis. My days as a hoopster had come to an end much sooner than I had ever anticipated, my dream of playing division one college basketball dashed. But leaving the court was just the first wave of devastation; I needed to rediscover purpose and meaning in my life.

Just three years earlier, at the age of nineteen, I had been diagnosed with a rheumatoid arthritic condition that most often attacks young men, ankylosing spondylitis. My back, which ached and stiffened both preceding and following the diagnosis led me to wonder what, if anything, would ever fuel my fire again. Until then, my life had been solely about athletic prowess and physical feats. And those around me—those closest to me—knew I would need to find something to put my considerable energies toward, and it would have to be something significant and worthwhile. But two years later, I was still struggling to accept my condition and, even more so, my place in the world.

One day, I turned on PBS and watched a special about the reintroduction of wolves to Yellowstone. I had been going to Yellowstone with my family my entire life. Having grown up surrounded by mountains, lakes, and wildlife, I had always appreciated our nation's first national park, but now it took on new meaning for me. Yellowstone's gravitational pull became so strong that it reached me in the extreme south-western corner of Utah, where my new dream and vision for life came to me during a sleepless and windy night as I camped in Zion National Park, among a cathedral of desert rock outcroppings. I would become a National Park Ranger in my beloved Yellowstone. My mind raced with the newly inspired hope of donning the iconic Park Service uniform. Nothing had felt so real—so true and right—since my time on the hard-wood. Fifteen months later, after a fateful camping trip to Yellowstone and some uncanny timing, I was hired. I was a Yellowstone Park Ranger!

I spent the next three summers working for Brian Suderman, the park's North District supervisor, in Mammoth Hot Springs. While few things have ever given me the pride I experienced donning the flat hat and Park Service uniform during those summer months (especially at the peak of park visitation), even after three years, I knew I hadn't yet reached full Mammoth Ranger status. I was still a migratory visitor myself.

There was something about being a local ranger—someone who lived year-round in or near the park. I wouldn't call it arrogance, but perhaps it was a certain "knowing" that the locals seemed to possess. While most of the staff consisted of summer employees from around the country who departed as soon as their season ended, there were a few seasonal rangers who spent their winters in the Gardiner area. They were akin to the players on an NBA team who had reached the playoffs; while making the squad meant something, it wasn't until you reached the postseason and become a battle-hardened vet that you really began to warrant respect. These were the soldiers who had been to war, while the rest of us were green and deemed less worthy. Such words were never voiced—but they were implied. Each time one of my fellow sum-mer vagabonds excitedly left the desk at the Albright Visitor Center to "manage" a small group of docile cow elk with their calves and a few raggedy spike yearling males, it paled as child's play in the face of real ranger work.

Following my third summer season, when I was asked to return for a September weekend to provide additional help at the Visitor Center desk, I discovered what I had been missing—and why those rangers who stayed throughout the year acquired that heightened status.

For three consecutive summers, I had witnessed the precipitous drop in visitation that began around the 15 of August, so I was shocked when I drove up the hill from Gardiner to Mammoth for the first time in mid-September. While park visitation as a whole remained well below the summer numbers, you'd never know it by the crowds that had descended upon the park's headquarters. Why? They were there to get a taste of elk-inspired frenzy.

Much like the scene at bear jams, the big glass (camera lenses valuing well over $9,000) was out—so much so that, at times over the course of the weekend, it looked more like a staged photo shoot than a wild Yellowstone experience. The Park Service had, of course, unknowingly brought this upon itself by manicuring and watering the nonnative Kentucky bluegrass that abounds in the developed area around Mammoth Hot Springs, encouraging the elk to rut in the relative safety of a heavy human presence.

Each June, during calving season, I had observed pregnant cow elk choose the security of the lawns surrounding the Mammoth Hotel, Chittenden or Pagoda Buildings, medical clinic, or Albright Visitor Center to give birth to their young, opting to deal with pesky bipeds, asphalt, and vehicles over coyotes, wolves, and bears. While the constant gawking and pushy tourists had to take a toll on wild animals like elk, they instinctively knew they had the option of charging a two-legged to get them to back off—a tack that didn't always work with the predators adept at taking their calves.

I came to think of the whole thing as a sort of elk orgy. While thousands of elk performed similar rituals across the Ecosystem, the plush and comfortable accommodations at Mammoth seemed akin to the Playboy Mansion of elk ruts, inviting the participation of Yellowstone's most famous bachelors.

I had heard of the legendary #6 and #10, but it wasn't until that first September weekend that I actually witnessed these noble specimens. Both animals had a quiet confidence about them, perhaps born of the knowledge that when it mattered most, they would capture their quarry and dominate the largest of harems. And that they did. Over the course of the summer-like weekend, with temperatures in the midseventies, they both stood back, chilled in the shade, using little energy as they watched numerous smaller bulls wasting valuable calories to protect their newly acquired group of females—females who were not yet ready to mate but appeared to enjoy the attention.

Though little actual sparring took place over the course of my forty-eight hours back in the park, the repetitive chorus of bugling elk hung in the air; and for the first time since a fat, three-hundred-plus-pound black bear walked across the terraces one June morning earlier in the season, Mammoth pulsed with a wild heartbeat.

Throughout the ranger ranks, the reputation of Mammoth takes on a life of its own. While it provides unmatched convenience in regard to its proximity to Gardiner, Livingston, and Bozeman, the mere fact that Mammoth is home to all the brass, the bosses, the headmasters makes most interpreters choose other, less political and more wild places to work, such as Canyon, Norris, or Old Faithful. I, too, had considered moving to a more remote part of the park, perhaps Fishing Bridge, along the shores of Lake Yellowstone, upon graduating from college, but my loyalty and desire to continue working for the man—Brian—who gave me the chance to live a dream relegated such thoughts to mere fantasy.

And while Mammoth reflected a somewhat Disneyland-ish feel throughout the summer months, any doubts as to whether I wanted to return to Mammoth the following fall vanished after getting a short taste of the elk-induced chaos that accompanied my two-day retreat to my sacred Yellowstone. Over the course of my senior year at the University of Montana, I had difficulty getting that weekend out of my mind. The buzz of working the Albright Visitor Center information desk had lost its luster, and even roving the Mammoth Hot Springs didn't carry the same level of excitement that it once had. Standing between a group of excited visitors and a band of edgy elk not only carried a new level of responsibility, it provided an opportunity to better understand the behavior of one of Yellowstone's wildest residents.

While I had yet to become a seasoned vet, at the age of twenty-five, my wife and I made the bold decision to purchase a house in Gardiner after we graduated. We were bound and determined to make a career living in Yellowstone. My reputation as a passionate, inspired, and edgy interpreter had begun to grow, but I still hadn't become the real deal—not without having spent an entire September working as a "conflict resolution specialist" in the global headquarters for elk–human relations. I was putting up good numbers, but they were regular season stats. The elk rut represented the playoffs to that pinnacle of Mammoth Ranger status.

We spent our fourth summer in Yellowstone living in a 900-square-foot bungalow on "Dog Shit Alley" (a.k.a. Fifth Street) in Gardiner, just five miles north of Mammoth where doggy bags are not a cultural norm. The commute was lovely, and I traveled to work each day more confident than ever that my dream was achievable. This was really happening. The permanence of owning a house symbolized my commitment and desire to spend many years wearing the green and gray. And each fall, I would know the brief taste of glory I experienced the previous year as part of my autumn ritual.

Though every fall I worked as a ranger in Mammoth Hot Springs would provide stories and vivid experiences of unruly elk behavior, none would ever match my first full autumn season—in 2005. This would be the fall that big bad #6 was tranquilized and de-antlered for the first of two consecutive years, after his fits of rage led to thousands of dollars in property damage. It was a wildly controversial decision—one that left me frustrated and enraged. Most visitors assumed it was our job to manage the elk during their rutting season, but the elks' wild spirits were impossible to control. What we were responsible for was keeping tourists and photographers at bay, allowing the ancestral instincts of one of the Northern Rockies great symbols of wildness to play out undisturbed by human presence.

It is my opinion that those traveling to the park during the testosterone-filled rutting season of the elk—or that of the bison, bighorn, or any other critter for that matter—are doing so at their own risk. They are choosing to enter a wild and unpredictable, possibly dangerous environment. We humans represent the intrusive paparazzi camped out on the elks' front lawn, interrupting their primal instinct to mate. And if a tourist's car door is damaged as the result of a bull's natural display of aggression, then so be it. What an incredible memento and story to tell back home—the ultimate souvenir.

But when temperamental #6 responded to his reflection in the back window of a minivan with an attempt to punch it out—day after day showing pathetically little regard for the rangers attempting to control his outbursts—the park had had enough, and the decision was made to cut off his antlers. In my mind and heart, this was akin to cutting off the arms of the heavyweight champ. For a while, #6's instincts told him he was still the biggest, toughest elk in Mammoth, but his antlerless skull said otherwise. After attempting to spar in defense of a harem, he left town dejected, leaving the rest of the bulls to deal with Mammoth's #10 on their own.

There are multiple reasons why the boys from Yellowstone Center for Resources may feel the need to dart an elk, but most often it is because something is stuck in their antlers—literally. Stories abound of elk getting their antlers entangled in Christmas lights, badminton nets, or even the metal chains of a swing set. Whatever the cause, once handled by park personnel, from that day forward, a silver-dollar-sized piece of yellow or orange plastic with a number emblazoned upon it will dangle from the elk's ear, acting as a reminder of his embarrassing encounter and need for intervention.

During the months of September and October, on a daily basis, some poor citizen of Mammoth, groggy after being kept up most of the night by the echoes of clashing antlers (sounding like wooden sword fights) and screaming elk, will walk down the steps of their back porch and onto the path leading to their place of work, only to forget the presence of the very animal that kept them up half the night. These wild encounters can lead to pulled hamstrings and any other number of injuries—the result of the mad sprint that often accompanies an unexpected meeting with one of Mammoth's resident elk.

Rangers from the interior like to talk as if those of us who work in Mammoth experience an inferior level of wildness, but they miss out on dumping a mug full of scalding coffee on their green wool pants as they frantically scramble back up the steps of their residence—steps that elk have been known to climb in pursuit, or in order to eat the potted flowers. Though perhaps a less wild setting than other districts throughout the park, it is akin to the Old West days when an outlaw wearing a black hat would swoop into town, charm the women, and scare the hell out of all other residents standing in his way. Fall in Mammoth represents a rough and tumble time of year.

This was the feeling I got whenever #10 began to exert his power. An old bull, with a widespread and massive girth to his 7 x 7 antlers, it took me a while to figure out what #10 was all about. He had entered Mammoth early that season, during the last few days of August, but once there, he simply sat back, under the shade of a large tree, day after day. He seemed to study the situation, identifying his rivals while they wasted valuable energy posturing.

The first cold snap in September seems to trigger the bigger bulls' aggression and sense of urgency. And that was certainly the case my first full autumn.

The nineteenth of September had been a cold, autumn-like night, with temperatures dropping into the low thirties and a chilly morning haze hanging over Mammoth. Now, at 8:30 A.M. on the twentieth, I had thirty minutes before I had to be at the Visitor Center desk, and I decided to go for a quick rove through the area, which seemed devoid of people. On my way down the steps, I ran into Marc, a mentor and friend, who was on his way to lead a 9 A.M. walk. He decided to stroll with me down to the chapel, which sits at the end of the historic buildings originally built to house the military back in the late 1800s and early 1900s.

While I had enjoyed the first three weeks of September and the daily interactions with lazy, resting elk, like a soldier who had trained for months but hadn't seen combat, I was ready for action. I hate making all of these war analogies, but the US Army inspired the modern-day ranger uniform, and I was ready to earn my stripes. Still, I was completely unprepared for what was about to unfold.

Marc had worked in the park for over a decade and warned me that this—that first cold morning of September—was the day sparks would begin to fly. Much as I would on an overcast morning when I planned to fish with blue-winged olives after work, I began hoping that the clouds would hover over the northern reaches of Yellowstone all day, keeping the temperatures cool and the elk active. I didn't want to miss any action during my four-hour stint in the Visitor Center (answering the same mundane questions I had been responding to since the middle of May).

Marc and I engaged in a short discussion about our roles within the park and where we saw ourselves in the future. Marc always challenged me, as I hadn't really thought about doing anything else with my life since I put on the park ranger uniform. I relished the days when I looked on the work schedule and saw that I was closing down the Visitor Center with Marc. He didn't wear the same rosy blinders that seemed so prevalent with the other interpreters. He, too, took great pride in wearing the iconic uniform, and was—to me—everything a ranger naturalist should be: inquisitive, thoughtful, intelligent, knowledgeable, articulate, and charismatic. As interpreters, we represented the face of the park. If skilled, any given naturalist could be seen speaking to dozens of visitors several times a day, whether it be during a day talk outside the Visitor Center, a terrace walk at the hot springs, or a campfire talk.

One subject Marc and I had discussed on multiple occasions is why other divisions, such as Law Enforcement, have a somewhat holier-than-thou attitude toward our division—the Interpretation Division. Led by the best Chief Ranger in the business, the unflappable Tim Reid, there are still a handful of LEs who represent the old-school ranger, carrying a firearm and possessing the knowledge to provide interpretation for visitors after pulling them over, but classics like Tim, Eric, Kevin, Brian, Colette, Rick, Joe, and Keith have become the exception. The rivalry between LEs and interpreters reminds me of that between the Clippers and the Lakers: we both share the same arena, but the interpreters represent the Clippers in the Park Service hierarchy.

Even our strategies in dealing with the elk represented two starkly contrasting styles. While most interpreters remained passive, strictly dealing with the visitors, instructing them to keep their distance from the elk, LEs were much more aggro, scraping shovels on the asphalt, waving their hands wildly, yelling, clapping, even throwing milk crates to disrupt the elk in hopes of reducing conflict with humans.

Marc had experienced these tactics the night before in dealing with an LE after he had managed the people gathered around one massive bull and his harem of more than twenty cows for several hours. As the bull grew more agitated throughout the evening, Marc continued to create greater distance between the hordes of people and the band of elk. But soon upon arrival, one of the Mammoth LEs opted for more "proactive" tactics, and that was that—because they have ultimate control when the safety of people are in play.

Marc remained agitated the next morning as we walked toward the chapel, both of us adding fuel to the LE–Interpretation rivalry, believing our way to be the better of the two. I think Marc got a kick out of my fire as I told him what I would have said to the LE if he had come and taken over the jam I had been managing. Though both divisions ultimately work together, striving to protect the resources while keeping the visitors safe, there is an unacknowledged turf war between many of the Park Service divisions.

Just as we rounded the guardhouse—the first building erected in 1891 by the US Army during their thirty-two years of military occupation—we saw a smaller bull, with deformed antlers, in the middle of the grassy field. He had an ear tag but neither of us had field glasses in hand, so we crept up on him as quietly as possible. One of the ungulate biologists had told us earlier in the season about a young elk that got its antlers caught in a swing set and deformed the hell out of them while they were in velvet and somewhat malleable. If this was the guy we were looking at (#47), this could be our glory moment—a chance to report to the elk study crew that we had found the youngster they were looking for, and that he was alive and well.

Had we been trained in the same manner as LEs, we might have looked around more before approaching the lone elk as we attempted to get a solid look at the number dangling from his ear. Rather than breaking the twenty-five-yard distance rule by at least fifteen yards, we would likely have seen the massive rack of #10 barreling our way.

"Holy shit!" I cried to Marc, as we both jumped back ten yards and watched at close range as #10 sprinted toward the elk with the funky antlers, running him off. By now, we unknowingly had a small group of camera-toting touristos in the parking lot, watching the events about to unfold.

I don't know what was running through Marc's mind at the time, but I know mine simply froze, shell-shocked by the athletic grace and power that #10 had just displayed. This wasn't the same elk I had watched sit under the shade of a tree for much of the last three weeks. It was game time. After trotting behind the scraggly elk for fifteen additional yards to make sure he had received the message, #10 flung himself around wildly, lowered the immense rack protruding from the top of his skull, and began to run at Marc and me with the same zeal and passion that sent #47 crashing through the sagebrush.

I had spent much of the spring in a walking boot cast, recovering from a wicked case of spondylitis-induced Achilles tendinitis, and though I had ridden my bike up the steep incline from Gardiner to Mammoth over two dozen times in preceding months, I hadn't run with such haste since before my tendon flare. As I sprinted the twenty yards to the guardhouse, I prayed my Achilles wouldn't snap, leaving me writhing in pain as 900 pounds of #10 threw me around like a rag doll.

I ran toward the front of the house while Marc opted for the rear. When I turned and looked back, #10 was hot on my heels, closing in for the kill. Like a wolf pack that looks for something abnormal in the gate of an elk, causing them to lock on to that one injured animal like a fighter pilot readying to score a hit, #10 must have noticed the hitch in my sprint, because he opted for me instead of Marc.

The rest was a blur. I assumed I'd be safe if I made it to the front porch of the guardhouse—that #10 would stop at the edge of the grass—but as I ran across the old, creaky wood of the deck, I heard hooves beating the surface in hot pursuit. Now I had really messed up. I would have been better off in the open field, getting raked and kicked until someone came to my aid, but I had put myself against the wall. My only hope was to bust through the front door of the building—if I found it unlocked.

The closest friend I ever made while working with the Park Service rangered with me that summer at the Albright Visitor Center. He had shared the guardhouse with two other roommates over the course of the summer, and the door was always unlocked. But he was a pot-smoking hippie from southern California, and protocol might have changed since his departure back to Humboldt State University for his senior year. If the door was locked, it wouldn't be pretty. In those few hurried moments, I envisioned the thick, daggerlike antlers of #10 busting through the tissue in my back and pinning me to the wall of the building.

I reached for the rickety old screen door, almost ripping it off its hinges, then lunged for the round doorknob of the inside door, closing my eyes and gripping it tighter than anything I had before, in my entire life. The door flew open and I fell inside, slamming the door just in time to stop #10's attempt to follow me right inside the house. My adrenaline had never coursed so strong. I felt sweaty and shaky, excited and terrified—all at the same time.

One of my buddy's old roommates stepped into the hallway in his boxers, a surprisingly calm look on his face.

"What the hell, man? Number 10 chase you?"

Apparently #10 hadn't been as docile as I'd thought during his three-week visit to Mammoth. According to this confident young man in his skivvies, he, too, had been chased back into the house on a number of mornings and evenings in previous weeks. I simply hadn't been around at the right time of day to see #10 display his aggression.

But now I had experienced it firsthand—and I was hooked.

How insane. After working the Visitor Center desk all summer (a sometimes tedious duty that becomes a mild form of torture during the final thirty minutes of a four-hour shift), this was incredible. This was what I envisioned being a ranger was about! Though I didn't help anyone, I felt heroic, accomplished—like one of the vets. I had earned my first stripe that day and would go on to acquire many more over the course of the month.

Before leaving the guardhouse, my young companion (who had shown nothing but tolerance for my interruption of his lazy Sunday morning) said, "Looks like you have a little fan club out there." I looked out the front window. To my horror, I observed half a dozen visitors laughing and recounting what they had just seen. It must have been quite the sight, watching a ranger run for his life.

I tried to go out the front door, but when I opened it, #10 lowered his head and charged again. My shift was about to start, so I decided to exit out the back to get the desk before any of the onlookers could run down to the VC to share their story of the incident. They wouldn't recognize me without my hat and jacket on. I could listen and nod, and then tell them that this kind of thing happens all the time.

Still riding high from my close encounter, once at the desk, I couldn't wait to get back outside; #10 appeared to be flexing his muscles all morning long. Every hour, one of the rangers on rove would come in with some semi-epic story of #10 charging a group of people—nothing as dramatic as my experience, but he still appeared to be in rare rutting form.

Over the subsequent years, I was blessed with many other #10 encounters but none quite like the first. My wife liked to theorize that he recognized my voice, because it got to the point where he always seemed to arrive nearby when I was giving a talk.

I remember one warm October day a few weeks after our first rendezvous. He began to approach while I presented to a group of twenty middle school students from Portland, Oregon. With no female in sight—and assuming he wouldn't come toward a group of people that large—I continued my bear talk as he approached. Then I noticed the eyes of one student who stared right through me, a look of panic on his face. I turned around, and there he was, head lowered, running our way. We ran through the grassy parade grounds in front of the Mammoth Hotel until we reached one of the fences blocking off a sinkhole.

Once there, we darted and moved in unison, attempting to stay one step ahead of the big angry elk, on the opposite side of the box-shaped fence.

Lucky for us, Ranger Keith, who seems to get the biggest joy out of managing the elk of any of the Mammoth LEs, spotted our struggle from the comfort of his sedan, turned on the lights, started hollering through the speaker, and rushed in his vehicle to our aid. The commotion finally caught the attention of #10 and sent him scurrying toward the VC, with Keith close behind. This time, I had narrowly escaped an antlered encounter with #10 and a large group of schoolchildren. Number 10 was raising the stakes.

I still have the notes written to me by each individual student, thanking me for saving them from the big elk wearing the "10" tag. While I like to think my action of ushering the students and teachers behind the fence may have helped us escape harm's way, I believe the notes were really intended to thank me for facilitating such a grand, wild, and unforgettable experience.

On that cold September day when I first encountered the wrath of #10, I had spent the rest of my shift tending to his overly aggressive needs by yelling and hollering all afternoon, in hopes of keeping his antlers intact. All I could think about was the fate of #6 and how I wouldn't allow that to happen to #10. But that meant remaining diligent and on our toes—and keeping our most intense encounters to ourselves. We had to keep the visitors at a safe distance, for if we lost #10, we lost another piece of Yellowstone's wildness.

Four years earlier, my life changed forever when Brian told me I was hired. And while I will never forget that first day wearing the green and gray, with the golden Park Service badge on my left upper chest, it was that wild autumn day in Mammoth, when I first experienced the zealous nature of an elk famous for his antics, that cemented my place in the history of Mammoth Rangers. That was the day I became battle tested, hardened, and fully aware of the responsibility and duty of a naturalist, which extends far beyond our ability to give a charismatic presentation.

Number 10 awakened my senses and showed me the power of purposeful actions. But the original numbers 10 and 6 aren't the first elk to excite the Mammoth community and inspire visitors from around the globe, and they won't be the last. Still, I like to think they were pioneers—bold, brilliant, brave representations of the animal kingdom who allowed us to experience their power and zest for a moment in time.

Number 6 has now passed, and it is believed that the old bones of #10 still roam the Northern Range. Soon, he too will be gone, but his legacy will always survive. For every time I pass the guardhouse as I guide a vehicle full of clients, I tell the story of that cold autumn day. And when I revisit Mammoth each fall in the years ahead, my head will turn with the sound of each bugle and each crashing hoof, in hopes of catching one last glimpse of an old friend with a bright yellow ear tag—the original "10."

7

Ranger Field Journal: A Sampling

May 15, 2007

After another early morning up at Swan Lake with no sign of the female grizzly and her sole surviving yearling cub, I was en route to the Lamar Valley when I stopped by the VC to pick up Sean, one of two other Bear Education Rangers on Yellowstone's Northern Range. Yesterday, I had hoped to set up shop at Dorothy's Knoll lookout—with aspirations of finding a grizzly busting into the elk carcass we spotted on Mother's Day—but these hopes were shattered when I was directed to spend a full day answering questions (of little relevance to the wild Yellowstone occupying my mind) at the Albright Visitor Center. It is hard to imagine how many hours I've spent working the information desk at the Albright VC over the course of the past six summers. Though I relished the opportunity to stand behind the information desk, sporting the prestigious NPS uniform, answering questions, making people happy, and helping plan their trips during the first two—or even three—summers I worked for the Park Service, the charm has worn off. And now, in my second season as one of three Bear Education Rangers in Yellowstone National Park, the roadway constantly calls to me.

On our way out to the valley, we stopped by the Hellroaring Overlook and talked with Jim and his wife, Joellyn, a committed and caring couple from Iowa in their late sixties. The wolf-watching scene in Yellowstone has a very eclectic and interesting cast of characters—a story in and of itself—and I have to say, Jim and Joellyn are two of my favorites. They are dedicated, kind, and sincere; and like so many of the wolf-watching regulars, they have found their own sense of community while tracking Yellowstone's top dog. They also seem to be appreciated by the trailblazer and patriarch of the wolf-watching community, Rick McIntyre, a man I am convinced knows more about wolf behavior than any other two-legged walking the earth.

Jim and Joellyn had seen a few pups and two adults a few hours earlier, from the grand and sweeping overlook, but things had been slow ever since the wolves meandered into the forest and out of view. I told them of my plans to visit the carcass I had seen two days earlier, sure that there would be bears or wolves on it by now, and they confirmed reports of a grizzly on the carcass earlier in the morning.

Though I enjoy watching wolves—especially when the hordes of followers of the recently reintroduced animals aren't loudly conversing—it is hard for me to ever pass up the opportunity to observe a grizzly bear. So much of our time as Bear Education Rangers is spent with roadside black bears that the chance to work grizzly bear jams always remains at the forefront of my mind. And while it is impossible not to marvel at the Serengeti-like scene we witnessed as we traveled the road through Little America on our way to Slough Creek, with numerous bands of bison and pronghorn grazing the rich green grasses, we passed through the herds of ungulates more hastily today.

The waters in the Lamar Canyon remained high, hurried, and turbulent, creating violent explosions of white frothy liquid as the river crashed through the narrowly constricted canyon and met the seemingly immovable slabs of house-sized boulders spread throughout the river bottom.

No matter how many times you enter the Lamar Valley from the west, the sight of Saddle Mountain, leaning off in the distance, and the glacially carved valley floor—dotted with cottonwoods sporadically yet perfectly placed along the banks of the river, and swallowed by a sea of grass—inspires a sense of holiness and wonder for the passionate onlooker.

We could see from Fisherman's Pullout that a dozen or so cars were parked ahead, and my hopes that we would soon be observing a grizzly remained high. One of the biggest challenges of driving our government-issued Toyota Prius was finding a place with enough clearance to park, but the Yellowstone gods must have been rewarding me for my patience and (generally) good spiritedness with the visitors at the information desk the day before. Just as we were about to pass the large pullout perched atop a hill overlooking the western part of the valley's floor, a sedan pulled out, and we swooped in.

Soon after arriving at Dorothy's Knoll, we were rewarded with a view of a griz feeding on the carcass, which he had dragged into a large jumble of downed, river-washed cottonwoods. But the tangle of deadfall made the viewing difficult. If it were not for the congregation of ravens perched on the outstretched limbs of the skeleton trees, finding the spotty patches of brown feeding on the carcass would have been a challenge.

We spent the next several hours with a big group of visitors watching the grizzly, who popped his head up from time to time as ravens, one red-tailed hawk, and a bald eagle soared overhead. At times when the grizzly was out of view, the topic of conversation switched to the avian community—specifically the patience of the ravens, who seemed ready to perch as long as it took to get their turn at the bloated cow elk.

There were reports that a wolf was still in the area, and after two hours of interpreting to the visitors the complexities of bear ecology and politics, a lone wolf appeared on the banks of the Lamar, opposite the grizzly marooned on an island in the middle of the river. By its behavior, I estimated this to be a young wolf, curious about how to get a chance to gorge itself on the carcass he or she clearly was determined to enjoy; yet its coloring had me wondering about its age, as it was neither black nor gray, but somewhere in between.

When the grizzly detected the presence of the wolf, who seemed intent upon lingering around long enough to test the waters, he finally rose from the carcass and began walking around the small island, giving us our first full view of this impressive animal. Any ideas the loner wolf had of feeding on the carcass quickly vanished when the grizzly swaggered around the dead elk, making it clear he intended to stay.

While not the most efficient (the mountain lion reigns supreme in their solo ability to take down prey four times their size) or the most productive (the well-oiled machine of a wolf pack sifting and sorting their way through a herd of elk in search of a weakness are top dog in this regard), grizzlies are the scavenger of all scavengers, bullying other predators with their brute size and strength. Wherever there is a carcass in Yellowstone, March through mid-November, there is bound to be a bruin dominating the prized possession at some point. Park biologists have observed one male grizzly fending off more than twenty wolves on a carcass, clearly showing the canine and feline community who's the king of the mountain.

Though I could have watched that bear all day, we had to attend a meeting with Law Enforcement at the Lamar Buffalo Ranch, which would turn into an event all its own as one of the more personality-rich and newly appointed rangers held center stage. We Bear Education Rangers work under the division of Interpretation, providing a bulk of the education at most wildlife jams, and we are fully capable of managing vehicle traffic until the LEs arrive to take over the mundane task of standing along the road while repeatedly waving one's arms to keep traffic moving. I couldn't get my mind off the wolf–grizzly interaction that was likely unfolding a few miles downstream, but I always welcome the opportunity to be brazen and outspoken among the LE crowd—something they clearly don't expect from a "peaceful" Interpretive Ranger. I love the shock factor when a fresh-out-of-FLETC (Federal Law Enforcement Training Center) LE tries to flex his newly acquired muscle and swag by arriving at a jam and promptly acting like my boss (since interpreters are low men on the ranger totem pole in the eyes of many LEs); and I respond by holding court, rousing visitors by dispensing my bear ecology wisdom with the flow and pace of a modern-day rapper.

Though this meeting was much more bearable than most of the others I had shared with our rivals from Law Enforcement (largely because of the presence of Brian Chan and Colette Daigle-Berg, the Northeast and Tower District Rangers, and two of the finest to wear the uniform), I still struggled to bite my tongue when the machismo bantering neared its climax. Many of the seasonal LEs liked to remind us tree-hugging interpreters of their intensive training, as well as our inferiority when it came to the ever-important Park Service chain of command. Managing a bear jam really isn't rocket science; and while the idea of taking charge and commanding respect remained a mystery for some of the more docile of my interpreter brethren, I have seen many an LE poorly manage a jam, failing to recognize the desire of the animal to cross the road, and therefore, never creating the necessary opening within the vehicle corridor to allow the bruin to follow its desired course of travel.

A growing number of LEs throughout Yellowstone cringe at the thought of standing along the park's roads managing bear jams all day, instead preferring to pull over visitors (often cantankerous in the process), but the crew of Brian and Colette are quite the opposite. They are both old-school vets who smile, work jams themselves, and expect their understudies to follow the protocol they have set forth, which includes willingly spending a day with a roadside black bear and a large cadre of awe-inspired visitors.

The Tower and Northeast Entrance LE crew have a reputation throughout the Park Service circle for being more wildlife and visitor oriented than other members of the same division, largely due to the inspiring legacy of Colette's leadership. And though the area's two above-mentioned leaders are certainly a big reason for the more hands-on approach to Law Enforcement, the relative isolation and lack of an Interpretive Ranger brigade forces the LEs of the park's grandest setting to wear multiple hats. There are a few LEs at Mammoth Hot Springs (Rangers Keith, Joe, and Eric being the exception to the norm) who seek out the opportunity to spend time among rutting elk in the fall and grizzlies roaming the roadways of Swan Lake Flat in the spring; but most prefer to let the noncommissioned, non-gun-toting ranger naturalists deal with these visitor-intensive tasks.

And then there is Kevin Dooley; never have I admired a Law Enforcement Ranger more. Hailing from New Jersey, Kevin is the quintessential park ranger who looks and acts the part. I first met Kevin the summer before receiving my dream job as a ranger naturalist in the park, while camping at Slough Creek. He went out of his way—as he seemingly always does—to stop by our camp to strike up a conversation. At six foot one, Kevin is thickly muscled yet lean and athletic. He has the stride of someone who has spent much of his time on a horse, and his horsemanship is, indeed, a sight to behold. Amiable and personable, I've never met a visitor, local, or fellow NPS employee who didn't admire and appreciate Kevin's welcoming demeanor and passion for the park. Whether perched atop his steed, hazing bison back into the park; traveling with a load full of supplies to the Elk Tongue Patrol Cabin in the third meadow of Slough Creek; or working an early season bear jam along the shoulderless confines of Calcite Curves, Kevin is quick to show his toothy grin and impart some unique piece of natural history knowledge.

I had hoped that Kevin would be at this meeting. We had developed a strong relationship of mutual respect that seemed to influence other LEs who, like me, admired Kevin's style and abilities. Though I believe he was on year ten of his post in the park, Kevin always rolled with the punches, even when doing work I imagined he didn't fully buy into; he never lost that childlike enthusiasm we all share when first putting on the green and gray. Perhaps it is because he is from New Jersey that he awoke every day with a smile on his face and a blessed feeling for his wild Yellowstone home, where he had developed a deep sense of place.

As the final discussion neared an end—a discussion regarding hazing roadside black bears who weren't cooperating—I couldn't help but wonder where in the wilds of Yellowstone Kevin was at that very moment. Probably watching a grizzly on a carcass, with a lone wolf waiting his turn, eight miles into the backcountry along the meandering waters of Slough Creek, his most visited early haunt. Knowing I would soon be relegated to a boot cast due to reinjuring my Achilles, my heart ached at the thought that I would not be exploring the glorious back-country and wild waters of Yellowstone for many weeks to come, in the magic season that is summer. I would simply have to find alternate ways to uncover the wild pulse of the park.

May 16

Today would be the most eventful of my early season. As has been my morning routine, I started the day venturing up to Swan Lake Flat, and again failed to see my griz and her cub. I am starting to feel snake-bitten, as I have only seen her once since the first of the month, and that was over a week ago. Her movements and appearances were so unpredictable last spring; and with the lack of snowpack in the high mountains and the abnormally warm weather, which will inevitably dry out the grasses and sedges earlier than normal, I am concerned that I won't see much of her this year.

I am always perplexed at how this area can be so prolific and rich with wildlife at times, and yet on other days, such as this, there can be a lifelessness about this high meadow habitat that rests so beautifully at the foot of the Gallatin Mountains' most impressive peaks.

New to the role of Bear Education Ranger, Sean traveled with me to the flats in hopes of working our first big Mammoth area jam of the season. But after an hour of watching the reflections of Antler Peak, Quadrant Mountain, Dome Mountain, and Mount Holmes shimmering on the waterfowl-packed waters of Swan Lake, we returned to the Visitor Center, where Sean had the dreaded shift at the information desk. I continued east for another rendezvous with the Lamar.

Driving by the Hellroaring Overlook, I was shocked to see it empty, not one car occupying the small lot that has been home to a dedicated cadre of wolf watchers for most of the month. I instinctively surmised that something had happened overnight. Later in the day, I got reports from the wolf watchers that the pups, who had drawn so much attention in the previous weeks, were moved early that morning by the adult wolves in the pack, and were now out of sight. This gives me mixed feelings. Having the wolves in sight has been a source of great interpretive opportunities, helping my eight-hour shift pass with more purpose and meaning on the days when bear sightings are few and far between. Conversely, I won't have to feel guilty when I drive by a parking lot full of visitors—consisting mostly of dedicated and sometimes overly attentive wolf watchers—who will gladly provide interpretation for the uneducated visitor when I would rather drive up and down the roughly five miles of road between the Twin Pullouts and Calcite Curves, on either side of Tower Junction, in search of a black bear sighting and subsequent bear jam.

When I arrived at Tower Junction, I checked in with Dooley over the radio. He had returned from the backcountry and was working a bear jam near Rainy Lake. I let him know my intention to spend the day back at Dorothy's Knoll if there was still solid bear activity. Hearing our chatter over the Park Service radio, Brian Chan (the Lamar District Ranger, whom I like and respect very much) called and told me I would have a great interpretive opportunity in the valley since there was a large group of people in one of the sizeable pullouts.

I drove by a horde of visitors piled into the Fisherman's Pullout. They were apparently watching wolves from the Slough Creek Pack on a carcass in the river, just off the road, so I could begin spitting some of my bear knowledge to those visitors more enchanted with the larger of the four-legged carnivores.

Just the day before, when Sean and I were working the same pullout with a group of visitors and one of the new Visitor Use Assistant

Rangers—John, a passionate and personable retiree from Boston—
we encountered an intense visitor who excitedly entered the pullout
when he saw the plethora of spotting scopes and binoculars focused on
the river bottom. But his excitement quickly turned to disappointment,
as he had no interest in watching the animal that represented the top of
the food chain in the Ecosystem, instead choosing to narrowly focus on
his obvious obsession with wolves. Always one to enjoy the shock
factor, I responded to the wolf-centric visitor's frustration that we were
"only" watching a member of the *Ursus* family with: "Hell, wolves are
just big dogs. Bears, on the other hand, are the most fascinating animals in the world," which prompted John to quickly add, "Folks, that
is Ranger Michael Leach, one of our less opinionated rangers in the
park."

I can't take credit for the line, "wolves are just big dogs," as this
was one I learned from the bear boys during my first year as a Bear Education Ranger. Yellowstone has always been a bear park, and in many
ways, it always will be. But the new kids on the block have taken the
park by storm. Wolves appear to be the sexier of the two critters these
days, creating a buzz all their own. On the road coursing through the
heart of the Lamar Valley, wolves have stolen the show and created a
friendly wolf–bear rivalry between the two camps. But even before I
became associated with educating visitors about bears specifically, I
observed as a wolf watcher (and sometimes the people watching the
wolves are more fascinating to study than the wolves themselves). And
because the wolf craze became so great, many wildlife enthusiasts were
becoming only wolf aficionados, ignoring the beauty and wonder of the
grazing bison, stalking sandhill cranes, and roaming grizzly that breathe
life and diversity into the region. To each his or her own, of course, but
I've come to believe it is the balance restored—the completion—that the
wolf reintroduction has brought to the Greater Yellowstone Ecosystem
that is the most powerful part of the story.

While I have great reverence for the wolves and find their reintroduction to be one of the most important and historic achievements in the
history of the park—and the entire Northern Rockies for that
matter—I do tire of the wolf-centrism that sometimes dominates the
wolf-watching scene. But truth be told, without the wolf reintroduction, I
don't know if I would have ever become a ranger in Yellowstone; I was

deeply inspired by it, and moved to action by the hatred and vitriolic anti-wolf hysteria that followed their homecoming. It was after watching a documentary chronicling this anti-wolf sentiment that I decided I wanted to advocate on their behalf. I saw this as a modern-day civil rights movement and found purpose in fighting for their right to exist.

Hailing from North Idaho, I had heard the tired old slogans—"The only good wolf is a dead wolf"; "Shoot, shovel, and shut up"; "Smoke a pack a day"—and to me, this was an issue of morals and values over science and biology. The hatred that led to wolf extinction never entirely vanished, and the federal government's reintroduction reignited the fire smoldering within countless communities throughout Idaho, Montana, and Wyoming. We had a moral responsibility to bring wolves back to the park, and by learning all I could about the critical role wolves play within the Ecosystem, I felt I could become a champion of their cause—a loud instrument in the pro-wolf orchestra, striving for cultural change and acceptance of *Canis lupus*.

Like most wolf watchers, I, too, had become consumed by learning the numbers, habits, and roles of as many individual wolves as possible. I became an active and willing participant in the soap opera unfolding on the legendary stage of the Lamar. But now, I'm less interested in the life story of individual wolves, and more intrigued and inspired by the simple fact that wolves once again roam the landscape. I love simply knowing that wolves are prowling the Yellowstone Ecosystem, bringing integrity back to the entire region.

With that said, I must admit that I can never resist listening to wolf ambassador and sage Rick McIntyre, one of the great storytellers of all time, holding court in front of an awestruck group of visitors. No matter how many times I have heard one of his stories (or have attempted to act as if I were somehow less in awe now that I play for the same Park Service team), I, like all the visitors, am still entranced by one of Rick's riveting yarns about an individual wolf—or better yet, the lineage of each individual sprawled out before us. Even when I'm in the middle of interpreting, or simply talking to a visitor, if Rick begins telling a story, I stop my jabber and bend my ear in his direction, in hopes of acquiring some of his wolf wisdom.

But it was still early in the season, and I would have an entire summer to learn from Rick. In the meantime, I was itching to share the knowledge I had accumulated over the last several months with the old-school visitors who wanted nothing more than to see one of Yellowstone's grizzlies. Today, I would be the only Park Service personnel in the pullout, so I would be able to dust off some of my bear facts, stats, and behavior as I readied myself for the daily grind of Tower area bear jams that were soon to come. It was shaping up to be an idyllic day.

When I arrived at the pullout at 11:30, the heat beating down on the pavement felt like that of a July afternoon, but this did not stop what appeared to be the same bear—the one who had laid claim to yesterday's carcass—from grazing up and down the meadow before us. On this sweltering afternoon, the need for post-hibernation calories, coupled with the richness of the grasses, spring beauty, clover and dandelions, clearly outweighed this bear's need to regulate its core body temperature. Food will drive a bear to endure extreme amounts of discomfort. This guy needed to work the low elevation grass while it still had nutritional value, because the grasses would lose their succulence at a rapid rate if the high temperatures kept up. As of today, the Yellowstone River drainage was at 36 percent of its annual snowpack, while the Madison Range sat at a slightly more dismal 29 percent, all of which speaks to a difficult year for the rich vegetation so vital to a bear's survival.

I never have an easy time leaving a site that has a grizzly visible, but today was even more difficult, as the bear continued to graze— visible to the naked eye—well into the afternoon. But I had to get back to Gardiner for a basketball camp I was running early in the evening. After saying my good-byes to the visitors, I began working my way back to Mammoth.

Soon after I dropped down into the Fisherman's Pullout, I saw that Erin (one of the new—and beautiful—wolf-study crew members) had a circus of sorts on her hands. The pullout parking lot was full, with two-dozen tripods and, by my estimate, at least $75,000 in lenses occupying a third of the asphalt. There were three wolves across the road, but the lenses were still focused on a carcass, which I was seeing for the first time. I couldn't believe how close it was to the pullout. These photographers had the opportunity of a lifetime: a carcass within fifty meters of their position and wolves willing to walk across the road to feed, despite the multitude of camera shutters rattling and buzzing in the parking lot less than half a football field away.

Erin is a biologist by training and didn't appear to relish the visitor contact that would be a big part of her summer gig. But she seemed talented, committed, and hopeful that she would land a full-time position within the ranks of researchers, and this was the best way for young biologists like her to get their foot in the door—to make a good impression on Doug Smith and Dan Stahler, who lead the wolf-study team. While Erin appeared gentle and quiet, she had a presence about her that warranted attention. Dark flowing hair, olive skin, and the build of someone who cared about her physique—all added to her mystique. Though she clearly had the attention of every LE on the Northern Range (and perhaps even the admiration of those donning a wedding ring), she carried herself with humility. This was not always the case with her predecessors—fresh-out-of-school biologists eager to land a spot on the most famous wolf-study team on the planet.

As I passed through, I leaned out of my window to ask if she needed help, and she responded, "That would be awesome," with a deep breath and sense of relief (I think it was still her first week or two on the job). After bringing me up-to-date on what was going on, she told me of the vision that kept occupying her thoughts as she scrambled up and down the asphalt each time a member of the Slough Creek Pack attempted to cross the road: there was a blind rise where the wolves were choosing to cross, and the last thing anyone needed was one of the wolves getting pulverized by a speeding vehicle. Managing a disaster like that certainly wasn't how she had envisioned her first days on the job. And as I saw how close to the road one of the gray wolves lay (within feet of the pavement), I instantly conjured up the same haunting concern.

Erin told me the gray near the road was the alpha male of the Sloughs—the same wolf that crossed in front of my vehicle back in February, while I was guiding a couple from New Orleans. It had been an amazing sighting. We had just come through the Lamar Canyon when, from the north, a hulk of a wolf slowly and confidently crossed in front of us. Later that afternoon, as the snow howled and flew, we watched the same wolf copulate from roughly six hundred meters away. Now, the wolf that had captured my heart months earlier lay in harm's way.

Was he too confident? Was he becoming habituated to humans? Or was he simply utilizing the elevated observation perch to keep an eye on the carcass and the remaining members of his pack, who continued to scavenge what little meat remained?

The answer didn't matter; his safety was first and foremost. And after watching the sixth car cruise down the hill completely unaware of the 130-pound alpha, I had to find a way to slow vehicles traveling eastbound while also keeping them from stopping if they did notice the wolf. Though my initial thought was to drive my car up to where I could manage traffic, there was no shoulder between the parking lot and the rise in the road (near the wolf), and the Prius's clearance was too shitty to park without a sizable shoulder. So I limped my way there on my bad Achilles.

I was no more than ten yards out of the parking lot, where hordes of visitors had spent the entire day, when the big alpha wolf took note of my movement and began to stand up. I could just see it now: all the defensive and self-appointed wolf police—visitors who had been watching the wolves since first light—failing to see the predicament he was in and freaking out that I had disturbed him. But then my thoughts turned away from the visitors and toward the wolf himself. I had not felt the least bit threatened by the hefty alpha, but as his attention on me intensified, my heart rate quickened.

Though the wolf didn't approach, he certainly perked up as I walked by him, showing more curiosity than I felt comfortable with—especially with one-hundred-plus human eyes watching my every move. But I will never forget the richness of his eyes as we peered into one another's soul for a split second. I waved for Erin to let one of the cars through so I could move alongside it, using it as a shield for the remainder of my walk to the top of the hill. I was not worried that the wolf would attack, but if his curiosity drew him toward me, I planned to get big—try to scare him—which I very much wanted to avoid with the ever-growing crowd of spectators.

It was an experience I will never forget. To be in the presence of such wildness at such close range, without any intellectual thoughts of what the wolf represents, or of its impact on the Ecosystem biologically or ecologically; to instead be in a situation where, for a moment in time, we were the only two who existed—to share that time, that in-this-momentness with such a soulful creature—is something I will forever cherish.

May 17

It's Thursday, and today I had to attend yet another meeting with LE. Unlike our bear jam meeting, this meeting was led by Doug Smith, head of the Yellowstone Wolf Project, and focused on wolf management. The meeting was timely, considering the events that unfolded all day yesterday, with the alpha male of the Slough Creek Pack setting up camp right beside the road. Doug and a group of LEs had contemplated a series of aversive conditioning (shooting cracker rounds in the wolf's direction) earlier in the morning, but Doug decided against it after arriving at the scene. While the wolf was closer to the road than they would have liked, he concluded that the wolf was not demonstrating what Doug would consider bad behavior.

I'm not one to enjoy meetings of any kind, but like most interpreters, I do savor any opportunity to listen to Doug. It's not that I believe— as many awestruck interpreters do—that the man walks on water simply because he is the head of the Wolf Project. But I very much respect his style, confidence, passion, and demeanor, which are non–Park Service in nature. As I have for Dooley, I have great respect and admiration for Doug, and I can't fathom any other two-legged more fit to be the alpha dog of the most celebrated and scrutinized wolf study in the world.

I first connected with Doug the year before, after I had done a series of interviews for film crews as the park's first internet ranger, earning the nickname "Hollywood" among some of the rangers (sometimes said with affection, sometimes with a slight hint of venom). Turns out Doug has long been known as "Hollywood," as he, too, appears comfortable in front of the camera. And like me, he even seems to enjoy the opportunity—a trait frowned upon by purists.

Today's ranger meeting was more engaging than most simply because of Doug's presence and brevity; however, due to the ego antics of one of the older newbies yearning to express his breadth and depth of knowledge in front of the head of the Wolf Project, the meeting went longer than scheduled. When I saw a chance to get the hell out, I made my break.

Dooley had already left to respond to a bear jam at Elk Creek, and now we were getting a call about a large jam building at Rainy Lake. I quickly got on the radio with Colette, the Tower District Ranger, and volunteered to help. She obliged by sending me that way, and as I was walking out the door, another call came in saying that we better hurry; a visitor was reporting a bear tearing the hood off a vehicle. Now, all but the wolf-obsessed few, still enamored by Doug's charisma, scrambled out the door and to our government vehicles. There wasn't a need for all of us to respond, but this was shaping up to be one of those can't-miss moments we yearn for.

When Brian Chan, Dooley, Colette, and I arrived, I was shocked at the scene unfolding, which looked like it was straight out of the '60s (from 1931 to 1969, Yellowstone averaged forty-eight bear-inflicted human injuries and over one hundred incidents of property damage per year before the implementation of a new bear management program aimed at reducing human conflict in 1970). The bear that visitors like to call Rosie (I call her "the black with two red ear tags and two yearling cubs,") had her front paws on the hood of an SUV, her yearlings following suit. It wasn't until we hazed her and the cubs away from the road that we were told the driver struck a deer earlier in the day. As members of the bear family, who have the keenest sense of smell of any animal in North America, and being habituated to people, the three bears were attracted to the leftovers on the grill.

I was bummed I didn't have a camera with me to document what I had just witnessed. To make my error worse, Mom and cubs returned two more times throughout the day. It simply amazes me, with the profusion of lush vegetation throughout the area, that a little blood can be such a strong attractant—such is the power of a bear's nasal membrane.

In pursuit of more tasty offerings, Mama Bear returned to mount Dooley's front bumper, searching the truck's grill for spattered bugs. Those of us who remained in the area hazed her again, this time throwing and rolling rocks in her direction while yelling. She fled into the meadow below the road, and we assumed all of the harassment had moved her on to greener and more natural pastures.

Just as I was about to leave the scene, Greg Reed, the bear ranger from Canyon, arrived. He had hurried over Dunraven Pass after following the events over the park radio. Greg—one of my all-time favorite interpreters—was bumming because he hadn't worked a jam in two shifts. Though Tower was not part of his typical beat, like the rest of us, the thought of experiencing a moment for the memory bank was too much to pass up.

It had been over an hour since we last saw Rosie, and the rest of the rangers had returned to the road, leaving Greg and me. I, too, was beginning to think we had seen the last of the fearless black bear and her cubs for the day. But then, on the verge of giving up, we spotted the fat black female working her way down to the road, cubs following right behind.

We rushed out of my vehicle, where we had spent the better part of an hour catching up, and got in position to manage the traffic that would surely follow. Unfazed, the famous female, who had spent much of her life around people, walked right past Greg and me, completely undisturbed—on a mission. She locked her sights on Greg's vehicle, which was parked in the same spot as the one that had rewarded her two hours earlier, and proceeded to climb onto the hood of the government rig. At one point, all six of the front paws searched the hood of the vehicle, with mother and both cubs appearing to eat a few bugs before they wandered over to my truck (my supervisor had taken my Prius for the day). Failing to find a scent worthy of their interest, the three began working their way back up the road, in the direction they had arrived.

When Dooley and his seasonal backcountry cohort arrived, we all grouped together to yell and clap the gregarious bears off the road. One cub did respond by climbing a few feet up a tree, but in general, they ignored our aggression. We all watched as Rosie and her cubs called it a night, meandering through the mixed lodgepole and fir forest, returning to their place of refuge. The roads now quiet, another eventful day in Tower's bear-rich world was behind me.

On the drive back to Mammoth, the fate of Rosie weighed heavily on my mind. I am starting to worry that these bears are becoming too habituated, and this is a concern—not because I believe the bears will injure anyone but because they are more likely to be hit by a vehicle the more they linger along the park's roadways.

People who have experienced the bears of Yosemite always express great concern about any bear like Rosie who demonstrates such tolerance of humans; but in Yellowstone, habituation is not always a negative. There is a big difference between a human-habituated bear and a food-conditioned bear. A food-conditioned bear is one who has developed a taste for anthropogenic food sources, such as garbage, birdseed, dog food, and other scented items, like cooking grills and grates. A human-habituated bear is one who has lost its natural fear of people, but this varies in degree.

Stephen Hererro, author of *Bear Attacks: Their Causes and Avoidance* (Lyons Press, 2002), writes about Avoidance Reaction Distance (ARD), which differs for each individual bear. The fact that a bear has a shorter ARD and a greater tolerance for humans is not always a problem in the relatively protective confines of Yellowstone. While a habituated bear is more likely to be hit by a car or fed by an uneducated visitor, there can be positives to bear habituation that, when not combined with food conditioning, sometimes outweigh the negatives.

But this certainly wasn't the case with one of Yellowstone's most legendary roadside bears of the last twenty years. Two sixty-four, a female grizzly, delighted thousands of park visitors during her lifetime. She roamed the flats of Swan Lake each spring, scavenging winter-killed elk; and in early June, she killed elk calves in front of hordes of stunned photographers and wildlife watchers who had come to get a glimpse of her hunting prowess—and willingness to exercise it in close proximity to the road. Over the years, 264 carved out a roadside niche where she would graze the grasses, biscuitroot, and yampa with her three different litters. The first bear jam I ever worked was August of 2002, when 264 walked within thirty feet of me as I held up one side of a barricade with bear biologist Kerry Gunther—in an effort to create enough space for 264 to cross the road. It was at that moment that I realized I wanted to become a Bear Education Ranger in Yellowstone; 264 was my inspiration.

But on a summer day in June of 2003, 264's life came to a sudden and tragic end when she was struck by a truck, breaking her spine and paralyzing her lower body. In an attempt to save her, the Bear Management team rushed her to Bozeman, Montana, but it was quickly determined she would not survive. With a dark cloud hovering over the northern reaches of Yellowstone, one of the greatest bears to ever walk the hallowed grounds of the world's first national park was put to rest.

Two sixty-four's story clearly represents the negative side of bear habituation. Another black bear was hit and killed in Yellowstone that summer, leading to an energized discussion of what is acceptable bear behavior. But the flip side to those deaths is that roadside habitat represents well over fifty thousand acres of suitable habitat for bears—habitat utilized by subadults and females with cubs, while the dominant males tend to occupy the biggest, wildest, most untrammeled habitat in the Ecosystem. We have built roads through some of the richest bear habitat in the entire park, and for those bears willing to tolerate people—to have a shorter ARD—the benefit of the succulent vegetation and lack of dominant males in these areas can be significant.

While speeding cars represent a very real hazard, there is absolutely no way to downplay the value of the bear education that is facilitated by bear jams—ultimately leading to bear conservation. People will only fight to save what they love and only love what they know; and this love and knowing is unfolding every summer day at bear jams throughout Yellowstone National Park. That said, I still worry about the fate of Rosie and her cubs, and don't want to see another bear in Yellowstone end his or her life on the asphalt.

One thing is certain: it is going to be an interesting summer when Rosie kicks off her two cubs, who have little fear of people. I hope my Achilles will hang in there so I can enjoy what is to come. . . .

May 23

I returned from Missoula today for the afternoon session of training. I'm always shocked by how few local Idaho, Montana, and Wyoming rangers there are, as most of the folks packing the room hail from east of the Mississippi. Though it is day three of the long training session, there is an electric energy in the room full of veterans and rookies. The rookies have a naïve and nervous excitement about them; while the veterans walk with a quiet confidence and sense of peace that they are "home," clearly grateful for the honor of another summer representing Yellowstone National Park. And here I am, in a fucking walking boot cast.

I had held out hope the entire drive to Missoula that my orthopedic doctor would simply opt for giving me an injection of cortisone, which is always tricky when dealing with anything near the Achilles, but she decided to play it safe and relegate me to the boot cast for much of the summer. My heart ached more than my leg. I, too, had arrived with great excitement and anticipation for another summer of rangering in the park, but now I felt as if my bubble had been popped. Feeling the energy in the room made my pain all the more difficult.

I received reports from a few different people late in the afternoon that someone had been mauled by a grizzly in the Hayden Valley. The next morning, the one and only Jim Williams (one of the backcountry rangers) read me the press release, and I immediately thought of Jim Cole. Later that morning, I found out Mr. Cole was indeed the man mauled. I can't say I was surprised, but I was saddened. He already has such a bad reputation around the park (and probably earned it), but you never know if you can trust such rumors.

This time last spring, I was just getting to know Jim Cole. And though he is definitely brash and arrogant, I have to say that I kind of like the guy. He was kind enough to draft a mock journal page for me so I could emulate his journal style, which he shared with me one day when we were speaking about field journaling.

Reports are that his face was ripped off after encountering a female grizzly with cubs out along Trout Creek. He had walked out pressing his palm to his face—otherwise, the skin covering his facial bones would have simply hung as he walked the three miles from where the incident occurred. Days had passed since his life-and-limb encounter with a protective mother bear, and I know nothing of his condition other than he is stable.

I can't imagine what will become of Mr. Cole if he is no longer able to wander around the backcountry of Yellowstone. Though his eclectic and sometimes confrontational personality made some enemies in the park, and while he clearly needs to discover a less intrusive way to experience the grizzly bear he so reveres, he has now been mauled by grizzlies in both Yellowstone and Glacier National Parks. I'm afraid that he will die of a broken heart if he can't continue to walk the depths of this wild country.

June 7 (Gardiner)

After the driest and warmest May I have experienced, the rains yesterday brought rejoicing not only in Yellowstone Country but all over the state. In fact, it has looked all day as if the clouds may again empty their contents on the still thirsty grasses surrounding Gardiner, but I have yet to see so much as a drop. Even so, the grounds around town are saturated with water we desperately need.

Yesterday was about as wet as I have ever seen things in Livingston. My dear friend Allison, in her second season as a ranger naturalist in Mammoth Hot Springs, had accompanied me to the Garden City, and we were on our way back from Missoula when we arrived in Livingston to a steady downpour that inundated the streets and low points of the wind-tattered town. The rain had begun early in the morning in Lolo and continued all day across the southwest part of the state. I don't think the rain followed us; it was already there—already wherever we went—giving the rivers, mountains, and valleys an overwhelming barrage of H_2O.

I have really struggled the last three weeks since hurting my Achilles. I have such a difficult time dealing with being laid up in a boot cast, unable to observe the daily changes that occur this time of year in Yellowstone. Though my first reports of an elk calf came on the morning of May 24 from a park visitor, and my wife, Crystal, reported a similar sighting only days later up in Mammoth, it was just today that I saw my first elk calf of the season. It was a spindly little thing—lightly spotted, thin, and gangly. At first glance, I thought the little bugger was injured, reminding me of the elk calf two summers ago that limped around most of the summer with a broken front leg. But then the long back legs of the calf begin kicking like a rodeo horse, as if something was nipping at its heels, and I could see all was well with this little one.

And these weren't the only reports. I heard of bighorn fawns in the Tower area the week of May 21, and then, on her way home from work, Crystal spotted several ewes with fawns dancing up the precarious slopes below Osprey Tower in the Gardner Canyon. Several days later, on the 31 of May, I witnessed my first bighorn fawns of the year in the same area. And on our way to Cody—which turned out to be a very eventful day—Crystal and I watched the alpha male of the Slough Creek Pack cross the road around 11 A.M., then caught sight of three rugged members of the Mollies Pack just west of Sedge Creek, near Mary Bay, around 7 P.M., two of which had the most distinctive colors I have ever seen on a wolf: black tails, black faces, and brown bodies. Earlier that day, I also spotted my first Canada geese goslings of the year at the same place in the park that the first sighting has occurred every year—on the grassy banks of the Gardner River in the Chinese Garden area.

On June 3, while driving to Columbus for my first basketball tournament as head coach of the varsity boys' team at Gardiner High, a half-dozen pronghorn fawns showed themselves between Livingston and Big

Timber, on the south side of the road. We also spotted one later in the afternoon, as we were passing the airport; the female and one fawn were crossing the flats near the Stephens Creek road. Two of the three prong-horn mothers with the fawns had twins.

After two days of summer basketball, I was relieved to be back in the comfort of my home, admiring the magic summer light illuminating the Sepulcher foothills. As I was taking out the garbage last night, I noticed a huge moth tightly grasping the weathered cedar of our fence— the most amazing moth I have ever seen outside of the island of St. Maarten. I quickly called my neighbor Randy to come check it out, and he identified it as a cecropia moth, the largest moth in North America.

Even from the confines of a boot cast, restricted from exploring the rivers and mountains that haunt my daily reveries, Yellowstone's wonders remain accessible to an uninhibited mind.

Just before dark tonight, I went to see if the moth was still there. It hadn't moved an inch. And I took Crystal out to marvel at the intricate beauty of the fat, juicy bug.

8

Wild Entrapment

I first met Travis Wyman on a hot and arid August day in Yellowstone National Park. I had known of Travis and his work in the Yellowstone Center for Resources' Bear Management Office, but in my five summers working as a ranger naturalist in a park legendary for its bears, our paths had never officially crossed. It was my first summer as a Bear Education Ranger, and we had reached the peak of the late-summer doldrums that take the bears of Yellowstone to the high country.

While there had been a drought of bear jams in preceding weeks, there was no shortage of visitor traffic, so I started each day driving the winding road from Mammoth to Tower, hoping to spot a bear foraging the roadside vegetation. Along the curvy section of road from Calcite Overlook to Tower Fall as I approached a sweeping meadow full of downed, dead (but still standing), and live Douglas fir trees, where black bear sightings were a daily event throughout the summer, a man in uniform waved me down. It was Travis.

Excitement rushed through me as I pulled in behind his government truck. I hadn't seen Travis at a bear jam all summer, so I knew this must be something big—no ordinary event.

Tragically, I was right.

Though we didn't know each other, I thought I sensed relief on Travis's face when I stepped out of the car. Perhaps it was simply seeing another NPSer, as it became immediately clear that we had a crisis on our hands.

En route to dealing with a bear wandering through the Canyon campground, Travis had been the first on the scene. Within minutes, more men and women dressed in uniform arrived; and within an hour, it seemed every able-bodied Park Service employee had been directed to assist the search and rescue taking place along the precipice of the Grand Canyon of the Yellowstone.

For the next hour, Travis and I stood at our post at the farthest point of the Calcite Springs Overlook, peering into the gorge that constitutes the northernmost reaches of one of North America's most magnificent canyons. Our assigned duty: watch a barely distinguishable figure far below for movement—any movement.

An extensive recovery operation was in progress. The body below us was that of a woman who had just taken an unthinkable fall of more than eight hundred feet. Knowing she could not have survived, our hearts ached for the victim and her family. Travis's and my feeble attempts at conversation felt distant and distracted, almost surreal.

Two years after that unsettling first meeting, Travis and I were reunited. Travis, whose stepfather is legendary backcountry ranger "Action Jackson" (for speaking out against park policy that put bears and humans at risk), grew up in the wilds of Yellowstone, spending many summers in the historic Thorofare Ranger Station, the most remote dwelling in the lower forty-eight. He began working in Yellowstone in his late teens, and even after seventeen years of sporting the Park Service uniform, Travis's love and enthusiasm for the Ecosystem remains inspiringly high.

One might expect that our shared experience the sad day we met combined with our shared love for wildness, Yellowstone, and bears to be the catalyst that formed a friendship so strong it has led our families to share Christmas Eve together at Mammoth Hot Springs every year (the Leach-Wyman tradition). Ironically, it was our mutual passion for sports—in particular basketball—that ultimately brought Travis and me together.

Travis was in his second year as the assistant varsity basketball coach at Gardiner High (Gardiner is a Yellowstone gateway community crazy about its hoops), and I was just beginning my first year as the head coach. It was clear from the first week of practice that we were going to make a good team; but while I sensed he liked the energy, passion, and spirit that I brought to the program, I wasn't so sure what Travis thought of me and my knowledge of—and burning love for—bears.

There is a somewhat dysfunctional relationship—or total lack thereof—between the different divisions in Yellowstone National Park. Yellowstone is such a massive park that if it weren't for our annual meeting to start each summer season (where all rangers working in the Interpretation Division come together for an intensive three-day training session), I would have no clue as to who works in the same division in Grant, Fishing Bridge, Old Faithful, Canyon, Madison, and perhaps even Norris. So the sheer size is a definite factor, but then there is also the cultural makeup of the Yellowstone Center for Resources, which keeps its staff an island unto themselves.

If you are not a biologist, it's a hard culture to break into. Part of me had no interest in even attempting to do so, but the truth is, I found the work they did "over there" absolutely fascinating. Wolves, bears, bison—all the sexy stuff that I lived and breathed—that's what members of this auspicious fraternity focused upon.

And then a miracle happened. Even as one of the park's Bear Education Rangers, I had never gotten any play with the Bear Office folks; yet now, as the head high school basketball coach, with Travis as my assistant, doors were beginning to open.

As our morning practice got started the day after Thanksgiving, Travis mentioned that he would be journeying down to Old Faithful later that day in an attempt to trap a malnourished black bear wandering around the snow-covered landscape and complex of buildings that surround the world's most famous geyser. He invited me along. While I had a newborn at the house, as well as my folks and sister visiting, this was an amazing opportunity to get into the park's interior, to look for and possibly trap a bear, and to kick it with my new assistant, who was growing on me each and every day.

I hadn't been on the interior park roads since the first Sunday in November, when, under cover of darkness, my dad and I returned to Gardiner from our annual foray to the haunted waters of the Madison for our yearly fly-fishing adventure. Now it was late November and the roads were in flux—not enough snow for oversnow (snowmobile) travel but too sketchy for a traditional four-wheel-drive vehicle. But it didn't matter. Thanksgiving season or not, I felt more like a little boy on Christmas morning. Though I had worked my share of bear jams over the course of the last two summers, traveling in the presence of the man who is summoned whenever there is a bear crisis in the park would be an unmatchable treat.

As agreed, I met Travis in the YCR (Yellowstone Center for Resources) parking lot an hour after practice. We had both transformed ourselves from sweat-suit basketball garb to rugged, outdoor regalia. Travis wore his Carhartt-style, green Park Service pants with a pair of knee-high leather winter boots, a black turtleneck under a gray Park Service shirt, a charcoal-colored wool vest (the type the local outfitters and Montana Fish, Wildlife, and Parks personnel wear), and an older green NPS fleece bearing the golden Law Enforcement insignia on the right sleeve.

Walking to Travis's work rig—a beat-up, white Chevy Silverado pickup with sixty-seven thousand miles on it and a winch to haul carcasses off the road, to one of the park's many carcass dumps—I slipped, grasping at the air in an attempt to recover, before falling hard to the ground. While I caught myself, it was one of those quick and sudden jolts to the spine that leaves you with a stiff back for the remainder of the day. With the swagger of a man clearly in his element, Travis ambled to the driver's side door of his rig as steadily as a good horse walks a slippery trail he's traversed hundreds of times.

The interior park roads had been closed for several weeks now, but the roads that remained open around Mammoth also had a strange desertedness about them. Maybe it was the cold temperatures or the layer of snow covering the pavement, but something was keeping visitors out of the park during this holiday weekend. The small cadre of dedicated wolf watchers in the Lamar Valley might be the only ones bold enough to endure the freezing temperatures.

After a short drive to the Upper Terraces, where a gate barricaded further travel into the park, Travis stopped, turned off the engine, and slid out of the driver's seat. It was like watching an old cowboy getting out of his truck to open the barbwire gate to spread the hay that feeds his cows. Travis is a big boy: six foot one, 235 pounds, and stout. He played baseball in college but has the look of a linebacker or a wrestler. Thick-boned, he has muscled legs and a back that resembles the trunk of an Engelmann spruce. And his forearms appear to be under constant tension, hardened by the pressure of opening traps, handling bears, and butchering carcasses.

After casually sliding his key into the lock at the barricade, he let the chain drop and dangle from one end of the extended pole while he walked the other end open. That simple act constituted for me one of the great joys of being an employee of the NPS in Yellowstone National Park. Even though I seldom used the keys for work purposes, there was a certain romanticism knowing I had the option of doing so. I jumped out of the truck as Travis returned, no words spoken. He climbed back into the driver's seat and pulled the truck through the opening, barely bigger than the width of his steed, as I shut the gate behind him, blocking the mysterious winter world of Yellowstone's interior to the next journeyman with keyless luck.

While Travis tended to sit back at practice to absorb everything before entering the fray, he took on a different personality when we crossed the Park Service barricade. It became clear that he was most comfortable—in his element—in the mountains. Though we were still in the vehicle, there was a wildness to the heavily rutted roads and lack of human presence. Trav reminded me of some of the guys I had played basketball with in the past. Put the uniform on, and come game time, they went from quiet and reserved to confident, almost cocky. Travis had worn the esteemed uniform of the National Park Service for so long that I imagined there to be a familiar comfort to the itchy shirt and stiff pants that had adorned him for almost two decades.

Expertly negotiating the sketchy road, he proceeded to tell me how their office received a call from an LE (Law Enforcement Ranger) at Old Faithful earlier in the week, informing them of a grizzly cub wandering around the area alone. If the report of the grizzly COY (a cub of the year) turned out to be true, he would almost certainly perish. A grizzly cub should weigh between sixty and eight-five pounds by November of its first year, and the report had this bear being much smaller. Add to the small stature the fact that a grizzly cub typically stays with its mother for two years, and this bear was in big trouble.

Travis informed me that after driving down the day before and searching the area for the grizzly cub, whom he hadn't been able to find, he'd come upon a black bear cub rummaging around a collection of empty dumpsters. According to Travis, "The little guy was climbing all over the bear-proofed dumpsters like some kind of monkey."

Shifting his efforts to the black bear cub, Travis had pulled an aluminum culvert trap down from Mammoth and piled hay inside it, in hopes that the approximately twenty-five-pound cub would follow its natural urge to bed down and go to sleep.

When we reached Swan Lake Flat, wind funneled off the summits of the Gallatins, pounding the windshield and rattling the hood of the truck. Only twenty-five minutes earlier, we'd left a clear sky in the high desert of Gardiner, but now we traveled in a blinding whiteout. The gale blew snow across the road, creating massive drifts, which Travis expertly navigated. Not long after we entered the lodgepole pine forest near Indian Creek, the skies started to clear again, and by the time we reached the ominous flanks of Roaring Mountain, it had become a bluebird, early winter day on the Yellowstone Plateau.

An enigmatic beauty surrounded us as we drove along the banks of the Firehole River in this winter environment. By now, Travis's forearms had to be fatigued from the constant pulling of the rutted road, which became worse with each mile traveled. But soon the snow froze, creating a hardened track for our truck's wheels to roll through, finally taking away the need to constantly correct the wheel.

We shared many life stories and a lively discussion the entire way to Old Faithful. What typically takes an hour and fifteen minutes in the summer took us two hours on the treacherous fifty-one miles of road.

Visiting Old Faithful between seasons was an otherworldly experience. Driving around the complex, we craned our necks, looking for any sign of the little twenty-five pounder. As we were driving around the historic Old Faithful Inn, a lone man wandered out of the building. He seemed excited to see someone with whom he could strike up a conversation and went on to tell us about the problem with the boiler he was trying to fix. It felt like a scene out of *The Shining*—so desolate and harsh, with this lonely maintenance worker, probably in his fifties, laboring to keep one of the most famous structures in the National Park system from freezing to death.

After fulfilling the pleasant man's need for human contact, as well as our desire to hear if he had seen the bear, we continued the hunt on foot. When we finally came upon tracks—just the right size and shape— we followed them around the inn and then forged on, to continue in the bear cub's path of travel. Not long after, we spotted him.

When we first caught sight of the young chocolate-brown black bear, he was perusing the sparse vegetation along the northwest wing of the inn, scrambling up and down the steps, and eating rose hips, which remained a viable food source due to the southern exposure and warmth radiating off the building. I was astonished by the size of the little guy. He was literally a small ball of brown fur, with long, pointed ears disproportionate to his head. While he was clearly underweight, he appeared full of life. But he was completely unfit for hibernation. If we were unable to help him, he would surely starve to death.

After locating him, I followed Travis's cue and quickly worked my way back to the truck. Since he hadn't cooperated with Travis the day before, we'd come better equipped this time—with the hindquarter of a mule deer. Our goal was to get him to the culvert Travis had set out the previous day. One would think this would be an easy bear to trap, as his need for food should have surpassed any antihuman sense his mother had taught him.

My adrenaline soared at the thought of taking the cub back to Mammoth. Travis, on the other hand, remained cool and calm. This was old hat. It wasn't that he didn't deeply respect the cub or wish to help the little guy. Travis had simply captured so many bears—including four-hundred-pound grizzlies—that there was a visible sense of routine to the task at hand.

The thing I quickly observed about Travis—and have since learned to greatly appreciate—is his creative knack when it comes to deriving a solution to a bear-related problem. After studying the bear through field glasses, Travis grabbed the front quarter of the mule deer he had left in the trap the day before, which had gone untouched, and began to slowly and confidently walk toward the little tyke. When he'd gotten within fifteen feet, the cub finally reacted by vocalizing his displeasure. At that point, Travis grabbed the end of a ten-foot rope, which he had secured to the ankle of the still-hardened section of deer, and like a bait fisherman hoping to entice a shark, simply tossed the quarter toward the frightened, confused cub.

Watching this interaction fifty feet away, from the cozy confines of the truck, I could see there was a deliberate method to Travis's actions. Once the meat hit the ground, he began walking quickly to the road, never looking back—with bear cub in pursuit. While the cub remained reluctant to get too close, his sense of smell had clearly overwhelmed all other reasoning.

When Travis reached the truck, the bear cub stopped twenty feet short of it and stared with intense curiosity as Travis circled to the back tailgate and adeptly executed an overhand hitch, securing the end of the rope to the ball on his bumper. Calmly, as if he had done this a hundred times before (which I suspected he had), Travis walked his slow, cowboy gait back to the door, climbed in, and started the engine. The four-wheel-drive turning radius of the government-issued Silverado surprised me as Travis spun the steering wheel hard to the right and we slowly began traveling down the road, in the direction of the trap.

Had it not been so heart-wrenchingly pathetic, it might have been a comical sight. I sat on my haunches on the front seat, facing the back of the truck, watching as the front quarters of a road-killed mule deer slid back and forth, dragging behind us—the raggedy cub trailing its every move.

As it turned out, Travis hadn't devised this plan solely in hopes that the cub would come barreling down the road in pursuit of the meat. It was as much intended as an effort to stimulate the bear's incredible capacity to smell, which, by most calculations, is seven times that of a bloodhound and twenty-one hundred times that of a human.

We continued to the culvert trap, put the meat inside, and began a long and uneventful wait. It was already late afternoon, and we didn't want to travel the hazardous roads in the dark; time was running out. And it soon became clear to Travis that the cub wasn't going to cooperate. At least not today.

With only an hour and a half of light left, Travis made the decision to abandon the mission once again. He didn't show anger, disappointment, or even frustration; it was what it was. While I don't think he relished the idea of driving the frozen, rutted, shitty roads again the next day, I could tell he loved that he was interacting with a member of the *Ursus* family long after most had gone to sleep. He wasn't about to bat an eye at journeying back to Old Faithful again the next day. For Travis, any day in the field was better than punching data and numbers in the office. Whether it was to retrieve a collar, re-trap a study bear, or help an abandoned cub make it through winter, this passionate bear biologist lived to be in the field. And while he may not have said as much, it was clear that he relished the opportunity to find this orphaned cub a winter's home.

The drive back to Mammoth was magnificent. The wind let up, and the western horizon danced with different shades of pink and orange alpenglow highlighted by wispy clouds, their colors amplified by the setting sun. Again, it took two hours (we could have driven to Missoula in the four hours we'd spent in the truck that day), but the time couldn't have passed faster. I actually felt a hint of disappointment as we arrived back at headquarters.

A few days after our Thanksgiving adventure, Travis finally trapped the runt of a bear with the aid of Old Faithful LE, and on the slightly thawed, still heavily rutted road, pulled him back to Mammoth in the culvert trailer.

For the next few days, the cub—who had frantically scrambled throughout the grounds of Old Faithful Inn in a struggle to survive—received buckets of apples from the trees out at Stephens Creek in an effort to help him consume the calories necessary to make it through a very active hibernation. Since park policy dictates that the disturbance and interference with wildlife remain minimal, the decision was made to transfer the scrawny little guy to the Stephens Creek area, where it was hoped he would hibernate for the winter.

But he still needed lots of caloric supplementation before his body would begin the physiological transformation to hibernation mode. So Travis and his boss, Kerry Gunther (another kind and impassioned bear biologist, who has extensively studied Yellowstone's bears), continued to bring apples to his nest until they felt he was ready to sleep. Because bears don't shut down to the extent of other members of the hibernating community—metabolically speaking (they can be easily aroused during hibernation)—the only hope of survival for our twenty-five-pound cub was a continual "dumping" of food, which is how Travis described his job preparing the cub for hibernation. They had to dump food on the little guy to get him as plump as possible, bringing him two-dozen apples a day, with elk quarters thrown in for protein.

Finally, after his weight had tripled, they took away the food to trigger the physiological changes necessary to induce hibernation. It was Christmas Eve.

One day, weeks after the bear boys, Travis and Kerry, felt the bear cub no longer needed nutritional supplementation, Travis invited me up to visit the little cub who had captured my heart and imagination since I first saw him wandering around the wintery landscape on the barren grounds of Old Faithful. Now that Travis and Kerry no longer supplemented him with food, their visits had decreased in frequency. This would likely be one of Travis's last walks to check on the cub, who had clearly become a mission for him.

As we headed out that day, I wondered how they knew when the bear no longer needed their support. What I learned is that not every decision is based upon a scientific formula. The reality, in fact, is quite the opposite. Many decisions are dictated by the years of experience of folks like Travis and Kerry, and their best guess—another thing that amazes me about these two dedicated Yellowstone bear experts, and something that makes them irreplaceable.

We had just completed a midweek 6 A.M. basketball practice on a cold January morning. I followed Travis in my truck out to the point where we would start our short walk.

I'd had trouble getting the bear off my mind for weeks; my wife, Crystal, had heard me speak of the little roughneck often. So with my baby girl, Kamiah, just two months old, strapped to my stomach and cocooned in my parka, the four of us—Crystal, Kamiah, Travis, and I—began the walk through shin-deep snow for a short visit with a black bear cub gripping to life. The bitterly cold wind hustled off the slopes of Sepulcher Mountain and slapped us in the face.

When we reached the bear's first winter den, I was surprised to see it protected by a wire enclosure. Bales of hay had also been stacked around it, intended to discourage any predators from disturbing what everyone hoped would be a deep winter's sleep.

One of the reasons I have grown to love Travis is his devotion to the bear—a reverence that we share, and one that deepens our bond and friendship. He made it clear ahead of time that today's visit would only be a quick look, as he didn't want to stress the little guy any more than necessary.

Travis lifted the door on the cub's manmade den and, without a sound, dark rich eyes peered back into mine.

For me, it was a life-transforming experience.

Kamiah had experienced her first of many bear encounters (inches away from an eight-hundred-plus-pound captive grizzly) two days before her birth, in her mother's belly, as I worked with members of a film crew on a short bear-education piece—so her nickname, "Boo Bear," is fitting for my Yellowstone wild child. Though she had no idea what she was seeing this cold winter's day, I like to believe she felt it—that there was power in that moment. How could there not be? She was looking into the eyes of something wild—a spirited, orphaned bear who had overcome all odds by remaining alive, strengthening the pulse of Yellowstone in the process.

I thought back to the day we brought our little cub home from the hospital in Bozeman. She wasn't yet forty-eight hours old when, passing the turnoff to our house, we drove her through the grand and historic Roosevelt Arch. We took pictures in front of the Yellowstone National Park sign, and then walked her out to a meadow where I had witnessed wolves, bison, bears, pronghorn, bighorn, elk, coyote, and deer. I believe the presence of these symbols of wildness breathe their spirit into the landscape.

After placing a blanket on the cold and hardened ground, I laid down my bundled daughter and said a prayer. I prayed that she would endure the obstacles she will undoubtedly face with the grace, strength, and courage that embody the land, health, and spirit of Yellowstone.

On the day that we visited the orphaned black bear cub—sleepy now and ready to hibernate—just like the day two months earlier, when my newborn daughter rested on the sacred ground of Yellowstone, I experienced a moment of spiritual tranquillity; pure, innocent, resonant. Though brief in time, it was profound in nature; it changed me for the better.

That would be the last I would see of the Old Faithful black bear.

Or would it?

Perhaps, when making my fall treks up to the summit of Electric Peak, while sauntering through the thick whitebark pine just over the ridge where I last saw him, I will see him again. And maybe, if I'm lucky, I will once more look into the eyes of a wild animal whose life story I will never fully know, but who once deeply touched and inspired my own.

9

Christmas In Yellowstone

Ever since I was in my teens, the idea of spending a Christmas in Yellowstone sounded like a dream. After injuring my back and hanging up the basketball kicks, I felt lost—in search of new dreams while mourning the old ones. Without the game that had played such a pivotal role in my life, I struggled to find my identity. Then one day, I read about the opportunity to celebrate Christmas at the Mammoth Hot Springs Hotel. Inspired, my high school sweetheart, Crystal, and I made a valiant effort to make this dream come true, but that year, we failed. A few years later, however, my new bride and I ventured east along I-90 for a three-day stint of cross-country skiing and wolf watching on Yellowstone's Northern Range. Largely because of this and other trips to the park, I rediscovered myself, and uncovered new hopes for the future.

Although I had been visiting the park since my days as a toddler, that short journey in January during my second year at North Idaho College gave me my first taste of winter in Yellowstone. And it is hard for any wilderness aficionado not to love Yellowstone's longest season. The crowds are long gone and a stark feeling blankets the landscape. Sluggish and unhurried, the frolicking wildlife and raging rivers that will spring life back into the countryside when warmer temperatures return now meander and retreat. But don't let the cold temperatures, deep snowdrifts, and all-consuming silence scare you away from experiencing the joy of this winter wonderland.

Before graduating from the University of Montana, Crystal and I purchased a humble little 1920s bungalow in Gardiner. After signing the papers—entitling us to thirty years of debt counterbalanced by a lifetime of memories—I remember how excited I was as we walked along the reemerging waters of the Bitterroot that warm April day. "This year, we will finally celebrate Christmas in Yellowstone," I declared.

And though we haven't spent all of our six Christmases since moving to Yellowstone's doorstep in the glorious grasp of the Gardiner Basin (due to the birth of our daughter, Kamiah, and family gatherings in Lolo, Montana—a starkly different, yet powerful place), over time, the Christmas holidays in Yellowstone have provided rituals we will forever cherish.

This year, in typical Yellowstone fashion, after a long spell of bitterly cold temperatures (-20°F was not uncommon, with highs rarely reaching 0 degrees) and dry weather, with barely any white garnishing the hills surrounding our home, we awoke on Christmas Day to a dusting of snow. Each year, the feel of this holiday varies, depending upon the snowfall; and with the snowpack below 75 percent this Christmas, Yellowstone's Northern Range certainly didn't have the aura of a winter paradise. But regardless of snow depth, the last week of December in the world's first national park always produces winter recreation opportunities to fulfill the traditions of even the most demanding Yellowstone purists.

In our tradition, on Christmas Eve, we load up the Tundra and venture up the often sketchy road from Gardiner to Mammoth. After passing through the North Entrance station—cheerfully decorated with white icicle lights—the truck's two beams of light lead us up the windy and precarious hill to the park's headquarters in Mammoth Hot Springs. This time of year, the road is typically barren of wildlife, but every so often, the eyes of a bighorn sheep, mule deer, elk, or bison will catch the glare of our headlights and send a sudden bolt of excitement—reminiscent of summertime—through passengers in the vehicle.

Once through the fog lingering around the Chinese Gardens, just south of the 45th parallel, the remainder of the two-mile climb unfolds quickly as we anticipate the festivities ahead. Our first stop is always the Mammoth Hotel, where we stroll into the exquisite Map Room to listen to our dear friend—and guardian angel of our little girl—Randy (or "Doons," as she calls him) work his magic on the keys of the grand piano, to the delight of the Christmas regulars. Then, after a few carols shared with these recognizable strangers (it's funny how the faces with whom we have sung for years are familiar but the lives unknown), we skate on the soles of our shoes across the ice rink of a parking lot to the dining room to meet up with Travis Wyman and his family.

In the Leach-Wyman tradition, we share a holiday meal at the Mammoth dining room with my assistant basketball coach and bear management specialist; his wife, Beckie; and their two children, Parker and Marley, who are the best of friends to Kamiah. While the menu changes from season to season and year to year, depending upon the head chef, we can always count on a belly full of beef, bread, salad, and trout by the end of the evening.

This year's Christmas was taken to another level entirely, as Kamiah, who turned two in October, was letting us all know about her desire to open presents from Santa. Boo Bear, as we like to call her, symbolizes what makes a Christmas in Yellowstone an experience beyond anything else I have ever known. While the visitors in summer sometimes detract from one's appreciation of the natural wonders that abound in Yellowstone, there is something about the pure joy and peace radiating from each man, woman, and child during this special season that confirms what one already knows in their heart: we are truly blessed to share this special time on a sacred landscape. Unlike other seasons where I venture far and wide in hopes of avoiding the presence of talking two-leggeds, on Christmas Eve at Mammoth Hot Springs, the company of my fellow man and carolers adds richness and abundance to a unique and unwavering experience.

On Christmas morning, after the spiked eggnog has worn off and the presents have been unwrapped, running into a jolly family ambling along the Upper Terrace Loop is part of the beauty of venturing out on skinny skis in pursuit of a little exercise—four thousand calories still bloating your belly from the previous night.

The snowpack was thin at best this Christmas (and only worsened with the lack of snowfall in the days leading up to New Year's), but the track was fast, the skies clear, and the hot springs flowing, making our annual Christmas Day ski as memorable as ever.

Still, it is not the ski tour that sparks the greatest memories of a winter holiday spent a mile above sea level in the middle of the Rocky

Mountains. It is, instead, our pilgrimage to a spot like none other—a spot with scalding waters surging out of travertine caverns and flowing into the ice-cold Gardner River. A place known as the Boiling River. It is always crowded on Christmas Day, but the free-spirited, swim-suit-wearing river rat can more often than not find a spot to his or her liking. I feel for those who missed the opportunity to gingerly dip a tired and achy body into the hot and cold waters of the Boiling River this year, because the experience has been as good as it gets. I cannot remember a December with more pockets of hot water and fewer pulses from the cold Gardner River to interrupt your winter serenity.

Perhaps the most amazing phenomenon of bathing in the Boiling River is the way your aching muscles suddenly feel supple; and how, even on the coldest of winter days, your expanded blood vessels keep your body comfortably warm while walking the quarter mile back to the parking lot with your towel draped around your neck. Is the Boiling River magic? Well, if you consider the definition to be "any art that invokes supernatural powers," then I would have to answer yes. The hot water surging into the curvy ribbon of a much-revered trout stream, at the base of the mysterious sandstone bluffs of Mount Everts, is as fine a natural canvas as exists in Yellowstone National Park.

Yes, indeed, wild wintery magic exists for the Yellowstone believer. And it's there to be experienced by all those adventurous enough to take the plunge on what will inevitably become a spiritual journey; perhaps even, as it has for my family, becoming a ritual. Celebrating Christmas in Yellowstone.

10

Ode to #6

It has been a sad week here in Yellowstone Country. One of our most beloved and fierce warriors of the Northern Range was found dead just north of the park over the weekend. Visitors from all over the world had come to admire and respect his fervor and zest for life. On Sunday, February 8, his body was found within a few hundred yards of the main drag running through Gardiner. After slyly avoiding another late-winter hunt, a mishap while jumping a fence in town apparently took the life of an animal who will go down in Yellowstone folklore. Perhaps no other recent icon of Yellowstone National Park has displayed more audacity than this big old elk, known simply as #6.

Each autumn—beginning in late August, thanks to the high elevation of this region—roughly one hundred elk, including cows, calves, raghorns, and satellite bulls, congregate in and around the park headquarters at Mammoth Hot Springs. In response to this massive gathering of ungulates, roughly a dozen bull elk descend upon the area in hopes of passing on their genes to as many willing cows as possible. The less dominant bulls may be successful in assembling small harems, ranging from three to ten loyal females, but two bulls have come to rule the elk orgy that follows the busy summer season in Mammoth: numbers 10 and 6. Known simply by their ear tag numbers (anytime the resource managers in the park have to sedate and capture an elk, it receives a numbered orange or yellow ear tag), both #10 and #6 have reached legendary status among visitors and residents of the Mammoth/Gardiner area.

For years now, on any given day in late September or early October, it has not been uncommon to see big #6 with a harem of thirty to forty females. With the exception of #10, few other bulls in the region seriously contested his dominance. Many have tried to sneak a few females from his harem, and even acted as if they wanted to battle, but when it came down to #6 displaying the aggression necessary to defend his flock, most competitors simply fled. A pretty mild-mannered guy for nine months of the year, he'd spend most days peacefully grazing the tender spring grass in the Lava Creek area, or calmly sitting below a particular apple tree each winter—one in the heart of Gardiner, just off Scott Street. During the height of the rut, however, in my seven years as a ranger naturalist, I have never seen another elk create more havoc and show more warrior spirit than #6.

For me, the news of the fifteen-year-old bull's tragic and untimely death triggered tears and plenty of memories. Despite my title as Bear Education Ranger, my duties were diverted each fall to the suddenly bustling metropolis of Mammoth's elk show, which enveloped the historic district. And though my closest calls with any animal in the park or elsewhere remain two encounters with #10, #6 dominated my autumn as I worked to keep the people at bay. I would watch with glee as the big old elk tore up grass, chased intruders (two- and four-legged), and on numerous occasions, mashed the front grill of a rental car. In fact, his antics were so outrageous and notorious that in the fall of 2005 and 2006, the Park Service ordered his antlers cut off—an action that not only robbed this much-beloved animal of his glory but also his means of defending himself in battle with other bulls. Despite the thousands of dollars in property damage that #6 was credited with and his continued acts of aggression in subsequent years, the public outcry and support for the old guy was so great that in the autumns that followed, the Park Service declined to take further action.

In 2008, my last fall working on intermittent status with the Park Service, a story worthy of #6 began to circulate around the Mammoth staff. Though his guilt was never proven, the facts were that an elk with a massive rack and an aptitude for damaging valuable property had raked the hell out of the park helicopter, leaving his mark on one of the most expensive resources in Yellowstone. Number 6 was later seen calmly strutting on a hillside above the helipad. The sentiment among most of us was that this proud elk may have finally achieved retribution for the humiliating and endangering removal of his antlers years earlier.

As we celebrate the life of #6, one last image of the hulking brute comes to mind. It was a cold and foggy afternoon late last February. I was on the big black bus with my boys from the Gardiner Bruins basketball team (whom I have the privilege of coaching), on our way to Livingston to play our rivals from the Shields Valley in a challenge game that would advance the winner to state. We could sense that it was going to be a wild night, but none of us knew upon leaving Gardiner that we would be making history—that later that evening, we would participate in a game the *Livingston Enterprise* would headline "The Greatest Game Ever Played," and the *Bozeman Daily Chronicle*, "A Game for the Ages."

As we slowly drove down the main street in Gardiner, which had shut down in anticipation of the game, a massive figure stepped into our path of travel. He simply stood, stopping our bus in its tracks. With a slow tilt of his head, we were able to see the orange tag hanging from his ear. Almost in unison, with equal parts excitement and awe, we called out his name.

He stared at us for several seconds. Then he swaggered down the middle of the road approximately fifty yards before ambling off the highway, heading down the hill toward the river.

On that night—the night that eighteen young, nervous, impressionable boys journeyed north with my assistant, Travis, and me to participate in an event so beautiful and powerful that it will always be a part of who we are—the Gardiner Bruins boys' basketball team was escorted out of town by none other than an unruly, beloved, and magnificent legend of Yellowstone. Number 6.

11

The Story of the Kestrel

Late last night, as the light faded from clarity to what seemed to be a fog, I rode my bike down to the Devil's Slide overlook. The day before, I had been in a meeting with Glenn Hockett from the Gallatin Wildlife Association, where we spoke of the hypocrisy surrounding the agencies and NGOs (nongovernmental organizations) involved in the bison wars. There is a placard at the overlook that I am thinking I will need to vandalize in order to bring a sense of reality to the visitors who stop to read the half-truths found at this exhibit—on their way to God's theme park, Yellowstone.

The placard describes the migratory movements of pronghorn, bighorn sheep, and elk but fails to even mention the largest migratory animal left in North America—the bison. The agencies and NGOs who sponsored the roadside exhibit chose to leave out an animal that symbolizes the phenomenon we call migration. While reading the empty, vague words, I lifted my eyes to the expansive corridor on the west side of the river, and there, below the monument that the devil himself created, were three shaggy bison stoically perched atop a hill in defiance of the fanatical property owners on whose ground they stood.

One day, I will likely do my part as a free-spirited participant of democracy and civilly disobey the law, which tells me to leave the sign alone. But today, I decide, is not that day.

Wind is the one constant of any bike ride or fishing endeavor in the Gardiner area. On this mellow evening ride, the wind, which was raging days before, allowed the flag at the Forest Service office to hang limp—a cause for celebration. I hadn't traveled a quarter mile outside of town when I spotted what looked like an old rag in the middle of the highway. As I approached, I quickly realized I was looking at one of our winged community members—one whom I deeply respect—the American kestrel.

I dropped my bike on the pavement and hurried to the bird's side. Kneeling in the roadway (there were no vehicles in sight), I gently dipped the fingers of my right hand under its tail feathers and carefully moved up its backside until the bird's lifeless body rested in my palm. I then began to scan for the nearest sagebrush, which I found fifteen feet off the road, but this particular bush appeared lifeless and was no place to rest this pillar of the aerial community.

Inspired, I scurried up a steep, sandy slope to a rugged rock outcropping where sagebrush dotted the hillside. When I found what appeared to be the healthiest of all the gnarly bushes, I got down on my knee in the dirt and held the brilliantly colored bird in my hand as I said a prayer to the Creator for its spirit.

I had just begun the prayer when my words froze—my mouth open but no sound funneling from it. I realized I was holding a creation of stealth-like perfection. Admiring her rusty plumage, rufous back, and dark, black wing bars, I noticed her black talons were tightly curved, the way a man would desperately grasp at anything if someone were forcefully holding his head underwater.

Though nothing rested in its grip, I could imagine how many times the bird's talons had forcefully closed around the skull of a vole as it scavenged the earth in search of a morsel. It was a spiritual moment, holding the smallest of raptors—one I have respected for many years, since I grew accustomed to watching her hunting the meadows of our old ranch house nestled above Lake Coeur d'Alene.

Midway through my prayer, I stopped again, my heart rate increasing several beats. I began to study the body of the speckled bird lying in my hands and discovered that there were no apparent injuries—no blood, no gaping wounds. For the next few minutes, I thought I felt a heartbeat, a twitch, subtle signs of life. Perhaps this little warrior of the sky world was just shocked from bouncing off the windshield of a speeding car. But after several minutes of examination, I realized my hopes were mere fantasy.

As I finished my prayer for the kestrel, a large band of perhaps three dozen ravens, soaring in the thermals above, caught my attention. As I stood to walk back down the hill, I saw a large feathered mass from the right corner of my eye. I crossed the ten yards to where it lay off-trail. The critter's burnt orange tail feathers quickly identified it as a red-tailed hawk. Standing over the corpse, I wondered what would have killed such a strong bird, who, just like the kestrel, showed no visible signs of injury. Shaking my head in astonishment, I spotted what looked like yet another dead bird.

This time, I walked right into a massacre. In the next ravine, four ravens and a young osprey lay lifeless, all within twenty-five feet of one another. Again, there were no feathers scattered about, there was no blood—no damage at all to their seemingly perfect corpses.

Furiously, I concluded a two-legged culprit had to be poisoning an entire community of our winged friends, and a sudden urge to get back on my bike gripped me. I couldn't bear to see any more carnage. That is when the story began to rage like the swollen torrents of the Yellowstone River a few hundred yards below.

What first appeared to be a white plastic garbage bag thirty feet away transformed as I approached the noble head of a bald eagle, body intact and showing no signs of distress. Adrenaline coursed through my body, and my breath began to increase to the point of dizziness. I hadn't moved more than seventy-five feet since the end of my prayer, but my heart was pounding as if I had just climbed fifteen hundred feet in elevation on the bike.

Startled, I jumped a rabbitbrush to race for my bike. But before I had taken five steps, I stumbled upon the largest bird I have ever seen in my life. I knew only one species could be so massive—a bird that can be seen soaring a mile into the sky. Its dark brown feathers, bright yellow talons, and honey-colored head caused my lower jaw to drop. Aloud, in shock, I announced, "a golden eagle."

I fell to my knees and spoke aloud a prayer to the heavens, the kestrel's feathered body still engrained on my brain. I don't know how long I had been speaking to the world, but I certainly will never forget the sudden burst of wind that slapped the left side of my face and the back of my neck. Again startled, my eyes opened as wide as a blooming bitterroot. And what I saw next still seems a creation of my own imagination.

All of the lifeless birds began to rise as one, flying in unison, the kestrel held gently in the talons of the golden eagle. They continued to ascend in a thermal, soaring together, the body of the kestrel still lifeless.

The band of raptors and the four ravens were nearly out of sight when I saw something burst from the talons of the golden eagle and soar high above the rest.

My friend the kestrel was now soaring straight toward the summit of the sky, and the rest of the birds—who were lifeless minutes ago—parted ways. The ravens began to swoop toward the dump, the osprey back to its river perch, the red-tailed hawk to the edge of a meadow, the bald eagle to its branch in the cottonwood, and the golden toward the summit of Electric Peak.

My focus turned back to a faint light soaring toward the heavens.

They had all come together to celebrate the life of their friend. Together, they had lifted the limp body of the kestrel and restored its vitality for one last flight—to a place where her spirit will forever dance with the masters.

12

Bitterroot Paint

After a difficult weekend, today doesn't get any easier. It's a cold and blustery day in Gardiner, with temperatures hovering in the single digits and clouds hunkering tight to the eastern slopes of Electric Peak and Sepulcher Mountain. The time is 1:45 P.M., and the Creator is welcoming one of the great warrior horses into the Spirit World on this winter afternoon.

Hers is the story of a four-legged with a spirit like few others. She is a strong and determined paint named Moxy, and she has taught all two-leggeds blessed enough to participate in her journey the meaning of struggle and perseverance. Her ability to nicker and forge on in the face of immense hardship is a lesson to all of us as we navigate through this life of ups and downs.

While it feels as if she has been among us for a lifetime, Moxy only entered our lives in the last decade. Before coming to our family, she lived a life of neglect and suffering. One would never know this when in her presence, because of her gentle persona and strong character, but it quickly became apparent that the apparatus of greatest importance to a horse—her feet—were permanently damaged from the lack of attention she received in her early years.

Moxy's journey with the Leach clan began in the open pastures and tall grasses overlooking the Heart of the Lake in the ponderosa forests of North Idaho. It was here that she came to understand what the love and compassion of a guardian angel could do to ease the frustrations accompanying her handicap. Within weeks of wandering her new home range, Moxy discovered that she had been adopted by her guardian, and no matter how great her pain, the love of the beautiful woman with wavy blonde hair always made the struggle worthwhile.

After a few winters enduring the muck and moisture of her hilltop pasture, Moxy readied herself for her move to her final destination, a place she would always cherish as home. The journey over a pass of great significance to her family—a pass called Lookout—delivered her to the fertile valley of the Bitterroot. Alongside the meandering Bitterroot River, tucked away in an oasis of cottonwood and ponderosa, with the constant chatter and companionship of a diverse and eclectic group of winged friends, Moxy had found her ultimate paradise.

Though the time she spent in her new home was not without pain and suffering, it was here that her spirit finally felt at peace—here that her guardian's devotion and tender care comforted and protected her on a level no four-legged ever thought possible. And on this, Moxy's last day in the physical world, there is no doubt that her love of place, and her loyalty to her longtime companion and barn mate, Daisy, gave Moxy much strength in her struggle; but I know, in the end, her faith in her guardian angel, who dedicated herself to making her life more comfortable—and whom she eagerly awaited each morning, afternoon, and evening—gave Moxy the courage and mental fortitude to whinny each visit, pressing her soft, steamy muzzle to her angel's cheek in gratitude.

As I play with and feed my little spirit baby, Kamiah, yet another lover of Moxy—and, as the only Leach to ever ride the warrior horse, the only one in our clan to actually feel the great paint's power beneath her—my mind is consumed by all the lessons and blessings this ailing horse has shared with us. I think back to all my prayers to the Creator that Moxy's feet be healed and her suffering ended. I remember the Thanksgiving when we both suffered together as I lay beside her, my left arm around her neck as my right arm shielded my face from the freezing rain. I remember the many times I brought my medicine bundle to Moxy's side, rubbing her shins and feet in hopes that the bundle's power—combined with the sincerity of my prayers—would make a difference and lessen her pain.

So today, it was with great sadness and a heavy heart that I prepared for one last ceremony for an ailing horse resting in Lolo. Just before 1:30 P.M., I pulled out my medicine box filled with the most powerful, sacred medicine I know, and with deep thought and a strong spirit, filled a palm-sized seashell with sage and buffalo hair that I had gathered on a sacred journey with a man the Assiniboine call Medicine Warrior—a spirited, heartfelt man who helped me during a time of my own great suffering. We picked the sage on August 11, 2001, 365 days after a wedding ceremony the Leach clan will always hold near to our hearts.

With feather, shell, sage, buffalo hair, and matches in hand, I ventured into the frigid winter day without gloves or hat as an offering of suffering to the Creator. I slowly climbed the boulders in my backyard, which were covered in ice, and thought of the age when these great pieces of granite were deposited by the Pinedale Glaciation fourteen thousand years ago. The day they landed on this spot must have been cold and blustery much like today.

When I arrived at the altar that a holy man created for me beneath the lone tree gracing the hillside—a site overlooking my sacred Yellowstone National Park—I found my boulder and prepared my mind for one last ceremony to honor a critter that I have given more prayer and ceremony than any other living being. I pulled out an eagle feather that Medicine Warrior had given me as an offering during our 2001 quest and took four deep breaths, swiping the air with the feather toward my face and over my head with each exhale—an act of cleansing.

"Aho, Creator! I thank you for this day and for all that you have blessed me with. I say a prayer for the less fortunate; for the hungry; for all of the winged, finned, and four-leggeds who need your help, Creator. But this prayer, Creator—this prayer is for an incredible warrior horse named Moxy, who is with my mom in the Bitterroot Valley. I thank you, Creator, for blessing us all with being a part of this great horse's life, and give thanks for all of the lessons, love, and strength she has shared with us. Moxy has taught us how to live, one day at a time, and she has shown us that no handicap can define us; she has demonstrated what perseverance really means.

"Creator, I ask you to watch over Moxy and her guardian, my mom, on this day. Give them both strength. I ask you, Creator, to end Moxy's suffering and welcome her into the Spirit World, where she will feel no more pain, and will dance and prance with Sweetness, Teton,

Archie—all of the four-leggeds who are no longer with us. I say this prayer with all of my strength and all of my faith, Creator. Aho."

And though there was more, this is what I remember of my final ceremony for the paint that hobbled into our lives one calm summer day. I said a few more words and worked my way out of the wind, down to the deck behind my house.

Next, I said a prayer with the buffalo hair and added it to my medicine bundle, which dangled from my neck; then I lit several matches until the dried sage began to smoke. After clearing my head with the powerful essence of the sage, I pulled out my eagle feather and smudged once again, drawing the smoke with the feather into my face and stroking it over my head. After scampering back up the hill, I fanned the smoke away from me, toward the summit of Electric Peak, saying, "Aho, Creator. I ask you to take the spirit of this prayer and the power of this smoke over the summit of Electric; over the Gallatins, Madisons, and Tobacco Roots; through the Big Hole Valley; and over the Flint Creek Range, Garnetts, and Sapphires and blow it into the ear of Moxy, who lies along the Bitterroot in Lolo."

Before leaving my perch overlooking Yellowstone, I yelled four times: "Aho, Moxy! Aho, Moxy! Aho, Moxy! Aho, Moxy!"

After I said these words, I brought the smoke into the house and hurried to Kamiah's crib, where she had been put down for her afternoon nap but was not yet asleep. With the burning sage and the eagle feather, I said another prayer as I smudged her for the first time, pushing the smoke into her face and rubbing her cheeks, body, and head with the eagle feather. Though she couldn't understand what I was doing, there was a depth in her gaze as I gently brushed her skin with the velvety feather. My last gesture with the smoke was toward Kamiah's rocking horse, Moxy. I directed the final, lingering puffs all around it and then rubbed its feet just as I had with the real Moxy on many occasions. With one final flip of my wrist toward the toy horse and one final push of smoke toward Kamiah, I sounded one last "Aho!"

All of us who have come to know the power of Moxy are better off for being a part of her journey. Just before I sat down to write this tribute, I went back to my altar overlooking the wildest piece of ground that I know and said one final prayer. This time, I asked the Creator to keep Moxy in my heart so that I might use her journey as a tool to keep the dramas of life in perspective. Moxy may not walk this world with us anymore, but she will always live on in our hearts, our minds, and our stories. And I, for one, know that another powerful, strong, and determined female is now among us in baby Kamiah. May Kamiah always have Moxy's strength and spirit coursing through her—especially as she learns of the day she became the one and only member of our family to ride the great paint.

13

Only In Yellowstone

Only in Yellowstone could the first hour of one's day begin with such natural drama. While countless adjectives describe Yellowstone, "unpredictable" surely ranks at the top of the list. And this blizzard ravaging the northern reaches of Yellowstone Country couldn't have come at a worse time.

As is often the case this time of year, I stay up too late, oversleep my alarm, and in the morning, find myself frantically getting Kamiah dressed as I throw together her lunch and snacks for the day. Before moving to Yellowstone, I spent my entire life in the Columbia watershed; but now, the ol' Pacific time zone handicaps me. Turns out that one extra hour makes a big difference when the NBA playoffs are at their peak. Games that used to start at 7:30 P.M. Pacific Time, ending no later than 10:30 and getting me to bed well before my 11 P.M. danger zone, now start at 8:30. This puts me in the predicament of staying up for the conclusion of the game and slowing me down the next day, or doing the responsible thing by enjoying the first half and getting to bed at a decent time.

So you see, there are tradeoffs to living in Yellowstone Country. It's not all frolicking bison, wild trout, backcountry powder, and scenic vistas. We are in the midst of what feels like our seventh month of winter, and our Rocky Mountain time zone keeps us up later than we should be during the NBA conference playoffs.

After scrambling to get a light breakfast in my little girl's belly, I sat her in front of the television and told her I was going to start the truck—that I would be right back. But as is often the case with our adventurous nature baby, she wasn't having any of the TV, and instead followed me outside, into a raging snowstorm. With winds whipping both the falling flakes and the settled snow into a fury, it was difficult to tell how hard it was actually snowing. As I struggled to open the tailgate of my truck, my arms filled with fly rods for the third in a series of four fly-fishing tutorials I was going to be late for at the high school, I heard Kamiah's cry from behind the locked gate. Wearing her Seattle Supersonics sweat suit and kid-sized, yellow ball cap to commemorate the playoffs, she grimaced as snow pelted her face.

Just then, several inches of accumulation from my truck's roof came crashing onto the tailgate as it slammed down, so I dropped the fly rods and scooped up Lil' Stuff while I still could. With her giggling delightedly to be out of the storm's fury, I settled her in the toddler seat and cranked up the heat. Typical of Yellowstone Country, the first twenty minutes of our morning had already started in an eventful fashion.

But things were about to get downright strange—another adjective that describes many aspects of Yellowstone Country. First, there are the oddities that are the geothermal features, which abound throughout Yellowstone National Park and are not found in such density anywhere else on our planet. Then there are many of the people who call the Yellowstone region home. Now I imagine every region has its fair share of unique folks, but there seems to be a disproportionate number of unusual people in this part of the world. Perhaps it is the landscape that rubs off on residents after having lived here for a certain amount of time, but I also suspect Yellowstone's remoteness and otherworldliness attract more of this type than other places. And I'm convinced that enough winters in Yellowstone can turn otherwise normal people a little weird—this is another reason I coach basketball all winter. To maintain my sanity.

As I rushed out of the driveway and down the twisting road that leads to town, I felt my tires slide and brakes lock, and with a shake of my head (it is May, for God's sake!), I put the truck into four-wheel drive.

The drive from Gardiner up to Kamiah's day care in Mammoth takes about fifteen minutes. For seven years, when I worked for the Park Service, this constituted my workday commute—a commute that has to be one of the most spectacular in the world. Barring a complete whiteout, which was beginning to look like a possibility today, you can always count on stunning views of such natural treasures as the fast-moving Gardner River, stoic Rocky Mountain junipers, steep rocky outcrops with crumbly sandstone hoodoos, and the impressive Bunsen Peak. On any given day, you might also see migrating bison, large bands of elk, resident bighorn sheep, nesting golden eagles, soaring osprey, meandering grizzly bears, or wandering wolves. While it's not likely you'll see all of these animals on the same drive, the potential for such sightings tends to keep one eye focused on the narrow, curvy road, while the other searches for movement in the surrounding wilds.

But due to the weather, driving through the canyon this morning—where thick plugs of mud and massive boulders that descend during summer rainstorms often lead to road closures—I focused entirely on keeping all four tires on the road. On more than one occasion when I've been driving home late in the evening, after giving a program at the Mammoth Hotel or the Indian Creek Campground, I've seen headlights radiating up from the river bottom, after an impatient or impaired driver missed one of the sharp curves in the short canyon section of road.

As we climbed out of the juniper-lined river gorge and made the short descent into the Chinese Gardens, I assumed it was wolf watchers (a culture that often provides some of the earlier-mentioned strangeness) I saw piled into the largest pullout in the stretch of meadow road paralleling the river, just before the steep climb to Mammoth. But as I got closer, I recognized a number of white Park Service vehicles. One of three things could explain this: (1) they had nothing to do, (2) there was something extraordinary happening, or (3) they were concerned about visitor and/or wildlife safety.

It frustrated me to no end that I was forced to pass by without discovering the explanation for this influx of vehicles and bystanders, but I had to get Kamiah to day care and myself to the school. I slowed and scanned the western bank of the Gardner River, looking for the carcass we had seen two days before, which wolves and a grizzly bear had reportedly scavenged. That day, I had personally observed twenty-four ravens jubilantly tearing their beaks into the flesh of the winter-weakened elk (on average, twenty-nine ravens feed on every wolf-killed elk carcass in the park).

At first glance today, it appeared a black wolf was cleaning up what remained of the carcass, but a quick glimpse through field glasses yielded a lone raven—perhaps the largest raven in the world—triumphantly claiming his morning prize.

My curiosity quickly turned to anger as we approached the big turnout and parking area for the Boiling River, at the south end of the meadows, and saw three ghostlike figures atop massive horses riding our way. Why were three cowboys—one as strong and thick as a bull bison, with a handlebar mustache and weather-worn, ten-gallon hat—riding down the southbound lane on this wintry day in May?

My thoughts jumped to the disgraceful reminder of Montana's antiquated bison management policy that had taken place the previous day, when Department of Livestock agents killed two bull bison on the north end of Yankee Jim Canyon. Having seen Park Service officials haze bison lazily bedded down on the forty-yard line of the Gardiner High football field the day before that, I quickly assumed that the men on horseback were there to push bison deeper into the park.

I have developed a pretty good system for my drive to day care with my beautiful little girl. We spend the first half jamming out to K'naan or any other music with a strong beat that Kamiah can bob her head to; and then we talk for the latter part of the drive—about how much her Mommy and Daddy love her, and the events that will transpire throughout her day. But on this morning, the sight of those three macho cowboys embedded in my mind, and all I could think about were the bison that I have such a deep veneration for. I always refer to them as "the elephant of North America" and believe they may just be the greatest treasure Yellowstone National Park can boast of. And yet, we somehow continue to let ignorance and bigotry rule our management decisions regarding these magnificent animals.

Just as I could easily fill the next ten pages with my disillusionment with the Interagency Bison Management Plan, I could have consumed the next several hours of that morning thinking of nothing else. But I was about to send Kamiah off to the unpredictable world of day care, where sixteen two-legged toddlers create havoc each day for the angels that are their caregivers, and I always try to leave her in good spirits and feeling loved. So, I managed to push my fear for the bison back—at least temporarily. Moments later, however, after my daughter bestowed a good-bye hug and kiss upon me, I climbed back in the truck, my anger brewing again.

How can anyone buy the press reports that the two bison slaughtered yesterday were killed because of the brucellosis threat they pose to cattle in the area when, three days earlier, I witnessed several hundred head of elk—who, like bison, carry brucellosis—in the same pastures?

People seem to take offense when I compare wildlife genocides such as the wanton slaughter of bison in the 1800s to those of humans. I assume this stems from the fear and anger that someone would have the audacity to value nonhuman life on a level comparable to that of "soul enriched" people. But to me, it is clear that the same misguided hate that led to tragedies like slavery, disease-infected blankets distributed to American Indians, and the Holocaust now drives the massacre of the last wild, free-ranging bison herd in the lower forty-eight.

By the time I approached the Chinese Gardens, the snow was again lightly falling. I rounded the bend leading to the meadows, where all of the excitement had been unfolding a few minutes earlier, and to my astonishment, the horse carrying the old-school cowboy was standing in six inches of river water while the other two horsemen sat atop their steeds, eight feet off the river bank.

What the hell? My seven years of learning how to think like a Park Service employee finally kicked in and I realized that there must be a carcass in the river. That would explain all of the NPS vehicles hogging the pullout and the lack of wolf watchers. Park Service employees had flooded the pullout to keep the wolf watchers and other members of the public out while they hauled the carcass away from the road.

I slowed to a crawl as I passed by the scene—waving and saying hello to a few of the rangers I knew—and marveled at the brute strength of the horses and the skill of the riders as they dragged a water-logged elk out of the river. I could only imagine the hell that the riders would catch from the wolf watchers—not that an army of spotting-scope-armed wolf enthusiasts would stand a chance in a battle of blows with these three.

Many photographers and wildlife enthusiasts get riled up when the NPS goes against natural regulation policy and doesn't allow a dead ungulate to rest where it took its last breath. And while I often take issue with Park Service policy (as does any free-thinker with a heart), I have to say they have this one right. By leaving the carcass where it was—yes, across the river but only twenty feet from the road—they endanger scavengers and visitors alike. It's true that I'm not particularly fond of the common practice of moving dead animals to one of the carcass dumps, but I believe moving the carcass a safe distance from the road, where it still provides fodder for visitors and safe scavenging for wildlife, is a sound policy. So, my anger over the bison hazing had—at least this time—proved unwarranted.

I will never know what happened to an elk who, in death, no doubt attracted more attention than in life; but this is the story of Yellowstone. Unpredictable, strange, exciting. Yellowstone's splendor and magic rest not only in its abundance and overwhelming beauty but in its oddities and sadness—including its deaths. Though harsh, unforgiving, and often tragic, Yellowstone's workings display the cycles of life, a modern-day saga worthy of her legacy.

14

Hello Again, Old Faithful

This day is long anticipated by those of us who cherish the opportunity to journey into the depths of Yellowstone National Park before the craziness of summer begins. For the first time since the first Sunday in November (always an important date, for it marks both the closure of the park's interior roads and the end of the park's fishing season), the road from Mammoth to Madison Junction and on to Old Faithful is again open to the public. Though the park attempts to open this road by the third Friday in April, the spring snowstorm that descended upon the northern reaches of Yellowstone on the 15 of April threatened to delay the much-heralded opening of an old, rusted gate.

Though subtle, it truly is an event. Hundreds of times each winter, the creaky steel pole that spans the width of the road just south of the Upper Terrace Drive is swung wide by park employees as they move personal items to and from their winter living quarters. The Park Service—which in typical, bureaucratic fashion has some special terminology to make everything seem more important than it actually is—calls this mode of vehicle movement "admin travel." If one were not familiar with the ways of the Park Service, they might assume every employee with admin travel credentials carries some level of importance, but it is simply the title given to employee travel when the park's roads are closed to the public. Still, I have, on many occasions, experienced the joy, the feeling of importance, and the pure exhilaration of admin travel through one of these road closures, which abound throughout the extensive network of roads coursing through the world's first national park.

There is something empowering in knowing that you have a magic key that unlocks the wonders of America's sacred wilderness. Of course, anytime you utilize the barricade key, you are supposed to have a work-related reason to do so; but since I turned in my badges and keys yesterday—officially parting ways with the Park Service and surrendering my ranger status after eight glorious years to put all of my eggs in the basket of a new nonprofit, Yellowstone Country Guardians—I feel free to admit my love affair with parking my government vehicle in front of a barricade, slowly swaggering to the gate, gently turning the key, and swinging open a door leading to my own personal wilderness Shangri-la.

Even though there was seldom a reason, when presentations weren't imminent and bear jams weren't beckoning, the opportunity to swing open a barricade gate—field glasses resting on the dash—in pursuit of a bear sighting that only I would observe was a gift I will always treasure. Never before did I realize that something as small and seemingly insignificant as a gold key could be the source of such unfettered happiness.

This afternoon, the sun shines bright on the summit of Electric Peak as slender cumulus clouds stand still beside both its south and north ridges. The blizzard that raged through the Gardiner Basin just forty-eight hours ago, leaving in its wake a bulk of snow nearly two feet deep on the hood of my truck, seems a fleeting memory. And with the ceremonial swinging of a gate, thus opening the road to Old Faithful, there are new journeys to be had. First, I will venture back to my old stomping grounds atop the flats of Swan Lake in search of a female grizzly with cubs—a bear I spent many years observing and admiring. Then, when the feeling is right, I will load my little girl—who first strolled through the Upper Geyser Basin (Old Faithful's home) at six months of age—into the truck, and we will make her second pilgrimage to its haunting landscape.

Perhaps this is the greatest pleasure of residing in one place for any length of time. Whether it be the April trek to observe the drama of Old Faithful, the budding cottonwoods along my favorite stretch of the Bitterroot River, or the first sight of yellowing western larch in the mountains outside of my hometown in North Idaho, there is comfort in knowing that seasons will return, and with them, the traditions that give each of us our own sense of hope, ensuring that our lives will remain anything but routine.

15

The Hills Are Alive

Welcome to Yellowstone Country. Where a day that sees seventy-two degrees with a hint of breeze and deep blue skies may just as easily be followed by a day with highs topping out at forty-five, dark ominous clouds, and raging winds battering the side of the house. But today, one thing is certain: it is the middle of May and the hills are alive.

Though it takes somewhat of a discerning eye to see it—amid the massive outcrop that is Electric Peak to the west and the gaping mouth of the Black Canyon of the Yellowstone to the east—the arrival of succulent green grasses covering the hills around Gardiner, Montana, is always cause for celebration. In this small, rural, gateway community, we jump at any opportunity to celebrate. Take the high school basketball team, which I have had the privilege of coaching for the last four years. It's been a while since we've accomplished the difficult and daunting task of going to state, but when we do, the townspeople turn out en masse, with fire trucks roaring and law enforcement sirens blaring, to escort sixteen pimple-faced high school athletes through the short stretch of Highway 89 that constitutes Gardiner's main drag.

Unlike more metropolitan towns and cities across the Rockies, we don't have a big Fourth of July parade, and we are without galas for political elections, as we are unincorporated and have no mayor or other elected officials. And because many of us find too much to complain about as it is (the dearth of dining options, the lack of early summer tourists to fuel our economy, the abundance of late summer tourists driving us crazy, etc.), it is essential to find every possible opportunity to commemorate what makes living on the edge of Yellowstone National Park worth the six months of winter.

Unnoticed by those foreign to the Gardiner Basin, and simply ignored by folks too crabby to acknowledge their transcendent beauty, the grasses adorning the glacial hummocks west of town, at the foothills of Sepulcher Mountain, represent a festival of enormous proportions. While it may be as short-lived as two weeks during hot and dry periods (with the potential for as much as six weeks of vibrancy during cool and wet times), regardless of duration, the abundance of birds and insects that descend upon the usually barren hills add winged life to the now rich grassland on the edge of town—and in the process, create a carnival for those eager to explore.

Yellowstone's enigmatic nature is a major part of its charm. While there are numerous well-known treasures throughout the park that bring people from all over the globe to snap a photo, countless unrecognized and seldom-explored gems remain undiscovered to outsiders. Located in the middle of a banana belt of sorts, the abundance of scrub brush and prickly pear cactus that proliferate in the Gardiner area tell the story of a dry, high-desert basin. Because it is devoid of three-hundred-foot waterfalls, massive herds of bison, predictable geysers, and enormous mountain lakes, many visitors simply pass hurriedly through the northern boundary of the park—on their way to greener and more spectacular pastures.

Coinciding with the greening of the hills in the Gardiner Basin, the violent and turbulent waters of the Yellowstone, surging with snowmelt, become a playground for those seeking a taste of white-water rafting adventure. Thus, like the homecoming-queen big sister, unwilling to let her younger and less glorious sibling have her moment of praise, the river corridor pulsing with *mana* steals the show during the foothills' window of brilliance.

Like many other locals, I have been guilty of noting the return of life to the hills—and perhaps even celebrating this symbolic change in my own way—but never fully experiencing it. Acknowledging is one thing; participating is another entirely. You can watch the ball drop at Times Square from the comfort of your living room on television, but this certainly does not make you a participant in the gathering. You are merely a spectator of the crazed and drunken party.

It wasn't until my neighbor and dear friend Doons (as he is known by my daughter), invited me for a walk through what he called "The Magical Sepulcher Foothills Loop" that I fully participated in what I now call "The Hills Are Alive Festival." For many springs, he had heard me talk about my affection for the return of life to the hills around us, but he always told me that I needed to experience what he called "a walk in the hills" in order to truly understand the "magic" I'd admired from afar.

While I am well known for my love of superlatives, "magic" seemed a pretty bold way to describe the seemingly simple landscape on the edge of town. But then again, these are the same rolling hills that I have admired each summer evening around 7 P.M., when the light hits the folds and crevasses in such a way that the phrase "three dimensional" takes on new meaning, the somewhat drab daytime landscape coming to life.

So after several years of turning down Doons (a.k.a. Randy Ingersoll, the soulful and celebrated pianist at the Mammoth Hotel) and venturing to other, more exotic locations throughout the Ecosystem, I opted to take him up on his offer for a short, four-mile, off-trail hike that only he could lead. With twenty-eight years of experience exploring the northern reaches of Yellowstone, Doons understands this land more intimately than any person I know. And when I say exploring, I don't mean the way I venture around the Ecosystem. This man is a modern-day wanderer, in search of lost treasure and simple pleasure.

Now in his fifties, Doons has an energy and passion for sauntering off-trail in Yellowstone that I have only experienced from inspired fly fishermen dedicated to exploring new waters. One of the many things I admire about Doons and his love for Yellowstone is how authentic, pure, and almost childlike his romance for wandering remains. Therefore, I was not surprised to hear the excitement in his voice on a too-windy-to-fish afternoon in early June when I gave him a call and, somewhat guiltily, suggested, "Why don't we go explore those magical foothills you have been dying to share with me?"

Minutes later, I scooped him up at his house (the way most of our adventures begin), and he climbed into the truck with the same trekking poles, worn-out boots, and battered hiking pack that have accompanied him on untold outings over the years. Though I will be a bit vague in describing where we ventured, to protect the "magical" nature of Doons's private wonderland, I will say that we drove less than fifteen minutes before arriving at an undisclosed pullout. There, we shouldered our daypacks, looked around to make sure no one was watching, and quickly scurried up a dirt slope and out of sight.

Knowing that Doons can find beauty in the most innocuous of settings, I have to admit that I was a bit leery for the first quarter mile of our walk through the green grasses—though they were considerably enhanced by a profusion of wildflowers. I was also surprised by the steepness of the terrain that I had looked at for several years now, without ever setting foot upon it. As with any walk across a bed of moist grass and open terrain in Yellowstone Country, within minutes of starting our sojourn, we encountered a diversity of raptors, including two red-tailed hawks and a northern harrier. So even if Doons's treasures yielded little in the way of enchantment, the reward of soaring raptors on the wing had already made the outing worthwhile for me.

One of the things that struck me most while walking through this previously uncharted territory was the sparseness of the grass that looks so thick from below. But the busybodies of grasshoppers, bees, ants, butterflies, and countless other creatures of the insect world overshadowed any disappointment I may have felt from the lack of stems. While I knew it wouldn't last for long, the cornucopia of bugs made it feel like we had entered a Burning Man festival for insects.

Entranced by the life literally buzzing around me, I didn't notice that Doons had stopped, a look of mischief on his face. We had entered a small basin hidden and protected by steep, round mounds of dirt on each side. A modest spring coursed through its center, and—I gleaned from Doons's expression—this little oasis clearly housed something of significance. After leading me a few feet toward the edge of the bottomland, Doons instructed me to look around, then added "on the ground." I hadn't been looking for more than two minutes when my patience began to run thin. Just as I was about to ask him what the hell he had me searching for, my eyes landed upon a skillfully crafted arrowhead.

Doons has always had an affinity for the Native peoples of the West, and his desire to learn more about those who traversed his beloved Yellowstone knows no bounds. While I have logged hundreds of miles in the backcountry of Yellowstone, my footsteps are typically driven by remote trout streams, ridge walks, and mountaintop vistas. It is not that I don't have a deep reverence for the people who called this place home for thousands of years and hundreds of generations; I believe we can't have any true sense of place without a respect for and understanding of the people who came first to it. But the discovery of artifacts has never moved my spirit for exploration. I simply don't have the patience to walk slowly enough, with my head down and my eyes scanning the dirt, to discover remnants of human civilization—clearly a gift that Doons has aplenty.

Dropping to my knee and gently picking up this beautiful piece of work—sculpted from a chunk of obsidian most likely harvested twenty miles south from the point where I now stood—stirred both my heart and my imagination. Looking at the deeply rich black rock, turned into a treasured tool capable of cutting through the sinew of any number of ungulates browsing the area, I was awed by the craftsmanship and intricacy that made this weapon so proficient in the hands of a skilled and determined hunter. A chip in the upper right section of the arrowhead may have spoken to why this valued possession had been left where it now sat. With gentle care, as instructed by Doons, I placed the arrowhead back where we found it, going so far as to line up its edges in the very depression of dirt that it had rested in for an untold number of years.

We were off to a good start as far as I was concerned, and the next stop on The Magical Sepulcher Foothills Loop waited just over the rise. At the headwaters of the spring that gently meandered through the basin where Doons unveiled the arrowhead, we came upon an anomaly befitting of Yellowstone. Though I am by no means an expert in the power of description, I have always taken great pleasure in attempting to transport people—whether through the written or spoken word—to a place they can viscerally relate to. But Stop Number 2 on the loop seemed almost impossible to capture with words.

In a wash more reminiscent of the desert Southwest, the water coursed through a shallow but steep trench made of hard-packed clay before dropping off in a series of miniature plunges. Near the top of the wash was a small pond of sorts that acted as a catch basin for the water traveling through the ravine, feeding life to the small basins below. Off to the side of the pond, approximately fifteen feet away, was what appeared to be a large mud puddle, twenty feet in diameter. It looked eerily similar to the mudpots found throughout Yellowstone's interior, on the high plateau. And while this pot of mud did not boil with the release of gases, nor possess the acidic nature of car-battery acid, its quicksand-like viscosity made it a lethal trap for any living thing curious enough to test the muddy mess.

I grabbed one of Doons's trekking poles and attempted to poke and prod my way to the bottom, never meeting any resistance, even after six feet of pole had disappeared. There was something enchanting about the pool of mud that inspired a pure and uninhibited sense of wonder. While we could have explored this liquid enigma for hours, I knew my little girl would be waking up from her afternoon nap soon, and I hoped to spend the evening with her; it was time to move on to the next stop on the Loop, which was growing more magical with each step.

Before we left, I couldn't help but indulge my impulse to roll up my sleeve and dip my arm as far as I could into the abyss of our mud-riddled sanctuary. I quickly recognized why people pay one-hundred-plus dollars to have someone plaster mud all over their body; because the deeper I reached, the more soothing and intense the cold, thick mud became.

Ultimately, the thought of some mysterious life form living down there prompted me to release myself from the eerie "black hole." Within minutes, its dirt began to dry and crack, creating a full arm cast that, to be honest, caused me a little anxiety because it hindered all mobility. And as we ventured through the upper reaches of the foothills, nearing the Douglas-fir tree line, I stared frequently at the hardened glob entombing my limb. Slowly transforming from man to beast, the mud on my arm began to appear more and more prehistoric—more dinosaur-like in texture and color. I was beginning to shiver. As the wind picked up, the mud sucked moisture from my skin, making my arm feel as though it were submerged in a bucket of ice water. A small price to pay for the childish pleasure that an oversized puddle of mud had provided.

The marginal grassland now gave way to a plush carpet of succulence, filled with grasses, sedges, and wildflowers in the quarter mile leading to the dark and secret forest only one hundred yards away. Just as we topped out on a rise overlooking the entire Gardiner Basin, movement caught my eye in a stand of aspen trees to the southwest. We had caught the scent of elk ten minutes earlier but hadn't seen a single wapiti. That changed when we stumbled upon a herd of more than seventy cow elk zigging and zagging their way through the trees in a semi-frantic effort to escape our approach.

Thrilled by this abundance of wildlife just two miles (as the crow flies) from my house, it took me a moment to realize that Doons had stopped again. Though I didn't see anything out of the norm, I surmised that we must be at the third stop on his Magical Loop. Still focused excitedly on the legion of elk—some of which peered through trees to see what we were up to—I had completely missed the treasure he had led me to.

At the base of a pair of thick-trunked Douglas fir trees stood a tightly woven pile of slender sticks in the triangular shape of a tepee. I wasn't entirely certain if what I was looking at was the structure invented by the Native people across the region for its ease of set up, so I asked Doons, "What is it?"

The awe in his voice audible, he responded, "It's a wickiup."

While he could not guarantee that some summer park employee, infatuated by his latest reading of one of Tom Brown's survival books, wasn't the creator of this traditional structure, the location—overlooking an elk-grazing paradise and off the beaten path—led Doons to believe that this was indeed an original. Regardless of its authenticity, the crude and dilapidated shelter gave us reason to pause. And as we stood there quietly, I could not help but envision a husband, wife, and their newborn child waiting out a storm on a fierce spring day two hundred years ago, en route to their traditional bison hunting grounds. As with any of the treasures Doons bestowed upon me over the years, his words of high esteem were that of a sage: "We look but don't touch."

As we proceeded, insect life was on vibrant display in all directions, affording us a multitude of up-close-and-personal sightings of mountain bluebirds; chipping, vesper, and savannah sparrows; American robins; and countless other songbirds. Just as we were preparing to leave the dark recesses of the Douglas fir canopy, we watched a male western meadowlark land upon a gnarly piece of sagebrush and, to our delight, let out the harmonious song of the bird that, for me, most beautifully represents the spirit of spring in Yellowstone Country.

Walking along the tree line, heading north, we began our slow descent back to the road below. Before pointing our toes in the direction of town, Doons mentioned one last stop. Skirting a steep and rocky incline, we followed the jutting thumb of a ridge to its precipice. Though not so steep that we couldn't have continued, it was far from the easiest way down on our now tired and sore ankles, which are always the first to fatigue on any off-trail outing. For the first time, our route didn't make much sense to me, as we were venturing farther north from our destination, and into steeper and more rugged terrain.

Instead of dropping down onto the loose scree layering the sharp decline, we continued to follow the contour line that led to the precipice until we reached another terminal ending point. Doons was clearly searching for yet another treasure. After a few short minutes of searching, his shoulders loosened with relief as his eyes fell upon an irregularly shaped rock. He pointed to the object, which had been half swallowed by earth, and with the tender care of someone attending to a poor hiker with a neck injury, unwilling to move the massive rock before us, he gingerly brushed the exposed portion with his hands, great adoration radiating from his entire being. To me, it appeared to be a massive chunk of petrified wood, by no means an anomaly in Yellowstone Country but always a cause for reflection.

Though I would never have known without the knowledge and paleontologist's eye of Doons, my hands now rested on a portion of a dinosaur fossil. By its size, Doons theorizes it was a piece of a femur. And while I don't remember having any kind of infatuation with prehistoric critters as a boy (the presence of grizzly bears, bison, and wolves had always been enough for me), this—the most ancient of items I have ever touched—certainly carried more weight in symbolism than in its hefty mass. After a brief examination, with genuine awe in our hearts, we covered the fossil with dirt, ensuring it remained in the same spot where we had found it, just as we left the arrowhead in the same dirt it had rested upon for hundreds of years. Perhaps one hundred years from now, two wide-eyed explorers will discover the same artifacts that today allowed our imaginations to run wild.

As mysterious and magical as this four-hour walk in the hills had been, I was yearning to see my one-and-a-half-year-old baby girl. We decided to take a shorter, more direct line back to the road, where we could walk with relative comfort to the car. As is often the case, the more direct route, with loose footing and steep slope, led to many slips, falls, and a few tweaks of the ankle. But neither of us cared about our aching joints. We walked in relative silence, both of us still absorbing the wondrous and enigmatic nature of the green hills that sit at our doorstep.

Indeed, the return of spring has added life to the hills around Gardiner, but my journey with a friend among these rolling hummocks taught me that, while not always green, the enchanted Sepulcher foothills are always alive.

16

American White Pelican

In recent weeks, we have seen the return of the often-maligned American white pelican here in Yellowstone Country. My first sighting of a gregarious flock of white pelicans occurred the last week in April, on a big gravel bar just south of the Carter's Bridge Fishing Access Site, along the Yellowstone River. The homecoming of one of North America's largest and most impressive birds is frowned upon by many in the angling community—"fish heads" who, due to an obsessive level of fish on their brain, fail to welcome the awkward majesty of our winged friends, seeing them instead as competition (they share the same main quarry—trout). But for those of us who relish the opportunity to observe one of the oddest and yet most effective bird behaviors in the Northern Rockies, the return of the American white pelican represents a celebration of winged migration as well as admiration for a species with the dogged determination to overcome.

Many visitors to the Yellowstone region are shocked by the sight of a large band of high-riding white sailboats with long, orange, bayonet-like bills protruding toward the water's surface; or the spectacle of a half-dozen white birds with black flight feathers and a nine-foot wingspan circling high above in the thermals more typically occupied by raptors. Their mere presence somehow seems out of place, and yet the huge-billed pelican is a master of its Yellowstone River domain.

It seems fitting that one of the few places in the tri-state region (Idaho, Montana, and Wyoming) where a great abundance of this massive waterbird can be observed is on the waters of the longest free-flowing river in the lower forty-eight—the Yellowstone. Not to be confused with the brown pelican, which is found in marine habitats, where it focuses its efforts on saltwater fishes and sardines, the American white pelican is most often found in freshwater, where it consumes a variety of freshwater fish species. After wintering in the coastal lowlands of Mexico, the pelicans who visit our region each summer begin their journey northward with a brief respite on the waters of the Great Salt Lake in Utah, which is thought to be a major staging area before their final push to the trout-rich waters of the Yellowstone Ecosystem.

The animosity that many bewildered anglers feel toward one of the most efficient avian anglers in North America has a long history in the Yellowstone region. This hatred reminds me of the obsession many hunters and outfitters feel toward the wolf, primarily because of the canids' habit of killing elk. This anthropocentric point of view, which led to the near extinction of wolves in the United States, has also played out in the story of the Yellowstone pelican.

Established in 1872 as the world's first national park, Yellowstone quickly became one of our nation's first destination fisheries. The park's desire to create a world-renowned fishing attraction began in 1889, when the first nonnative trout were planted in many of the previously fishless waters (40 percent of Yellowstone's waters were fishless before the aggressive fish-stocking program). From its inception in 1889 to the conclusion of the park's fish-stocking efforts in 1956, over 310 million native and nonnative fish were introduced into the waters of Yellowstone National Park. But even with all of these efforts to create an artificially abundant trout population in the park, as early as 1917, numbers of cutthroat trout were declining in parts of Yellowstone Lake.

With the people-first ideology of the time—and I often wonder how much this has changed—managers in the park surmised that the only answer was to begin a push to reduce pelican populations around the lake. According to park historian Paul Schullery, in 1926, park managers visited Molly Islands in the extreme southeastern arm of Yellowstone Lake and crushed 200 pelican eggs they found. Over the course of the next two years, they visited the islands later in the year and killed more than two hundred baby pelicans. As is often the case with government agencies entrusted by the citizenry to protect our most precious resources, in 1932, public outrage ultimately helped bring a stop to this intrusive and brutal endeavor.

Knowing this history—the struggles the Yellowstone pelican population has endured over the years—has instilled in me an even greater appreciation for its wildness, which is often displayed by behavior that seems incredibly odd yet methodical. I remember the first time I observed the impressive hunting traditions of the pelican, for example. It was my second summer as a ranger naturalist based out of Mammoth Hot Springs. My sense of pride in representing the Park Service soared and inspired a palpable self-confidence. There was nothing I loved more on one of my lieu days than to explore the interior of the park I served. My father and I had been to historic Fishing Bridge, where we watched a depressingly small number of Yellowstone cutthroat trout spawning beneath it. On our drive back to Mammoth, we spotted a flock of large white waterbirds, which consisted of two separate bands of pelicans, each with approximately eight to nine clansmen.

For the next hour, we watched as one band launched its determined float down a four-hundred-yard stretch of the Yellowstone River, bills bowed toward the water, eyes keying in on any movement. Occasionally, we would see a bird dunk its head—bill first—into the current, and more often than we could believe, the richly colored pouch would fill with river water and a heavily spotted Yellowstone cutty. Soon after that group's departure, the next band or flotilla would follow, mirroring the activity of the lead group: Right before a set of heavy rapids, at the same point each time, the lead group would circle the water, apparently working to move fish toward the shore. And after a few minutes of dogged fishing efforts, the group would take flight in unison, landing back at their original starting point to lead the next procession downstream. We witnessed this impressive and seemingly orchestrated fishing procession repeat a half-dozen times before the ancient-looking birds, possessing a wisdom beyond that of two-legged anglers, moved on to another of their traditional fishing grounds.

I cannot watch such an inspirational, determined, and ancient act of wildlife precision without my thoughts returning to the human element, and our role as stewards and guardians of a mysterious and wonderfully wild Yellowstone. As lovers of Yellowstone Country, we must all continue to spread our profound affection for it and the wildlife—

winged, finned, and four-legged—that make its landscape so incredibly rich. We who have the opportunity to experience the random sighting of a pine marten scurrying across the road; the American kestrel soaring through the Hayden Valley, a field mouse in its clutch; or the simple flutter of a caddisfly emerging from the turbulent waters of Le Hardy Rapids—we owe it to Yellowstone to share these one-of-a-kind experiences. There is no doubt that our love for and connection to nature is deeply personal—perhaps more of a relationship than an experience. But just as our partners, children, and friends wish to be valued—to be told that they are loved—so, too, does Yellowstone. In order to survive for generations to come, it not only warrants, it needs this affection.

Working in the fly-fishing guide culture, I have heard many an angler sigh in anguish when discussing the return of the pelican. This lack of reverence for a friend's return to our hallowed waters has always left me with a heavy heart. But a heavy heart is not enough. We need not picket fishing access sites nor write letters of protest to those who would just as soon see the American white pelicans of the Yellowstone region lose their compass after returning to Mexico; we must instead have the courage to speak up and out on behalf of a feathered friend whose very presence reminds us of something primordial. We must have the audacity to spread the Yellowstone gospel and the profound integrity that this raw landscape continues to inspire.

Much like the summer tourists who visit Yellowstone National Park each year because of the traditions and friendships they have developed, so, too, do the pelicans return to our waterways. If we don't learn to deeply appreciate their return, might they one day choose more friendly neighbors who celebrate their arrival? Without an appreciation for their nobility, the pelicans of the past may opt for a new summer haunt, and perhaps we ourselves may become lost the next time we journey down the waters of the Yellowstone.

17

Summer Love Letter

After a welcome yet fleeting spring, which brought the return of our winged migrants from the south, blooming shooting stars, and the long-anticipated arrival of the lush green grasses that garnish the glacial hummocks separating the desert oasis of Gardiner from the rugged extremes of the Sepulcher foothills, summer has returned to Yellowstone. And when these rolling foothills to the southwest of Gardiner begin to lose their short-lived succulence and fade to a drab brown, the locals know we have officially moved into the season of bliss and adventure in the northern reaches of the Yellowstone Ecosystem.

Yes, our annual celebration of these brief three weeks of richness has come to an end, yet Yellowstone's season of abundance is at the height of its display on the plateau. Traveling the roads winding through our nation's first national park in mid-July often morphs into a lesson in patience (an endorsement for banishing RVs from the park's interior), but it also showcases what is right in our world. Whether it be the holiness of watching a female grizzly with two cubs grazing the grasses on the shoulders of Mount Washburn, the excitement of observing a pack of wolves in pursuit of a cow elk and calf in the Lamar Valley, or the thrill of hearing a thundering herd of bison as they gear up for the rut in the Hayden Valley, summer in Yellowstone allows us to experience something primordial—the very root of the source we all share.

Some wilderness purists proudly proclaim their preference to avoid the park during the craziness of summer, and there are surely ample wildlands to explore outside Yellowstone for those who haven't learned to appreciate the childlike enthusiasm of the visitors—visitors who will stop in the middle of the road and proceed to chase any four-legged worthy of a file on their digital cameras. But those who choose to stay away miss the mystical pleasures of traveling the park's roadways in the crepuscular hours of its most magnificent season.

I can hardly remember a summer without memories made within the confines of Yellowstone's 2.2 million acres of wilderness. It seems to me a rite of passage; what is a summer in the life story of a wilderness lover without a walk or drive through Yellowstone? Missing this opportunity seems akin to the sadness experienced watching the arrival of a solo sandhill crane, having lost its lifelong companion during migration. Perhaps the solo crane will survive—or perhaps it will wither away from a broken heart. I fear the same can be said for those who forego the chance to drive through the Hayden Valley on a brisk July morning, when the mist rising from the surface of the Yellowstone River shrouds the surroundings, and the hulky silhouette of a bison is one's only reminder that we are not alone in this world. Shouldering a pack and heading into the backcountry certainly adds a level of authenticity, richness, and excitement to a Yellowstone journey, but a simple drive with an open heart can yield similar results.

Take my drive home from a recent guide trip on the enigmatic Firehole River—easily the most unique trout stream on our planet. The early evening traffic subsided the farther from Old Faithful I traveled, and by the time I reached South Twin Lake, I had the road to myself. Windows down, radio off—the meadowlark, American robin, mountain chickadee, and ruby-crowned kinglet provided my music. Just north of Roaring Mountain, as I rounded a bend in the road, a goliath of an animal caught my eye.

Now, anyone who's known me as a guide or park interpreter knows I've grown fond of calling the bison "the elephant of North America"; at nearly two thousand pounds, a bull bison constitutes the largest land-dwelling mammal on the continent. This time, the comparison almost seemed inadequate.

I braked to a stop in the middle of the road to gawk at the largest living critter I had ever seen. And I know from my time working the Visitor Center desk that every good-sized bear, wolf, elk, or bison is the biggest anyone has witnessed; but this truly was the biggest animal I had ever laid eyes upon. It was an old and rugged bull bison. He had shed his heavy winter coat, and though he was lying on the ground, his massive proportions and sculpted muscles told of a warrior who had undoubtedly endured many battles and now traveled alone as the king of his terrain. It was, for me, a moment of deep reverence.

Minutes later, I nearly drove into a ditch before again hitting the brakes to stare in awe. The hillside, though an eighth of an acre in size and boasting only four of the summer wildflowers that abound throughout the region, displayed a density and stark contrast of flora that took my breath away. The tiny white flowers of the yarrow, the pink-flowered sticky geranium, the purple petals of the larkspur, and the silvery lupine—all created a vivid spread of summer splendor that I, for one, am grateful not to have missed.

Upon returning to Gardiner, I received a call from the fly shop: the salmonflies had finally reached town. This is the gala—the summer event—that occupies the winter reveries of all Yellowstone trout bums. For the nonfisherman, it can be disturbing to see the big, orange-bellied bugs swarming over the high bridge spanning the Yellowstone River. But for those of us who relish any opportunity to pursue a meeting with finned members of the river by way of the dry fly, the salmonfly hatch is the most epic of them all. Part of the lure is its sheer size and proportion. To observe a swarm of salmonflies migrating upstream (the only exception being the Firehole hatch, which actually moves downstream) is to witness one of the great marvels of our Western rivers.

Adding to the lure of "The Hatch," which typically occurs on the Yellowstone River between the first and tenth of July (depending upon weather and water level), there is the unpredictability of river flow and clarity. The hatch coincides with the tail end of runoff, often leaving it unfished on the Yellowstone because of high and turbulent waters still swollen from snowmelt. Salmonflies, members of the stonefly family, require swift, flowing water, and are most often found in cool, well-oxygenated, freestone rivers like the Yellowstone. The Yellowstone provides ideal stonefly habitat. Thus, anglers and guides can be found fishing big rubber-legged nymphs all year round; but the hatch brings out the competitive nature of the seemingly peaceful fly-fishing culture. Once the waters are fishable, an armada of drift boats accompanies this legendary phenomenon, and even the most reclusive fisherman—such as yours truly—is willing to endure the circus for an opportunity to cast oversized dry flies to overzealous cutthroat trout. For the avid dry-fly fisherman, the mere thought of a salmonfly hatch elicits images of fishful bliss.

Salmonflies undergo incomplete metamorphosis, passing through only three stages of development: egg, nymph, and adult. The biggest of the stonefly family, the salmonfly can live for up to three years in their nymphal stage before emerging as an adult. During this time, trout and mountain whitefish—the much-maligned and disrespected cousin of the beloved trout—are looking to take any nymph that happens to become dislodged from its rock hideaway into the current. But when the right cues encourage the nymphs to begin their journey to adulthood, they depart the protection of their underwater homes and in a mass exodus—typically at dusk—migrate to the shallows along the banks to begin crawling out of the water in search of streamside vegetation.

Soon after leaving the water, the large nymphs climb into the nearest willows, juniper, or grasses and cling to them until their nymphal shucks split open. (This is where the journey we all love begins.) A major bug orgy ensues in the riparian habitat, and as the day warms and the winds start to blow, the adults begin flying over the river. Some of the unlucky ones will clumsily fall into the water to be gobbled up by greedy trout. The egg-laden females will dip the black sacks trailing from their abdomens into the water to drop their eggs, which sink to the bottom, ensuring that the process continues.

This frenzy of bug activity can end as quickly as it starts, and within two days, the most primordial-looking of all aquatic insects will move on to waters upstream, in the Black Canyon of the Yellowstone, with a small cadre of dedicated followers. Though it is short-lived, it is a long-anticipated and truly heralded indicator of summer's arrival in Yellowstone.

No landscape in North America is under greater environmental and political scrutiny than Yellowstone Country. A place that inspires enduring love and spiritual significance, according to most ecologists, the more than eighteen million acres of the Greater Yellowstone area represent the last, nearly intact temperate ecosystem on our planet. The fate of a wild Yellowstone, which remains interconnected with the health of our neighboring communities, in many ways represents the fate of our wild planet. If we can't inspire a commitment to Yellowstone—if we can't protect, preserve, and nurture Yellowstone—I'm afraid we can't any other landscape. That is not to say that the protection of Yellowstone will ensure that other significant ecosystems are secure, but I do believe the loss of the ecological integrity and wild spirit of Yellowstone would mean the loss of the same elsewhere. But how can we nurture something we don't know and love? How can we know and love Yellowstone Country without celebrating its heartbeat, Yellowstone National Park, during its most glorious season?

The salmonflies have returned, the rivers swollen with runoff are clearing, the afternoon thunderstorms and accompanying rainbows are a daily occurrence, the bison are rutting, and the backcountry is calling your name. And with all of this, the magic of another Yellowstone Country summer begins. May those of you reading this summer love letter journey—in your own way—to the heart of Yellowstone Country, ignore the crowds, and rediscover the power and beauty of a wilderness that still inspires the awe and wonder that the paintings of Thomas Moran revealed in 1871. By remembering the glory of summer in Yellowstone, we give hope to the future of our planet's wildest places.

18

Fall Is In the Air

While it has always been my favorite time of year and is perhaps the most splendid of seasons in the Northern Rockies, for me, fall is also a time of reflection, celebration, and anticipation of what lies ahead. Yet another wondrous Yellowstone summer has gone by, leaving behind fleeting memories of dust plumes and guttural songs filling the Lamar River bottom, courtesy of rutting bison; seductively rising cut-throat trout lazily gulping foam grasshoppers; soaring ospreys casting winged shadows over deep, dark pools of liquid gold; and, of course, river and mountain adventures that fill our summer hours—and our winter dreams. The passing of summer in this part of the country is almost akin to losing a loved one. In my mind, it is honored and treated with devotion.

We can never get back those summer days; but we can rejoice in their memory by gathering for one last evening barbecue, with favorite drink in hand, to toast a fading sun beginning its descent behind the massive hulk that is Electric Peak. And as we reflect upon and celebrate the fish caught, trails walked, peaks bagged, and rapids run, we quickly recognize that we are being fooled by these eighty-degree mid-September days. Perhaps, for those in more southern latitudes, summer actually lasts until the equinox of September 22; but here, at over a mile in elevation, fall announces its arrival much earlier. Unlike the dog days of summer, when it is nothing to stay outside shooting baskets in the driveway in shorts and a T-shirt long after the sun hides behind the

Gallatin Range, now, within minutes of the sun's final descent, the temperatures plummet to where a fleece and hat feel more appropriate for a game of H-O-R-S-E.

During the week of September 7, the signs of fall gently reminded me that I will have to wait until next year for the long days and warm waters of summer. On a morning float from McConnell to Corwin Springs on the Yellowstone River, on the eighth, the water temperatures read a fishy sixty degrees, and the willows lining the gravelly banks of the longest free-flowing river in the lower forty-eight still held a dull green appearance. Two days later, the water temperatures had dropped to fifty-six degrees, and the willows dancing in the wind struggled to hold tight to their life support system—revealed by the deep yellows suddenly dominating the riverbank.

Now is the time when the mournful cry of the sandhill crane and the busy chattering of grasshoppers give way to the regal song of the Rocky Mountain elk. With the onset of cold nights and cool mornings, one of the most impressive animal displays on the North American continent has drawn visitors from around the globe to Mammoth Hot Springs for an up-close-and-personal encounter with rutting elk. I remember commenting to my father on the last day in August that, after one of the busiest summers in Yellowstone's history, Gardiner felt like a ghost town. But all it took was a drop in temperatures to bring the freakish behavior of Yellowstone's most abundant ungulate to the surface, and, as always, the tourists quickly followed.

The days are now drastically shorter, with darkness taking hold by 7:30 each evening. And though I am sure we will see many of the brilliant fall days that make October a treasured month by residents of this region, I have a feeling that this past weekend was our last chance to truly celebrate another passing season in summer-like fashion. After the single best hopper fishing season of my lifetime and the most productive summer of dry-fly fishing with clients on my books, I took two beginner clients—who had never so much as held a fly rod in their virgin hands—to experience a day of magic on the 'Stone.

Not being inclined to ruin a good thing by offering too much detail regarding patterns used and holes fished, all I will say is that we ventured into the depths of the Black Canyon of the Yellowstone with black-bodied bugs in tote. What ensued was fishing bliss. The water was low and clear, making our drifts from steep, rocky outcrops a visual extravaganza as one big fish after another welcomed my jubilant clients to the art of fly fishing.

Wind is easily a fly fisherman's greatest nemesis, and autumn made its presence known as voracious gusts threatened to blow us off our perch. On at least three occasions, my clients excitedly announced, index fingers pointing, the presence of a trout floating through the water. With delicate care, not wanting to embarrass them—or worse yet, diminish their enthusiasm—I gently told them that the golden, spotted entity gracefully flowing with the current was not a finned critter but a cottonwood leaf ripped from its stem by the winds charging through the canyon.

My summer-like day with these two beginner fly fishermen and the dozens of eager-to-please yellow-bellied cutthroat stirred me to commemorate the days of summer and ponder their brilliance. But the shedding of fall leaves is also a time for anticipation. What comes next? How bad will this winter be? Will you get an elk to fill the freezer? Will my Gardiner Bruins boys' basketball team pull it together this season? Will we make divisionals? How much will the wind blow?

All of these are reasonable questions to ask in preparation for the fall and winter that now lie ahead—well, actually, all but one. We know how much the wind will blow. The pulsing winds of autumn will begin to build speed and consistency as the days pass, as if in training for the constant winter barrage right around the corner. This, the most powerful common element (excluding the supervolcano, which is even more powerful but not so common, with approximately 640,000-year intervals) in Yellowstone Country, will tear at the still-green stems of the cottonwoods and yellow leaves of the willows lining the banks of the Yellowstone, littering the waters with paper-thin fish bayonets that will eventually gather in a pool of frothy water. Then the suds from the bubble line, swirling in sequence with the once-living leaves, will become a temporary home to an emergence of tiny, tack-sized mayflies (blue-winged olives, BWOs) that trout will greedily gobble up as one last source of surface food before a long winter struggle. And with the disappearance of BWOs, the snows will fly and winter will be upon us. But not yet. . . .

Winter is still many weeks away; and though the celebration of summer has been digested with the last bits of smoky chicken at the barbecue, the great awakening that fall brings this particular Yellowstone resident has now arrived. All summer long, when contemplating the hikes left undone and the fishing that I still hope to do, I am comforted by thoughts of how distant is the time when the leaves begin to fall, the waters cool, and the song of the elk rings through the meadows of a holy landscape. Such thoughts allow me to stay home to rest—to watch a movie or a mountain stage in the Tour de France. But I receive no such comfort when thinking of the dark days of winter lurking around the next bend.

The days shorter, the waters cooler, and the nights darker, this is a time we will never get back. I will never amble along the banks of the Gardner River or climb the flanks of Electric Peak or journey into the eerie wonders of the Hoodoo Basin again as a thirty-year-young man. Next year, I will be thirty-one—one year closer to the end of my walk on this earth. This story holds true for all of us.

So get out there—walk the earth, climb the mountains, stalk the elk, wade the big river, and pursue the trout. Because soon enough, the waters will be frigid, the mountains frozen, and the earth hardened. Don't wait until next summer or next fall; this is the last autumn 2009 we will ever know. Now is the time of our becoming, now is the time. . . .

19

Yellowstone's Gym Culture

Last night proved restless, as my fifteen-month-old baby girl, Kamiah, spent much of the evening and early morning tossing and turning, bouncing her heels off her bed and rattling the wooden bars of her crib—her nighttime sanctuary—which, in turn, sent shockwaves radiating through the wall and into our room, keeping me awake.

When she woke up for her morning bottle at 5:45 A.M., I realized her cries were not the only sound echoing throughout the house. A strong winter wind was hammering the east side of our bungalow. It must have been shaking the freestanding, semi-retired gate that keeps the dogs in the backyard—until it finally came crashing down at 6 A.M. I'd heard my wife let Maddie and Tucker out about half an hour earlier. Having spent many other mornings wandering up and down the frozen alley in basketball shorts, wind slapping my bare legs as I looked for our errant pooches, when I heard the gate crash, I knew what was in store for me.

Tired and sluggish from lack of sleep and the early morning dog pursuit, I didn't leave for the gym until around 10:45. I like to get there by 9 to ensure that I have solitude and then plenty of time in the office after the infusion of endorphins, which, for me, only exercise releases. But today, I took my time as I headed up the hill from Gardiner to Mammoth. There are usually very few visitors to the park this time of year, but it seemed winter visitation was more dismal this season than in winters past. If it were not for the wind—which continued to rage out of the southwest, funneling off the flats of Swan Lake, and steadily picking up speed and force as it descended through the canyon—today would have been a great morning for a bike ride.

It was hard for me to believe I had already ridden my road bike up the nearly one-thousand-vertical-foot climb to Mammoth twice this year—and it was only the first week of February. The new year had already given us a smorgasbord of offerings in a short five-week period. The first few days of January greeted us with warm temperatures, cloudy skies, and rare rain. Frigid temperatures replaced the moisture, making it a challenge to keep the house (with its drafty, single-paned windows) livable. We burned more wood during this one-week cold snap—where daytime temperatures struggled to climb into single digits, and morning and nighttime temperatures plummeted into the double digits below zero—than I can ever remember. There were times throughout the day that I had to wear a hat and sweater in the house, with the heat cranking and fire brewing, just to stay somewhat comfortable.

But after the harrowing northern winds passed (inevitably taking the lives of many four-leggeds throughout the Ecosystem), a winter heat wave—the likes of which I have never experienced in Yellowstone Country—quickly took hold. For a solid ten-day spell, we didn't see so much as a cloud here in Gardiner. And for several days in a row, the temperatures hovered in the mid- to high forties, with one day soaring to fifty-seven degrees. On those warmer days, without the dreaded wind, I rode my bike up the hill to Mammoth, easily making the two grinds up to park headquarters my earliest such rides since living here. During these rides, I could have easily fooled myself into believing that it was already mid-March, and that winter's tight clasp on Yellowstone Country was about to be replaced by the season of hope and new beginnings, which I always welcome with open arms.

With the exception of the wind, today reminded me of those welcoming March-like days that surprised us in January—and then left us all too quickly. After the ten-day stretch of bright blue skies and abnormally warm temperatures, a fierce northern wind blew back into town and returned us to a more predictable few weeks as the first month of the year abruptly came to an end. Monday's flurries, while short-lived, represented one of the heaviest snowfalls in recent weeks. Scanning the hills around the Gardiner Basin would lead visitors to the region to believe that there is a paucity of snow. On days such as these, when the sun rests high in the sky and the thin blanket of snow caresses the glacial hummocks around town, this desert basin must seem like a winter Shangri-la to outsiders.

I didn't know what to expect at the gym today since I was now flirting with the lunchtime crowd. I realize it's absurd to talk of crowds at the Mammoth gym in February, where there may be a half-dozen people during one of its busiest hours, but that's what happens to your perspective when you've lived here long enough.

Feeling pensive, I stepped out of my truck on to the sheet of ice that now dominates the parking lot at the Mammoth Hotel and shuffled my feet in order to stay upright to the steps of the Rec Hall.

As I stepped into the gym, I couldn't help but think about the phone conversation I'd just had with my dear friend Trevor on the winding road from the 45th parallel to the Rec Hall. Trevor had spent a month this summer in a mental facility, and has struggled for years with severe depression and back pain that only worsens his mental dilemmas. Last week, when I was really struggling with a lot of pain from my ankylosing spondylitis and frustration in relation to my new nonprofit, Yellowstone Country Guardians, I gave Trevor a call and told him it was his turn to talk me through a tough day, which I have done for him on countless occasions. Today, half serious, I said to Trevor just before I got out of the truck that perhaps we should both go check in to Warm Springs (the state of Montana's mental hospital).

Now, I found myself walking into a depressingly dark gym, where everyone is so worried about saving money that the white drapes (which eerily resemble those of a mental hospital) stay drawn to keep the heat in. I have often wondered whether the winter employees leave the lights off while working out because of their altruism and hopes of saving the planet. Or perhaps they do so in an effort to stay in their utterly depressive funk, which may also fuel them to visit one of the local taverns later in the day—the few establishments in Gardiner that remain open during winter.

No one is likely to label the Mammoth gym as a utopia of workout facilities, with its antiquated benches and dumbbells, and minimal equipment; but its simplicity is part of its charm. I will admit, however, that sometimes it's good to remind myself that my commute from my house/office to the gym happens to be one of the most treacherous yet inspiring five miles of paved road in the country. Often, upon arriving at the gym, I have to dodge the gregarious elk that meander between the hotel and its guest cabins. And on many occasions, I have pressed my face against the glass window framed above the dumbbell rack—one of a few not darkened with a curtain—to meet the confused gaze of a year-ling elk, standing on spindly legs, with his unimpressive spiked antlers radiating out of the roof of his skull.

There may not be any state-of-the-art equipment, flat-screen TVs, or personal broadcasts beaming from the cardio machines, but the sight of a staggering bull bison, a fleeting coyote, and the ever-present elk make up for my gym's lack of twenty-first century accouterments. Certainly, the basketball court, likely built in the 1940s, is a major plus. Before I hit the weights, I always get a good warm up by flipping the ball to myself and, if only briefly, returning to the game of my youth. Still today, twelve years past my prime, there are few sounds that give me as much simple pleasure as the snap of the net after I cleanly swish a shot from eighteen feet.

Whether it be back pain—which isn't all that common anymore for me—or simply fatigue (almost a daily battle), there are many days where I struggle to find the inner motivation to push myself through my workout. I guess I must still possess the intense self-discipline of my playing days, because I rarely remember leaving without completing my routine. But these are the times when that "little something extra" of a newer, more modern gym would really help. That simple built-in TV in your own personal cardio machine can distract you just enough to push through the thirty minutes (or more) of boredom on a stationary ellipti-cal; or that attractive twenty-something brunette on the treadmill next to you—she can propel a person to new heights. With the exception of summer, however, when such a rare visual treat is more likely to occur, no such external motivations exist during most Mammoth workouts.

And despite the motivating factors that are common in gyms all across the country, the negatives of those environments far outweigh the positives for me. Walk into any reputable gym in any decent-sized city in the United States, and the steady flow of vanity is hard for many compassionate thinkers to tolerate. Conversely, I know that most city-type gym rats wouldn't be able to appreciate the simplicity of the Mam-moth gym. But I can honestly say that I will deeply miss my old-school and uninhabited workout facility when I eventually migrate to Livingston or Bozeman.

Another factor peculiar to Yellowstone adds to the funky—and to me, appealing—atmosphere of the equipment and facility itself. The people. Yellowstone National Park attracts a disproportionate number of one-of-a-kind employees; and while this is the case for all of Yellowstone's nongovernmental hiring entities, each summer and winter, the park concessioner—the largest employer in the park—seems to bring together the most unusual team. I would be surprised if any other employer in the country can boast of a more eclectic mix—foreigners, southerners, East Coasters, gays, homophobes, rednecks, hippies, young and old, and everything in between. Occasionally, I run into Park Service employees while working out, but generally speaking, they don't have the appearance of someone confused about their surroundings and purpose; and they typically show up after 5 P.M. Also, truth be told, for the most part, they are not "the gym kind"; so most mornings, I don't expect to see any men and women sporting the green and gray.

What I do expect is something unexpected. I would wager that I have witnessed some of the oddest gym behavior anyone has ever seen at any gym anywhere. Still, today may have broken all records.

The first thing that caught my attention was the number of people there when I arrived. Four bodies is a lot for a midday in February, but it turned out it wasn't just the bodies that surprised me; it was more about the souls holding up those four skeletons.

Today, most of the regulars happened to be frolicking among the weights and cardio equipment at the same time. The first and only person to greet me was a middle-aged, balding man with a barrel of a stomach, a stocky neck, and stump-like arms—Tom. Almost everyone who attends a gym has at least one body part they take pride in and try to show off, and for Tom, it is his biceps—which, for a seemingly nonathletic man in his sixties, are, in reality, nothing to bat an eye at.

The weirdness got going early, when I jumped onto the elliptical next to him and we began dreaming out loud of summer. "Mike," Tom said in his thick southern drawl, a heavy gold necklace hanging from his neck and looped rings dangling from his earlobes, "I was looking at a photo of a trail in summer yesterday with a friend, and it got me so fucking excited that I became sexually aroused."

I didn't really have a response for him, so I simply smiled, put my headphones in each ear, and went on with my workout.

I soon took note of the heavyset blonde guy, in his mid- to late thirties, who just began showing up in the last month. Nothing should come as a surprise in the park culture, but this guy seems extraordinarily out of place—the side of his head buzzed and the top of his skull flowing with long blonde hair, looking as if it were a horse's mane. And both of his legs are festooned with tattoos that seem paradoxical to one another; his massive left calf has a symbol of the Buddha next to the US Marine Semper Fi. I have never heard the man speak, so I don't know where he comes from. But for some reason, I suspect him to be a Texan.

The next person to catch my eye was a young man who, at first glance, looked very normal—even handsome. He was tall, with tightly cropped blonde hair capped by a snug black do-rag—a look more often worn by inner-city kids than lovers of Yellowstone. What stands out about this young man is his relentless narcissism. Between each set, he looks in the mirror, which in and of itself is not that uncommon. It's what he does while gazing at his image that borders on insanity. After each set, he hits his chest, grabs his crotch, and walks as close to the looking glass as possible. Then he proceeds to bump and grind with himself as if he were in a nightclub somewhere on the Vegas Strip. Staring intently, he puckers his lips, making love to his mirror image. Of all the characters I have seen in the gym over the years, there is perhaps no other so out of place as this young man in his early twenties. (And I can assure you he won't last another week here in Yellowstone.)

But wait. After roughly twenty minutes, the oddest of all the local gym rats walked in. I am guessing this eccentric-looking man is in his mid- to late forties; and according to Tom, his name is Jerry, and they have worked together for over a decade. Yet Tom says he can count on one hand the number of times he has ever heard Jerry speak.

Immediately upon walking in the doors, he beelined to the oldest, most out-of-date piece of cardio equipment at the Mammoth gym and—wearing the most restricting pair of Levi's he could possibly pour himself into—proceeded to race through a series of hill climbs. One of the things that strikes me as being the most odd about his cardio routine is that he always wears his spandex-tight jeans during it—even though he later changes into shorts. Also, he always positions his arms so that he is holding on to the middle of the screen, with his hands close together instead of letting his arms flow smoothly—the way they would if he were running. His hands seemingly handcuffed to the machine's computer, his upper body remains as stiff as a mannequin while his lower body races like some kind of crazed demon. Adding to the effect is the fact that the only thing moving above his waist is his blonde hair, flopping from side to side.

Like clockwork, after finishing up his usual cardio routine, Jerry walked over to the bench, peeled off the jeans, and reemerged with a pair of ball-hugging, gray cotton shorts that barely contain the roll of his ass cheeks. This, coupled with his skintight T-shirt (two sizes too small), calf-high white socks and white sneakers that have faded to gray over the course of the last two decades, and a personality as lively as dry mud, and you have one of the most unique workout comrades ever gracing a gym.

By this point in my workout, I begin to wonder whether there could possibly be any stranger gym experience in the country—and then the bizarre becomes the uncanny. With only five sets left in my routine, the doors to the gym crash open and in walks yet another regular, who like many of the folks who frequent the Mammoth gym, never opens his mouth to say as much as a hello. However, unlike most of the others who wander aimlessly throughout the gym, this hulk of a man in his late twenties enters on a mission each day. His typical attire consists of blue-and-white candy-striped pants, heavy black shoes, a tight T-shirt (covered initially by a worn-out, ranch-style jacket), and on some days, a limp but tall chef's hat on his head. When he wears his chef's hat into the gym, he always replaces it quickly with a brown skullcap, which makes me suspect he is hiding a receding hairline. His workouts are short but intense—he lifts more weight than anyone else I have seen in my five years working out at Mammoth. And when he is squatting these absurd amounts of weight, I have often wondered how his long silver chain—latched to one of his belt loops and hanging down to his thigh before wrapping back into his right-hand pocket—doesn't interfere with each repetition.

I think I have slowly come to understand his odd lifting behavior, however. For this pale young man with a raggedy blonde goatee, size is the ultimate goal. So instead of the more typical flow from top to bottom, his movements are short and erratic, building lactic acid in large quantities, and bulging his overworked biceps and thighs. Much like his personality (I have never seen him utter a word to anyone), his weight routine doesn't seem very well rounded. He focuses on his bulging biceps, then—as abruptly as he enters the gym—leaves without restacking any of his weights. A man on a mission.

The last to arrive during my workout today is a guy for whom I have always had a great deal of compassion. He is short and stocky, with an awkward gate to his step, and appears to be in his mid-twenties. I think he has some mental challenges; I have rarely seen him so much as move his smallish mouth. (True, the muscle-head chef doesn't talk to anybody else either, but I often see him mouthing something to himself.) Sticking primarily to the basketball court, this short, squatty kid, who is probably from Detroit (he is always wearing some kind of memorabilia, such as a cotton Red Wings or Tigers jersey, or a Pistons or Red Wings hat—and always matched with a pair of gray sweatpants), only opens his mouth in hopes of coaxing the poorly shot ball into the rim. Occasionally, I will observe him venturing out of his hometown box to sport a LeBron James jersey, but this is rare.

Today, I said hello to him twice, thinking he may not have heard me the first time, but instead of responding with a hello, he looked at me as if I were speaking a foreign language. Perhaps what captures me most about this dark-haired, nonathletic young man is not simply my instinct to look out for the less fortunate, but more his innate love of basketball and of Yellowstone. Unlike the others who come to the gym for a workout—often the result of some form of vanity—the little man from Detroit enters the gym with one thing and one thing only on his mind: busting a three-ball.

Some days, "Detroit" arrives wearing athletic shoes that will not scuff the floor and thus are acceptable to management; but most days, he seems to be taking a quick break from work and simply slides his shoes off. This says a lot about his character, because most of the knucklehead park employees I see shooting baskets on their breaks ignore the gym rules and play in their work boots, scuffing up the floor and trailing hard-caked mud in their wake. But not Detroit. He leaves his work shoes at the steps to the floor of the basketball court and slides across the slippery surface—always coated with dust—intently focused upon the ball rack, where he always grabs the one ABA-style basketball (with red, white, and blue segments).

Though he rarely stays long—on multiple occasions I've watched him leave the gym, dejected look on his face, when two or three people were already shooting—most days, if the court is free, he usually puts ten minutes of hard work forth as he stands at the top of the key and, with his right hand and no support from his left, proceeds to launch ball after ball at the front of the rim. More often than not, he does draw the iron; but often enough, the ball simply sails through the curtains behind the basket, and he is forced to scramble atop the stage in search of it. Sometimes he throws the ball with such vigor that I worry the backboard will give way and glass will come hurtling down, cutting his forehead and possibly leaving a mental scar that could keep him from further pursuing his great love of hoops.

Roughly an hour after arriving at the gym, my workout comes to an end. And as I depart, I like to take one last look around, just to take in the sights and sounds of a workout facility that, outside of a state institution, has to be the only of its kind. Driving the hairpin curves in low gear on my way home (so as not to brake and slide out if I hit a patch of ice), I often have the same questions about my workout cohorts and their pre- and post-Yellowstone lives. What brought these people here? How long will they stay? And where will their next stop be?

All questions I cannot answer, and in truth, hope not to answer—for that would take the mystery out of my workout reveries, where I often wonder whether or not the man next to me has the same love and reverence for Yellowstone that I have. I wonder if he is recently divorced, has lost a parent, has escaped from a mental hospital, or is perhaps on the run for a random and potentially violent crime. . . .

Not knowing their stories allows my mind to wander and my fingers to continue racing across the keyboard in search of answers— answers perhaps best left undiscovered, or lost to the winds and wilds of Yellowstone.

20

Winter's Loosening Grip

It's March 1 in Gardiner, Montana, and it feels more like the beginning of October. Though it is still supposed to be winter in our part of the country, the Gardiner Basin is barren of snow; and the rivers, which are running low and clear, are looking fishy, calling out to anglers across the region. We have also received our first reports of bears emerging from their dens, beginning the process of replacing a wildness dominated by cold temperatures and harsh winds with the wildness of the top-of-the-food-chain's return to Yellowstone Country.

After several weeks of brutally cold temperatures in December, the first and second months of this year seemed confused by the calendar. Typically January and February represent winter's most intense and trying time for the four-leggeds, who are simply trying to survive. Below-freezing temperatures accompanied by deep snows and fierce winds drive ungulates such as the bison, elk, bighorn, and mule deer to lower elevations outside of the park, where suitable grazing habitat exists.

But this winter's dismal snowpack has not led to the mass exodus of wildlife that we are so accustomed to seeing here on the north boundary of Yellowstone National Park. With not a cloud in the sky and balmy fifty-degree temperatures today, our backcountry ski outing this morning felt like we had been transplanted to the absurdly warm Vancouver Olympic venues seen on television the last two weeks. At 2,100 feet in elevation, the sticky corn snow slowing the world's greatest racers should not have been a major surprise in the wet Pacific Northwest; but at 6,700 feet, one would expect the Blacktail Deer Plateau on Yellowstone's Northern Range to be a winter wonderland on this, the first day of March.

Over the course of our short, two-hour ski tour, the track started glassy and iced over from the night's below-freezing temperatures, but turned into a sparsely covered mess of slop on the route back to our vehicle. And though these warm temperatures and clear days make life much easier for both the two- and four-legged members of the Yellowstone community, one cannot help but worry about the summer ahead.

At 70 percent and steadily dropping, our marginal snowpack—if not boosted by massive storms very soon—will mean a summer of raging fires, smoke-filled air, and warm waters leading to early fishing closures throughout much of August, dooming our fly-fishing economy and devastating the spirits of fishing gurus across the region. Though spring and fall are two of our greatest seasons, their hurried nature makes each year feel as if there are only two true seasons in Yellowstone Country: winter and summer. And while many relish the opportunity to play in the mountains all winter long, dancing like rock stars down avalanche-riddled slopes on fat-planked skis, for most of us blessed to call this region home, a summer spent navigating the area's wild rivers is what fills our souls.

Every time I ride a bus on a winter road trip with the basketball team or drive up north for a meeting or presentation, even when the roads are caked with ice, I cannot help but dream of tail-dancing trout at the end of my line and me on the other end, immersed in the cool August waters of the 'Stone. So the thought of a summer with water shortages and rivers teaming with trout struggling to survive causes major anxiety. Add to this concern the heartache of another basketball season come and gone, and one could easily see why this time of year is often a period of quiet reflection in the life of any Yellowstone Country resident—especially that of any head basketball coach.

Basketball is the king of sports in Montana for a reason. As much as folks love their football—especially the University of Montana's Grizzly Nation, with their top-five preseason rankings in the national poll each year—there are far more Montana youngsters who love to pursue deer and elk each autumn than those looking to strap on their helmet and pads in anticipation of a massive collision at the forty-yard line in a game of eight-man football (and with a crowd of fifty lining the side-lines). Track is another story altogether. With upwards of six meets each year, last year's Gardiner High track team only managed to participate in three events before the state tournament due to spring snowstorms pun-ishing the track venues.

Not only is basketball a fan-friendly sport but it happens to occur during winter. Each Friday and Saturday night in small, Class C towns across the state, townspeople from home and visiting teams venture into the warmth of a brightly lit gym to commune while the pride and joy of each community goes to battle, in an effort to represent proudly. Fortu-nately for the Gardiner Bruins boys' basketball team, this year was a huge success. Overachieving all year long, a preseason five seed in most polls, we jumped out early and never looked back, clinching the two seed on our way to an 11–3 conference record. But there was something strange about our journey to Butte this season for tournament play.

En route to the MAC (Maroon Activities Center)—home of Butte Central Catholic High School, where our district and divisional tourna-ment is played each year—we always make a special stop at Missouri Headwaters State Park, where I speak to the boys about overcoming adversity and prevailing through times of hardship. When it looks like we will face a team from one of the state's Indian reservations, I take the opportunity to help my players better understand and appreciate the Native peoples of Montana, which has led to tremendous events unfold-ing between our team and the Arlee Warriors and their fans from the Flathead Reservation.

But this year, while I was teaching the boys about the culture and spiritual values of many Plains Indian tribes in hopes of inspiring them to greatness, instead of dealing with blizzards and whiteouts as in years past, the usually frozen ground was soft and soaked with water. Instead of huddling together in an attempt to stay warm, our teeth chattering and our chins tucked inside of our jackets, many of us stood above the banks of the Missouri River at the convergence of three mighty bodies of water in nothing warmer than a sweatshirt.

Now our season is over; and rather than loading the skis into the truck and venturing up to Bridger Bowl for a month full of playing on the mountain, I am contemplating hooking up the drift boat to the back of my Tundra and journeying back home to the waters of the Bitterroot in pursuit of the wild trout—trout that I am afraid the lack of snow will keep me from getting to know come peak of summer.

I don't know where this winter has gone. With the exception of our winter ritual of packed gyms on wild nights against our rivals from Twin Bridges, Sheridan, and Shields Valley, the lack of snow makes me feel as if it never arrived. And though I am ready to welcome spring, and return to the saddle of my bike and the rowing seat of my drift boat, I can only hope that March and April will see the snow fly—and, for summer's sake, winter will extend its grip on Yellowstone.

21

The Fading Light of Summer

I sit at the desk in my poorly lit office with a heavy heart as I write these words. Everything is so cyclical in Yellowstone, and after the most hectic and busy summer of my thirty years walking this earth, the mere fact that I am once again sitting at my desk, attempting to write a short essay, says that things are indeed slowing down; fall is on the brink.

Just last week, I took my first twenty-four hours off with my family in over thirty-five days, which followed another arduous twenty-one-day stint crammed with guiding, speaking engagements, and Yellowstone Country Guardians (YCG) programming. With one commitment melting into the next, there was little time to get out and explore the wonders of summer in Yellowstone on my own. But with the encouragement of my family, I decided it was time to take a few days to refamiliarize my spirit with the land and waters that inspire me.

For much of the first three weeks of August, a gusty heat wave descended upon our part of the Northern Rockies, which made each day out on the water, rowing a drift boat, a windy inferno. The third week of August was marked by ninety-degree temperatures and the hottest hopper fishing of the season. But, as is often the case in Yellowstone, a dramatic change was on its way. By the 23 of August, temperatures plummeted both day and night; the rains began to pour; and with the apparent changing of seasons, a mass exodus of visitors ensued, emptying the once-full campgrounds.

Though this is often a cause for celebration for locals across the gateway communities of Yellowstone National Park as we begin to reclaim our towns, I cannot help but feel saddened by the cooling temperatures, cloudy skies, and lack of a line at the North Entrance gate; all mark the beginning of the end of yet another Yellowstone summer. While many cherish the winters in Yellowstone for their unsurpassed silence and solitude, I, for one, yearn for the summer months, when everything across the region feels full of life and abundantly rich.

Here is my recipe for a wilderness paradise: A warm, sunny day with temperatures hovering around eighty degrees; a wind of moderate proportions (we don't have a breeze in Yellowstone; it is always wind) gently swaying the tips of the lodgepole pines and dancing the leaves of a sprawling aspen grove; the ancient cry of a pair of sandhill cranes and the graceful flight of a northern harrier; the fragrant scent of sagebrush; the deep and guttural grunt of a bull bison in rut; and the methodical slurping of a pale morning dun by a sixteen-inch Yellowstone cutthroat trout on a slowly meandering stream.

Over the course of July and August, this description of my wilderness Shangri-la is almost a daily occurrence. So perhaps one can see why the twenty-five-mph winds, fifty-three-degree temperatures, and deep bank of clouds hovering at around seventy-five hundred feet—constantly threatening to rain and muddy up the waters of the Yellowstone River—make me a bit melancholy. Winter locks up Yellowstone Country for months on end, often leaving me yearning for warmer climates; but during the three months of summer, there is no place on earth I would rather be.

It is not that I don't love the shoulder months of summer—this couldn't be further from the truth. I can think of no better time to travel to the Lamar Valley in search of charismatic megafauna than April and May, and October has long been my favorite month in Yellowstone for a number of reasons. It is simply what the onset of fall represents—the passing of another summer in wonderland—that causes my serotonin levels to dip just a bit. Fall and spring in Yellowstone are short-lived and followed by much longer, more dramatic seasons—making their passing less dramatic. Where the end of winter represents a rebirth of sorts, the fading light of summer symbolizes a significant loss of a most glorious time. But the end of summer and each summer's adventures make me feel one year older and one year closer to the day when I will no longer be able to dream of seventy-mile hikes through the Thorofare, four-day fishing forays into Frenchy's Meadow, or the expansive view from the summit of any one of the hundreds of mountains I still dream to climb.

So forgive me if this essay isn't as uplifting as most; but since I recently turned thirty, every passing summer kick-starts a multiday midlife crisis. And the best therapy I know is to write—and explore. These past few summers, I have been so focused on guiding, and taking every speaking engagement and wedding officiating gig thrown at me— all the while planning for YCG programs that will enhance the lives of our youth and connect them to something far greater than themselves— that I have failed to reconnect with Yellowstone on an intimate level. Then the days start to get a little shorter, the mercury drops, and the winds that once brought hot air begin to bring bone-aching cold back to the region; and the desire to explore, which went unsatisfied all summer, suddenly grows urgent.

Though there will surely be a few summer-like days ahead, where a bike ride in shorts and tights or an afternoon of fishing in the sandals and shorts that I have donned for the last two months will still be an option, getting back on the bike in winter regalia or traversing the rivers in waders and boots will also keep my body young—and more importantly, my spirit joyful. This is perhaps the greatest gift that Yellowstone teaches us—the nature of change and transformation. While not as sudden as the change in light that I have witnessed over the course of the last ten days—which no longer has the vibrant summer vividness and seems a bit flat, with a little less pop—any season in Yellowstone takes us through the seasons of our own lives and gives us all cause for reflection.

I have often told youth from all over the country that when we stop growing, changing, transforming, and giving to the world around us, it is time to turn the lights out. Well, it appears that the light of another summer in Yellowstone is about to burn out. But with time and patience, summer will return to Yellowstone.

Our time on this landscape is a blink of an eye in comparison to the 2.7-billion-year-old granite in the Lamar Canyon, the 2.1-million-year-old welded tuff on the ridge of Mount Everts, or even the 500-year-old Douglas fir growing near Trout Lake; but the seasons of Yellowstone can still teach us much about our own life journey. Nature reminds us that there are mountain summits as well as deep canyons, and the tenderness of an Indian paintbrush is here to contrast the sharp pain of the prickly pear cactus.

Though Yellowstone's appearance may change from time to time, with dramatic forces such as the 1988 forest fire and the transition from one season to the next, in a world marked by technological advancement and rapid change, the knowledge that Yellowstone will always exist—and that another summer will return—is enough to give us hope that we will once again experience the quiet peace of sauntering through her most majestic season.

A full calendar year—the changing of seasons and the evolution of each individual season in the Yellowstone Ecosystem—represents, in many ways, our own transformation and growth from year to year. Personal growth is a fragile and sacred endeavor, much like the transformation of a wildflower from a struggling stem to a budding blossom. And while change can be difficult for us two-leggeds to deal with, often accompanied by anxiety and fear of the unknown, we will always have Yellowstone's cyclical nature to guide us.

22

Closing Out the Season

The day after the first Sunday in November, the splendid nature of autumn gave way to the doldrums of Yellowstone's longest season: winter. Almost everyone has symbols that represent the changing of seasons—events, holidays, something that guides them from one to the next. In the Leach clan, perhaps no other entry on the calendar signals the end of one season and the beginning of another as dramatically as this day. For me, it signifies more than the end of my two favorite seasons (summer and fall); it signifies the beginning of five months of quiet monotony. While there are many who relish the approach of winter with an almost cultlike fervor and excitement for each inch of fallen snow (largely because of the youthful exuberance that can perhaps only be felt dancing through knee-deep powder on two fat-planked skis or gracefully carving an ocean wave on a surfboard, the latter of which isn't a viable option for us residents of the Rockies), the onset of winter, the accompanying wind, and the brutally cold temperatures signal for many—including yours truly—the beginning of a depressive funk.

Regardless of which winter camp one finds oneself in, after the longest and most invigorating Indian summer I have experienced in my thirty-some years walking the lands of the Northern Rockies and Pacific Northwest, Yellowstone's inner calendar was mystically on point again this year. As if to emphasize this, the first Sunday in November 2010, which greeted us with yet another sunny day and temperatures hovering around sixty degrees, was dramatically followed by temperatures in the twenties and the first blizzard of the new season.

You may (quite reasonably) ask: what is my seeming obsession with the first Sunday in November? The answer: the first Sunday in November is the day they close the interior park roads, which remain blockaded until late April. Unlike many of the park's decisions regarding when to open and close certain roads (which often make no sense at all, such as the verdict to close Dunraven Pass weeks before any snow fell on the Washburn Range), the decision of when to close the park's interior roads appears to be more logical, because more often than not, by the first week of November, the snow begins to fly on the Yellowstone Plateau.

That said, you may still be wondering why this day holds so much significance for me. Well, it isn't just my inability to drive in comfort to the Grand Canyon of the Yellowstone for the next six months; it's that the road closure marks the last day of fly fishing in the park until Memorial Day of the following year.

For my overly active brain, one activity—more than any other— truly puts me at ease. Having the perfectly carved cork of the Twin Bridges–built green-stick resting gently in the palm of my hand, lightly caressed by my fingers as it quickly and repeatedly lifts and lowers—in the process, pursuing a meeting with a brilliantly colored and heavily spotted member of the trout family—is, for me, a form of active meditation.

Since the vast majority of the waters outside Yellowstone National Park remain open for the adventurous and dedicated angler willing to endure the falling snow and raging winds of winter, there are other mosques in which to pray; but the closing of Yellowstone's waters each and every year are, to this disciple of Norman Maclean's spiritual practice of fly fishing, akin to the doors closing in Mecca.

While I am sure some will find this comparison sacrilegious, in truth, my respect for others' spiritual beliefs knows no boundaries; I find spirituality to be a deeply personal affair. For me, Yellowstone is my sacred place, its mountains my temples, its waters my lifeblood.

Since my early years working as a ranger naturalist in Yellowstone National Park, my father and I have made fishing the final days of each Yellowstone fishing season a tradition. We've coined it "The Poor Man's Steelhead Run" because the last week of the season provides opportunity at reel-ripping browns, rainbows, and mountain whitefish throughout a specific few of the park's watersheds. Autumn is when the nonnative brown trout and native mountain whitefish spawn; and in their pre-spawn behavior, their feeding habits often become more aggressive—especially with the colder temperatures and cloudy skies that accompany the season. This can create the perfect storm for an encounter with what could easily be any fly-fishing angler's largest fish of the year.

Unlike the summer, when donning shorts, T-shirts, and sandals in pursuit of eight- to sixteen-inch trout on the surface is the norm, fall fishing is not for the faint of heart, requiring a more rugged, dedicated, and patient kind of soul. The temperatures during the Poor Man's can drop below freezing, the winds might be ripping, and snow is often fall-ing. Focusing on the bright orange of a strike indicator—with nickel-sized snowflakes obscuring your view as you walk along the riverbanks in your layers and waders—can be a challenge; but this is part of the appeal and charm of end-of-season fishing in Yellowstone.

The average onlooker traveling the road from West Yellowstone to Madison Junction, en route to an encounter with geysers, fumaroles, and bubbling mud, might consider the absurd number of fly fishermen in full regalia, hip deep in the cold waters of the Madison River, more than a little obsessive—and perhaps a bit delusional. And while more anglers than not will have little to no luck actually landing their trout of the season, pursuing the large Hebgen Lake brown trout running up the river to spawn—or the chance of hooking up with a feisty holdover rain-bow still residing in the river after moving in the previous spring—is all the temptation we need to embrace the challenging conditions and hours of casting to seemingly fishless water.

But for me, the opportunity to wade the waters of Yellowstone in November has far deeper meaning than the chance to encounter a deeply colored, golden-bellied brown trout, with its heavy round spots and severely hooked jaw. This is a time for reflection, a time of reverence—a time to thank the waters that have given me so much over the course of the last five months, fueling both my spirit and my imagination. And perhaps most importantly, it is a highly anticipated and celebrated time with my best friend, my father.

Every year since I left the Park Service in 2007, it seems my days actually fishing become fewer and fewer. My nonprofit, Yellowstone Country Guardians, continues to grow and its programs expand, at the same time that my guide services are in greater demand. But October has always been my time to fish—the time when my guide season comes to an end. With the growth of YCG's Yellowstone Leadership Challenge (YLC), however, my days of walking the river in October have been greatly reduced. And last year, I could hardly complain about missing the final days of fishing in the park, as my wife, daughter, and I immediately hopped a plane to Hawaii following the YLC for a much-needed family vacation. Yet I still remember standing atop my paddle-board, waiting for the next set to roll into Kalapaki Beach on the Garden Island of Kauai, and thinking of my beloved waters, aching at missing the Poor Man's.

This year, it looked as if I would miss yet another opportunity to quietly and patiently stalk the autumn waters of Yellowstone with my dad when we took a road trip to Seattle to visit friends and family the day after the 2010 YLC. The plan was for my wife and little one to fly back to Montana after our visit, while I would take a solo journey down the Oregon Coast in hopes of adventurous enlightenment. But when it was time to part ways, the thought of my girls heading back to Yellow-stone Country as I journeyed down the wet, dark edge of Oregon—that I was already a month too late to experience without a constant drench-ing—weighed too heavily on my heart. I changed plans (as I often do) and returned home with them. My new plan: take a week off to chase my Poor Man's adventure.

Upon returning to Gardiner, the drain of six months of constant movement and work finally took its toll, and I spent two days in basket-ball shorts and T-shirt, not leaving the house and rarely leaving the comfort of bed. But the clock was ticking, and I knew it. By Wednesday, I knew I better get after it, as there were only five days of fishing left in the Yellowstone season. No matter how badly my body was yearning for rest, sleep, and rejuvenation, my spirit needed sunshine, running water, and a tug on the end of my line.

I spent the first afternoon on my home waters of the Gardner River, and while I wasn't super motivated by the warm temperatures and blue skies (which typically don't make for good fall brown-trout fishing), I knew I would regret letting another day go by. My most memorable days fishing in the fall have always been cold, cloudy, and threatening snow or rain, so I was skeptical about whether I would do any good. But

I suspected my body would respond well to wading the hurried waters of the Gardner regardless of the fish count.

Another reason I love fishing in the fall is that it's not about the number of fish caught; what matters instead is the potential encounter with that one fish you won't ever forget. There are very few things in the fly-fishing culture that turn me off more than fish "counters." It has long been a sore subject, and I can as quickly lose respect for an angler who brags about the quantity of the fish he or she caught as I can gain great respect for the angler who humbly tells me of that one quality fish—or better yet, an angler who recounts the sight of an osprey dive-bombing into the river nearby, or any other observation of the river world. With that said, I have to admit to being pleasantly surprised by the number of quality fish that I met on that balmy, bright, first day of my Poor Man's adventure.

The next day, I decided I would take the spirit of adventure to another level entirely by waking several hours before the sun rose over the flanks of Mount Everts. Two hours after leaving Gardiner, I witnessed its first rays lighting up the waters of Yellowstone Lake as I made my way to Lewis Lake and the Dogshead Trailhead, nervously anticipating my five-mile hike to the largest backcountry lake in North America—Shoshone Lake.

Maybe I should explain. I wasn't nervous because of the strenuous nature of the hike through the lodgepole forest. What was causing me anxiety was my speculation about the number of vehicles I would see at the trailhead. Though not universal knowledge, more than enough locals and park employees know that the last few weeks of every season is the time to pursue Shoshone Lake's massive brown trout, as they migrate into the shallow waters of the Lewis Channel. The problem doesn't lie in a shortage of fish but in a lack of fishable water in the channel—the makings of a precarious fishing proposition, because one could easily walk five miles only to find anglers already anchored in the best holes, leaving the latecomer a few sloppy seconds.

Though the hiking proved brutal, with nine inches of four-day-old melted and refrozen snow dropping me to my ass on more than one occasion, my heart rate increased the closer I got to the lake's shores. As it turned out, however, my anxiety was of my own making. When I reached the tranquil shores of the clear waters of Shoshone Lake, there wasn't a person in sight as I walked down the outlet and peacefully worked my way along the channel itself, which is nearly devoid of fish for most of the year. There were footprints from anglers past, but on this cold, bluebird morning, the randomly leaping browns, raucous Clark's nutcrackers, and graceful bald eagles were my only company.

I am not one for in-depth fish stories, as I find that they are very personal—as intimate as sex. So you will just have to trust me when I state that my three hours of casting to spooky browns of overly large proportions was fall fishing bliss at its finest. Though my actual fishing time was relatively short (considering the ten-mile hike) and my river meditations were interrupted by other anglers (oh, the nerve of those bastards to hike all the way up here), I knew the fierce tug and violent leaps of brown trout rarely seen in the summer months would haunt my dreams throughout the winter months ahead.

The next morning, after a cold and sleepless night spent rolling around the back of my truck in the Lewis Lake Campground, with temperatures hovering around twelve degrees, I dragged my achy bones and tired muscles out of my sleeping bag—again hours before the sun would rise. Then I simply stood there, taking in the brilliance of a predawn sky lit by stars made even brighter by the cold temperatures, lack of artificial light, and eight-thousand-foot elevation.

With little in my belly, I ventured north, over Craig Pass, and into the fog rising from the warm waters of the Firehole River. Rarely reaching twenty mph over the course of the drive from Old Faithful to Madison Junction, my years exploring and leading walks in the park enabled me to imagine the bubbling mud, boiling waters, and vibrant colors of bacterial mats I was passing. Every so often, as I followed the yellow line bisecting the roadway, a massive solo bison would halt my progress; and in the mystical fog, its silhouette would remind me of the wildness I was traveling through under the darkness of early morning (while listening to Lady Antebellum on Sirius radio).

By the time I reached the road that parallels the Madison River, the landscape was once again reemerging from the grasp of fog and darkness, and the "goat show" that is the Madison in fall was already beginning. In the basketball coaching fraternity that is small-town Montana (better known to locals as Class C), we often refer to a game of disorganized chaos as a goat show. And though river etiquette is surprisingly good for the number of road-weary anglers, the entire concept of fishing in such close proximity to other fly fishers is all too often the case on the Madison, where there may be anglers in the holes above and below you—and it takes some getting used to. However, unless a real yahoo intrudes upon you, the abundance of anglers is usually tolerable, due in part to the knowledge of the size of what could potentially slam your streamer, grab your soft hackle, or gobble your nymph.

Along the road from West Yellowstone to Madison Junction, if you are willing to face the life-snatching cold of the early morning, you can stake out a hole, and once there, it will be yours alone. On this morning, temperatures had barely reached twenty degrees when I started rigging up and getting dressed. My waders were frozen from the day before, which made getting my feet into the neoprene booties a challenge, but not nearly as difficult as getting into my hardened boots. In the short time that it took to get my waders on, my hands had gone numb. And unable to get my heavily socked feet into the frozen boots, I hustled to the truck (which was still running just in case the cold got the best of me), and thawed myself and my boots under the hottest dashboard-blasting heat that my 100,000-mile Toyota could muster.

Minutes later, as I stood knee-deep in the Madison River—with the sun beginning its ascent, lighting up the block-shaped, rugged National Park Mountain and magnifying the steam rising from the river—a lone bull bison slowly rambled twenty yards behind my back. I could hear his breath, his feet crunching the hardened grasses. And I found myself amazed by his strength and seeming imperviousness to the cold. I was wearing everything in my guide bag, blowing hot air into my hands, yet still shaking. His beard and the thick, matted hair on the sides of his face were covered with frost. I reminded myself that he was built for these harsh conditions.

Magic moments such as these—that have so little to do with fishing but are facilitated by the pursuit of trout—are what make fly fishing more than a hobby or a sport. They elevate it to something akin to a religion, a philosophy, and a lifestyle.

On my way home, I stopped and fished both the Gibbon and Gardner Rivers, where the average fish may not have boasted of much heft but swam in waters that I had almost completely to myself. I connected with more of my finned friends in a few hours there than I would have all day on the meat run that is my beloved Madison.

Though it was only Friday, I was so moved by this day's experiences on my treasured Yellowstone waters that I decided it was the right day to end the season on. So I said a prayer to Yellowstone—to the rivers, creeks, streams, and all of the trout, wildlife, birds, and plants that gave me so much sustenance throughout the course of the fishing season. It appeared another season of fly fishing in Yellowstone had passed.

But as I always do, I called my pops to share what I had experienced over the course of forty-eight hours; and by Saturday night, he called me from his home in Lolo, Montana, to say he would be leaving at 6 A.M. to meet me at Madison Junction the next day—the first Sunday in November. The last day of fishing in the park for the year.

How could I say no?

A special romanticism hit me as I drove the roads to meet my dad the next morning—recognizing it would be the last time I drove this route, which I had traveled so often over the course of the last six months, until the following spring. Another season in Yellowstone had nearly passed. The grasses were shining gold and waving gently in a breeze that also swayed the tips of the lodgepoles.

Just before reaching Gibbon Meadows, I slowed to a stop and—awestruck—observed the largest bull bison I can ever remember seeing. Granted, it stood upon the high portion of the road, but its massive shoulder blades were level with the top of my Toyota Tundra. I reached for the buffalo drum given to me by an Assiniboine–Gros Ventre elder, whom I had considered my brother ever since we'd taken a spiritual journey together nine years earlier, and said a prayer for all of the bison, knowing the winter and politics they would soon endure.

While it seems my father is rarely on time for anything we do together these days—yes, even fishing—this, the final day of The Poor Man's Steelhead Run, has become like a religion to us. It was clear when speaking with him on the phone the night before that this would be as much a pilgrimage for him as a fishing foray. He came rolling in right on time, with a grin and an elusive twinkle in his eyes. After exchanging big hugs, laughs, and a little heckling, we headed off to our secret Poor Man's waters to put a closure to yet another season.

Having recently hit the thirty-year mark, I have found myself more reflective and contemplative. Though I hope to share another thirty years with my dad, I know that with each passing fishing season, we are one more closer to the dreaded day when he will no longer be able to wade the slippery rocks and heavy waters that he has come to master and love. Thus, I find myself more grateful for every minute spent—every fish caught—together. This day was no exception.

In fact, this day proved to be one neither of us would forget. This day would be for my pops. And this day would be filled with gratitude.

I had already experienced three days of fishing bliss and knew what these waters could produce; and while I, too, experienced magic and communed with more large fish in one day than I can ever remember, watching my dad hook into and land one large fish after another was something I will forever cherish. Just to witness his smile—his gratitude for our surroundings and his childlike enthusiasm as we shared the most amazing day of fishing either of us had ever experienced—spoke to the wild spirit of Yellowstone.

Since I began working in Yellowstone, my dad and I have shared many days exploring the waters along the park's road and deep into its backcountry, but this was my dad's first day of fishing in Yellowstone of 2010. He had generously taken a week off to be my right-hand man during YCG's first annual River Guardian Fly Fishing School in August, giving up our usual time fishing together; and now karma was returning with a vengeance.

After a feverish thirty minutes, in which I landed three fish over seventeen inches (including one foul-hooked in the pectoral fin that I chased for over 150 yards through shin- and knee-deep water before gently releasing it back to the dark and soothing waters of its refuge), I decided I had no need to meet any more finned friends. I made my way upstream to my dad, who wanted to fish a few more minutes. Not more than five minutes after meeting up, I watched his indicator dip violently. With catlike reflexes, he quickly yet softly set the hook. An explosion of excitement began.

It's almost a blur now, so I couldn't say how long it took before the fish of the day—a rainbow more than twenty inches and pushing four pounds—rested in my net. The little size-18 copper John sat perfectly on the outside of its massive fish lip, and with almost no effort on my part, was removed with ease. We admired this rainbow as if it were the most beautiful thing we had ever seen. Its deep red lateral line, perfectly sorted and rounded black spots, and muscled body was a work of nature's finest art.

Some may not understand why we go to such great lengths to pursue fish we don't even keep. And I am not going to attempt to convert anybody. Hell, better that you don't understand—less people crowding the water that way. But I will say, the reverence that we felt the entire day, catching fish and gently cradling them in our hands before watching their tails slowly and strongly sway from side to side, propelling them back to their desired lay; listening to the most soothing music that the earth has yet created—the constant hustle of a river moving over hardened lava flow over 640,000 years old—is for us a spiritual experience surpassing almost any other.

Driving back home to Gardiner that night, we rode in separate vehicles—as is fitting—both experiencing our own thoughts and meditations on what this day meant to us. When we got back into cell range after forty-five minutes of solitude, my phone rang.

"What's up, Pops?"

"How on earth could such a big fish eat such a tiny bug?"

Fascination. Inspiration. Wonder. How many activities lead to such visceral emotions?

Closing out the season on The Poor Man's Steelhead Run was a gift I shared with the most important man in my life. And though I was saddened by the passing of yet another season, no day lasts forever. But unlike the slowly eroding river rocks, the memories of this day will not fade with time.

One of my biggest fears in life is how I will cope with the dreaded day that I no longer have my parents to guide me and share the joys of life. Perhaps the greatest gift of the Poor Man's is the passion and zeal for life—the youthful exuberance and willingness to bare the elements it inspires in so many anglers. For that chance encounter with the trout of a lifetime.

The Poor Man's is, for many, including my father, a real-life Fountain of Youth.

23

Bison and Bigotry

With temperatures hovering around -20°F, I awoke this morning to blue skies and sun bathing the snow-covered landscape on the northern reaches of Yellowstone National Park. I look out my window and see a lone bull bison working his way up the Jardine Road. Why then, on this glorious winter day, does it feel as if a dark and lingering cloud hovers over the rolling hills surrounding Gardiner, Montana?

When I was growing up as a fourth-generation resident of the tri-state region (Idaho, Montana, and Wyoming), observing the elephant of North America, the American bison (*Bison bison*), was the highlight of many summer forays to Yellowstone. Having worked for the National Park Service as a ranger naturalist for seven summer seasons and as a wildlife tour guide since departing my post in Mammoth Hot Springs in 2007, I have witnessed firsthand the awe and wonder visitors feel when encountering a herd of wild Yellowstone bison. I continue to experience that same awe, even as I pick up my cell phone to call the Buffalo Field Campaign office in Gardiner and let them know of the lone straggler.

Bison management is the dark cloud that makes the northern boundary of Yellowstone National Park a depressing and oppressive place to live during harsh winters such as this. Long respected throughout the nation for its legacy in wildlife management, Montana's current approach to managing bison represents a deeply blackened eye that threatens to dismantle the Treasure State's reputation as a leader in progressive management policies.

While there has never been a documented case of a bison transmitting brucellosis to cattle in the wild, this has not stopped the failing and flailing members of the Interagency Bison Management Plan (IBMP) from spending millions of taxpayer dollars to haze, capture, and slaughter bison to protect the brucellosis-free status of the state of Montana. In February of 2004, Wyoming lost its brucellosis-free status; with back-page press coverage, Idaho's status was stripped two years later; and in 2008, after decades of stockgrowers warning that a loss of brucellosis-free status could destroy the Montana economy, their hyperbolic fear became a reality for ranchers under the Big Sky.

But guess what? Elk, not bison, were determined to be the culprits for all of these brucellosis cases. And though testing costs certainly increased for ranchers across the tri-state region, neither the largely tourist-based Montana economy nor the cattle sky came falling down—nor will they ever—from a loss of brucellosis-free status. Brucellosis just happens to be the smoke-and-mirror disease used to perpetuate the myth that Yellowstone's bison have to be aggressively managed. If this goat show (a Western term for clusterfuck) that is bison management had anything to do with the transmission of brucellosis, elk would be aggressively targeted too. And why not accept the common-sense proposal of dual classification throughout Montana, creating a hot zone around Yellowstone National Park that would acknowledge that brucellosis (in the words of the US Department of Agriculture's Animal and Plant Health Inspection Service, one of the five signatory agencies in the IBMP) "is a more localized problem"? Perhaps because such an approach makes too much sense.

As reported in a recent *Bozeman Daily Chronicle* article, area ranchers "get it" and are willing to live with bison. Why, then, can't the government agencies representing the IBMP begin acting rationally by practicing greater tolerance for an animal that symbolizes the wildness and ruggedness that Montana supposedly represents?

Yellowstone's most magnificent beast continues to be managed by politics and fear. The most recent management strategy—to allow twenty-five bison on land north of the park—is yet another mismanaged failure. For a pretty penny, the Church Universal and Triumphant (known to locals as "CUT"—remember Elizabeth Clare Prophet and her doomsday sect?) agreed to retire grazing rights on their thoroughfare of land extending north from the park on the west side of the Yellowstone River.

While celebrated by the NGOs who helped broker this controversial deal, IBMP workers on the ground were not optimistic this plan would work. True to predictions, just over a week after being released, the twenty-five bison that have been "poked, prodded, marked, vaginally violated, and all but dehorned," according to bison advocate Glenn Hockett of the Gallatin Wildlife Association, were already under assault from Montana Department of Livestock field agents.

Frustrated by the lack of cooperation on the part of the wild bison, who simply wouldn't stay put on the twenty-five hundred acres of Gallatin National Forest grazing habitat that promoters of the plan had hoped would contain the migratory animals until May 1, IBMP members recaptured thirteen of the twenty-five animals and released them back into the park. These released bison then surprised agents by crossing the Yellowstone River to commune with a band of bison being held at a quarantine facility—which should not have come as a big surprise to anyone who knows the behavior of this herd animal. One rogue bison, who refused to be hazed from private land, was shot. Not an illustrious start to the new plan, which had been touted by its creators as a great step toward resolution of the bison problem. Perhaps best put by Mr. Hockett: "I believe this will likely go down as one of the worst 'conservation' deals in US history, certainly in Montana history." It appears even the $3.3 million recently paid to CUT, on top of almost $13 million they received in 1997 for basically the same purpose, can't buy tolerance for bison.

Why are three-hundred-plus of Yellowstone's thirty-nine hundred bison currently crammed into holding pens at the Stephens Creek holding facility for simply following their ancestral instincts to migrate to lower elevations in search of food—a right all other ungulates in the Yellowstone Ecosystem are afforded? Why were the one-hundred-plus bison walking north into an oncoming storm a week ago Sunday hazed and captured when the band of a dozen bull elk and neighboring herd of forty cow elk—an animal proven to have transmitted brucellosis to cattle—were not bothered? Since this issue has more to do with bison competing with the sacred cow for grass (along with the bisons' fence-destroying abilities) than it does with any real concern over a disease that is fifty years past its time as a real threat, I believe there is clearly an elephant in the room that no one wants to address.

Gardiner, Montana, is the Selma, Alabama, of conservation wars in our nation today. I say this with great caution so as not to offend those who battled on behalf of equality for a beautiful people long oppressed because of the color of their skin. But I believe our current battle to gain greater tolerance and understanding for animals such as bison, grizzlies, and wolves requires the same passion, dedication, and leadership as the civil rights movements of the 1950s and '60s. Those who argue the election of President Obama signals that racism and bigotry no longer exist in our nation are delusional. While we have clearly become a more enlightened and progressive nation in regard to race, fear of the unknown still leads to hate and misguided policy.

Driving through the Paradise Valley early this morning was eerily reminiscent of a dark time in our nation's history. Let the dogs loose—the bison are out! With over three hundred bison already captured, another band of fifteen busted loose of the park under the darkness of night and -30°F temperatures. Does this seemingly innocent movement of roughly a dozen bison really warrant the deployment of an entire brigade of state agents? In the short fifty-one-mile drive north to Livingston, Montana, I witnessed eleven trucks and three horse trailers—representing Montana Fish, Wildlife and Parks; Montana Department of Livestock; and local sheriffs—caravanning en route to play cowboy with fifteen members of the Pleistocene.

I have often heard state and federal agents express the opinion that bison "don't fit" in a twenty-first-century Montana. There was a time in our nation's history when our government didn't believe whites and blacks were meant to coexist either, but many wise and determined leaders saw this racist nonsense to be unfit for a progressive and enlightened America. The question is not whether bison belong in a twenty-first-century Montana but whether we are willing to live in a state where intolerance for a magnificent and honorable animal—and not science—drives our management policies.

In my opinion, the Yellowstone bison debate is no longer an issue of wildlife management but one of social justice and moral responsibility. The bison management strategy that has sent 3800 wild bison to slaughter since 2000—simply for wandering across an invisible line in search of food—remains stagnant and archaic. How we will be evaluated by future generations as wildland stewards will ultimately be measured by how we respond to this challenge.

24

Teasing Seasons

While I have to believe that the spring-like weather conditions that have wrapped up the northern reaches of Yellowstone Country in recent days are a sign of the season to come, I am not fully convinced that winter has released its loose grip on the region. "Loose" because, for the last two months in the banana belt that is the Gardiner Basin, winter has failed to fully express its rugged nature. Regardless of the lack of precipitation, any winter spent in Yellowstone—even one such as this, where snow has rarely and sparsely fallen—seems long and drawn out.

If it weren't for the incessant winds and half-dozen snowstorms that interrupt our much-anticipated but short-lived spring each year, perhaps a light winter wouldn't feel so extended. But the two-plus weeks of below-freezing temperatures that locked up Yellowstone beginning the First of October makes this second week of March the sixth month since I last waded a river in pursuit of trout or pedaled a road bike without a cold wind cutting through my skin.

After experiencing countless snowstorms in April, May, and June over the years, I should know better than to think we have seen the last of winter. And while I fully expect and hope to see more snow fly in the weeks and months to come, it simply feels too much like spring right now to accept the idea that we still have several weeks of squalls ahead.

In the meantime, it has been a pleasure to break out the road bike and rig up the fly rod these last few days. The unrelenting winds of March let up just enough on Saturday for me to venture, wind at my back, up valley on skinny tires through the Gardiner Basin and into the dark depths of Yankee Jim Canyon. And earlier in the week, it was with great anticipation that I donned the waders with my dad and eagerly entered our traditional trout waters of the Bitterroot. Though it may still be too early to actually welcome the onset of spring, these symbolic activities represent our hopes, as members of the Leach clan, for the season to come.

But now there are new traditions unfolding as my life transforms like the seasons before me. After a day spent ripping up the garden in preparation for the crops that will add color to our yard and organic nourishment to our bellies, the sun descended behind the shoulder of Electric Peak. And with the departure of sunlight, the winds returned with a fervor. Though the temperature rapidly dropped fifteen degrees, my two-year-old baby girl was intent on continuing our game of soccer outside. It doesn't matter how tired I am, when my little Boo Bear asks, "Daddy, you wanna go out and play wit me?" it's on.

Gearing up in jackets, hats, and gloves, we ventured into the broken grasses of our front yard, and proceeded to kick and wrestle until the tireless winds changed her usually olive cheeks to the bright red of the tomatoes that will soon be growing in our garden. And thus, on this beautiful Sunday early in March, new traditions were born to symbolize the beginning of spring. The afternoon that began with a short meander along the banks of the Yellowstone River with my wife, Crystal; our nature-loving daughter; our black lab; and our Tennessee Treeing Walker Coonhound ended with a heart-pounding play session in the dry confines of our front yard, perched above the still sleepy town of Gardiner.

Entirely different from my tiring bike rides and thrilling dry-fly fishing on the 'Root (where, even in the presence of friends and family, my experience is almost entirely my own), my newly discovered welcoming of a spring with my greatest love—my little girl—somehow transcends the meaning of seasons, speaking to our shared transformation with the natural world. Unpredictable and unwavering, our lives and the seasons will come and go, and will present themselves differently with each passing year.

In the presence of love, when and how each season passes is of no importance. Instead, it is the beauty of each moment shared with a loved one or a loved place that makes our walk upon this earth uniquely ours—and yet immensely interconnected to the place we call home.

25

Chaos, Wind, and Harlequins

After a cool and wet May, the first two days of June greeted us with warm temperatures, sunshine, and lots of wind. The past thirty-one days of May represented the wettest month many of us can remember here in Yellowstone. While the accumulation of snow over a typical Yellowstone winter always makes this a harsh and unforgiving place to live, rain—especially on the arid landscape north of Yellowstone National Park, in the Gardiner Basin—is a somewhat random event. But this was certainly not the case for the past month, when my daughter seemingly lived in the bright green rubber boots that inevitably adorn her feet any day that showers unleash. And in Yellowstone, that's what showers do—they unleash.

The surging pulse of spring runoff, which occurs when the day and nighttime temperatures rise enough to begin melting the winter's snowpack, has yet to begin in earnest; but the rivers are already muddied and pulsing from recent rains, and ready to explode as temperatures continue upward. There has long been a saying here in Montana, Idaho, and Wyoming—somewhat corny perhaps but maddeningly true—that if you don't like the weather, give it ten minutes, for it will surely change. Today is perhaps as good a day as any to witness the high-elevation phenomenon that makes this such an unpredictable place to call home. At times, the blustery winds have reached a pitch so feverish they threatened to dismantle anything not tightly fastened to the house. For example, I'm scheduled to speak tonight to a small group of carnivore buffs, after which I have high hopes of returning home to watch game two of the NBA finals; but I fear that any plan to watch the Dallas Mavericks' attempt to tie up the series is delusional, as I will be shocked if our dish receiver withstands the brutal onslaught of wind this gusty afternoon provided.

With the upper Yellowstone River drainage sitting at a silly 226 percent of its annual snowpack equivalent and the mercury in thermometers beginning to climb, we will likely see historic flows scouring the river corridor and liberally overflowing the river banks, flooding the valley floor and bringing a renewed wildness to an already wild landscape. This past Saturday, the 28 of May, marked yet another chaotic day in Yellowstone National Park. Not accustomed to receiving such a generous amount of rain, the shallow layer of topsoil throughout Yellowstone's Northern Range can only soak up so much water before the land begins to give way in the form of landslides. That's what happened on the twenty-eighth.

I picked up my clients from Ontario, Canada, for what was supposed to be a routine wildlife watching tour in the Lamar Valley. At 5:20 A.M. (especially after being up preparing since 3:30), finding solutions to challenges can be difficult; but luckily, what we encountered blocking our path on the road from Mammoth to Tower, just beyond Blacktail Plateau Drive, was a series of car-sized boulders and recently uprooted conifers. This actually made decisions quite easy.

My only option was to put plan B in place. While this couple yearned to see a wolf in the wild, we would travel to Swan Lake Flat and hope for a random *Canis lupus* sighting while we searched for the female grizzly who had made headlines across the country last year, when she emerged from hibernation with not an excessive three cubs but an almost-unheard-of four. After turning around and heading to the flats, we scanned the area. No luck. Disappointment beginning to mount, we decided to move on in pursuit of a grizzly that had been hanging out around the Roaring Mountain area. Still groggy and prepping our minds to deal with the weather (which included snow flurries and a slight breeze), we rounded a bend and spotted a grizzly one hundred yards off the road—interestingly enough, nearing the Grizzly Lake Trailhead.

After we spent over an hour watching the ravenous, post-hibernation grizzly scour the grassy meadow covered with a fresh layer of snow—masterfully excavating the field in search of pocket gophers, grass, roots of all sorts, and if lucky, the occasional earthworm—he rewarded us with an up-close-and-personal encounter by ambling to within twenty-five yards of the road. Having worked an untold number of bear jams, I wasn't concerned by the proximity of this bear, in light of the size of the crowd and the determination with which he fed. The seemingly intoxicated photographers (giddy with delight at the bear's cooperation) were, for the most part, behaving themselves while wildly and somewhat frantically clicking digital SLR cameras that housed ridiculously large telephoto lenses. By my estimate, there had to be well over $150,000 worth of glass precariously perched on tripods on the shoulder-less edge of the road; and while none of it shattered, there were several close calls when novices used sketchy, albeit creative tactics to balance their cameras monopod-style—since they lacked room for the other two legs of their tripods.

Thrilled with the portraits they'd taken of the grizzly's large rounded head and snow-covered snout, my clients grew eager for our next stop. En route to the Hayden Valley, in hopes of additional carnivore sightings, we soon reached our second roadblock of the morning—all before the clock had even struck 7 A.M. This time, a truck and trailer had careened off the road, jackknifing before climbing Cardiac Hill on its way to Canyon, and in the process, forcing the NPS to close the road until plows could rid the asphalt of the roughly three inches of snow that had fallen overnight.

These are the situations where a guide has to get creative. Working as a ranger naturalist in the park, we were often told that we needed to be "expert generalists." While this is no easy task, the rangers who thrive in the complex and dynamic world of Yellowstone make a point of mastering a wide range of park-related topics. And while my expertise in regard to Yellowstone geology rests in the ever-changing wonders of the Mammoth Hot Springs, circumstances now dictated that I remember everything I had dutifully studied about the extreme environment of the Norris Geyser Basin as an eager rookie. We were about to embark upon a geological adventure.

Thankfully, my clients remained not only good-natured about the obstacles literally blocking our path, they were highly adaptable—their desire to photograph a wolf (a difficult quest to begin with) slowly fading with the odds of it actually happening. They had resolved to relish whatever Yellowstone threw at us. I must have had some good Yellowstone karma going on this day, because these are the clients you pray for when things go bad. After an hour of walking around the geyser basin, however, my cup of Norris knowledge had run dry, and we journeyed back to the truck in hopes that the road would be reopened. At this point, I planned to head back toward Mammoth (since it was still only 8:45 A.M.) to try to make it through the slide and out to the Lamar. But when we ran into a ranger who warned us that the road would probably not be cleared until later in the day, I decided we were better off heading to the Hayden Valley. (Side note: the road took five days to be cleared, leaving the goings-on in the Lamar to those willing to circumnavigate the northern part of the park or residents of Cooke City and Silver Gate.)

By Yellowstone standards, the rest of the afternoon proved uneventful. The snowpack in the Hayden Valley remained impressive. At certain spots, such as those near Grizzly Overlook, the banks of snow towered eight feet above the road. With winter still firmly gripping the Yellowstone Plateau, it felt as if the valley were asleep. While the landscape remained in the monochromatic shades of March, the scenery kept my clients (who by this time had become more like friends) engaged and enraptured.

I'd been hired to deliver more of a photographic wildlife safari, but I knew from experience that a good guide always remains adaptable, saving a few tricks up his or her sleeve for days like this. I still had my geology tour/talk of Mammoth Hot Springs in my back pocket, and I also planned on stunning them with the jaw-dropping, deeply inspiring Grand Canyon of the Yellowstone from Artist Point. Still, I felt I needed one more wildlife sighting to really close this one out; and considering the time of day and amount of snowfall in the Hayden Valley, I wasn't optimistic about finding any four-legged carnivores in close enough proximity for a 400mm lens. So I decided to journey down to Fishing Bridge and the lake, which remained locked in ice and shrouded by low cloud cover.

The lake area is always a great bet for spotting grizzly bears in early to mid-spring, though it didn't feel likely that we would see much on this wet and dreary day. The amount of snow made it feel like winter, but the temperature indicated the arrival of spring. And the Fishing Bridge general store was caught in-between, its parking lot under several inches of water, making a trip to refill the coffee thermos a sloshy endeavor.

After rehydrating, we came down to my last holdout of hope: spotting the elusive and rare migratory bird that descends upon LeHardy Rapids each spring. With visitation relatively low, the lack of traffic allowed me to make a lingering pass by the rapids named after a member of an 1873 exploration party attempting to map the river's course. When his boat capsized, Lee Hardy narrowly escaped the turbulent waters. Leaning across the lap of my client in the passenger seat, I stretched my neck, blue-heron style, hoping to get a glimpse of the prized waterfowl that's slightly smaller than a mallard, with a short gray bill, vibrant white stripes highlighting its chestnut brown flanks, and grayish-purple plumage—the harlequin duck.

According to Terry McEneaney's *Birds of Yellowstone*, there are less than twenty nesting pairs of harlequin ducks in Yellowstone National Park. McEneaney's book was published back in 1988, but I, for one, can attest to the fact that there are still very few places where one is likely to spot a pair of harlequins in Yellowstone. Two of the only reliable spots remain the swift water of Le Hardy Rapids and the hurried torrents below the Yellowstone River bridge, just east of Tower Junction.

To my delight, as I craned my neck and crossed my toes, no more than twenty yards from the bank, I spotted a pair.

More often than not, by this time of the year, one can walk along the frozen snow and ice layering the wooden boardwalk that leads to the viewing platform. But with the trail entombed with at least four feet of accumulation, we opted to view the ducks from the road, through the heavily weighted boughs of lodgepole pines lining the asphalt thoroughfare. In such a stark landscape, where the constant lodgepole shadows keep sunshine at bay and overwhelm the surroundings with snow and bone-aching temperatures, the mere idea of the frothy and pulsating waters of the Yellowstone beckoning an exotic winged migrant from the Pacific Northwest ignites the imagination.

Having heard no whispers of the harlequins' return, I was surprised and thrilled to find seven pairs in all. Always eager to welcome back any of our winged migrants, both for the color they bring to the landscape and what they represent—an end to winter—I savored the opportunity to again observe one of the lesser known but certainly noteworthy members of the Yellowstone community.

In typical Yellowstone fashion, our mere presence, with field glasses and cameras in hand, prompted passersby to ask what we had sighted. The response when I announced "harlequins" ignited our own little jam of the winged variety. The excitement convinced my clients that this was indeed a rare and notable sighting, and added to the success of what could have been a day I would have rather forgotten. Instead, it turned out to be one of those days that remind me there is always magic in Yellowstone.

With the presence of wolves, grizzlies, bison, elk, and a plethora of other charismatic megafauna, who would have thought that a feathered duck weighing less than two pounds, diving and scrambling for aquatic insects in the swift waters of the Yellowstone River, would be the wand that reawakened the imagination and curiosity of a dozen onlookers yearning for an encounter with something wild?

Yellowstone is full of wildness—perhaps more so than any other landscape in the lower forty-eight. But today, for two visitors from Ontario, Canada, and their humbled guide, the wildness within was most inspired by a chance encounter with a diving duck and its aquatic environment. So if you ever find yourself becoming too narrow in focus—too bear- or wolf-centric—remember the tiny harlequins and the enchantment that abounds throughout this Ecosystem when it's welcomed by an open heart and a fertile mind. Yellowstone will never disappoint.

26

Respect for Señor Blanco

In a rapidly growing Western landscape, the ability to assimilate to the local culture is a skill—and perhaps a gift—utilized by those who will one day inevitably add to our communities' diversity. There are certain cultural norms in small towns like Gardiner, Montana, such as driving through town with your steering hand high on the wheel, ready to greet each person passing by with a customary index-finger salute. These are the small things that help make Montana, well, Montana.

Having grown up in the tri-state region (Idaho, Montana, Wyoming), with four generations of family history here, there are many things about our culture that give me great pride; while there are others that need to be revised into a "new West" worthy of our children. Any young angler growing up under the Big Sky will likely be taught at some point about the inferior fish with the pea-shaped mouth and silver body—the mountain whitefish. Often described as the Rodney Dangerfield of the river community and considered a trash fish by many, this spirited inhabitant of our local rivers is maligned by spin fishermen and fly anglers alike.

Still, many newcomers to the region are shocked to learn of the "Montana handshake," which refers to the practice of squeezing the mountain whitefish's air bladder; or the famous "bank release," an all-too-common practice across the entire region referring to the simple—albeit illegal—act of tossing wild and healthy whitefish on the riverbank to slowly suffocate. Even in the guide culture I have been a part of for the last six years, the whitefish is often thought of as little more than a nuisance. Sadly, newcomers quickly learn to accept this discriminatory philosophy toward one of the Yellowstone Ecosystem's most common and abundant fish species.

Far too often, I have heard the argument that the mountain whitefish competes with trout as a reason for disliking the ugly stepchild of the river world; but this naively ignores the fact that both species have evolved over thousands of years, cohabitating the same streams long before we showed up. The Señor Blanco not only serves as a "canary in the mine"—indicating the health of our rivers and streams—but will eagerly eat a bead-headed nymph, thus providing ample opportunity at a tight line and fishing delight for the angler willing to target this lively species that is always ready to put up a good fight. As a fly-fishing guide and director/founder of a regional nonprofit that operates a River Guardian Fly Fishing School for high-school-aged youth across Gallatin and Park Counties, I have witnessed firsthand the joy and excitement felt by countless novice anglers upon hooking into the native Señor Blanco.

While the mountain whitefish may not leap and routinely rip line off your reel the way more "desirable" species such as rainbows and browns do, no one can contend that this vigorous member of the trout family—yep, that is right, Señor Blanco has trout bloodlines—doesn't put up a good fight. Every time new clients climb aboard my drift boat, the first thing I do after a brief casting tutorial is sit down and tell them that I have one rule: "All finned friends are treated equally. Meaning we will wet our hands and gently release every member of the finned community we have the opportunity to meet today."

And yet, hardly a summer day goes by on the waters extending throughout Yellowstone Country without a scrappy mountain whitefish enthusiastically taking the nymph or streamer of an obsessive-compulsive fly fisherman with a "trophy" trout on the brain—who, in his excitement, ignores the customary "Whitey head shake" sending shock waves pulsating up his line—only to have the disappointed angler exclaim, "Damn, it's just a freaking whitefish!"

Whether it can be explained by the tendency to overlook the iridescent colors radiating off the whitefish's scaled body; the perceived ease of catching this abundant species; or the presence of a rosy gill plate, pea-shaped mouth, and higher oil content (leading to a slightly fishier smell), the mountain whitefish has been dissed for far too long. It is time for a Whitey Revolution, and who better to lead the charge than the guides and anglers throughout the Yellowstone area?

In order to change an outdated cultural norm in our region, we must redefine what is desirable and what is not. Sexy is in the eye of the beholder. So next time you land a mountain whitefish, leave the played out "it's just a Whitey" jargon at home and show some respect to Señor Blanco.

27

Song of the Yellow Bellied

I have yet to hear my first western meadowlark of the year, which, for me, always signals spring's arrival. But the mountain bluebird sightings two weeks back by my mentor and friend, Executive Director of Montana Audubon, Steve Hoffman, while trekking along the park's Northern Range, were a clear sign. The fluttering wings of that mountain bluebird, combined with the warm weather of weeks past and the wet flurries now dominating the region, make it official: spring is here.

Just because I haven't heard my first western meadowlark of 2010—while my mom has been reporting their melodic call for over a week, three hundred miles to the west, in the Bitterroot Valley—does not mean they aren't already here. There are likely countless birders across Yellowstone Country who have seen and perhaps heard the Northern Rockies' winged announcement of spring, but the changing of seasons is a complicated and personal thing. After enduring yet another long and windy winter on the brink of a hill overlooking Gardiner, it matters not whether someone else has heard the long-awaited pronouncement of a new season. Until I experience this wilderness symphony myself, I remain in seasonal limbo.

And limbo is not where one wants to be after six months of winter. Some would think that the lack of snowfall this winter season would lessen its effect on one's nerves. But the accumulation of snow is seemingly irrelevant in judging the longevity and severity of winter months spent in the northern reaches of Yellowstone Country. The constant barrage of wind battering the side of the house eventually takes its toll on the spirit (and perhaps sanity) of local residents, thus making even the most modest signs of spring a much anticipated miracle of sorts.

Unnerved by the relentless wind, I ventured out of the office late this afternoon. Foggy in head after completing my fifth grant in thirteen days, I meandered my way to the kitchen, feeling like I had spent the entire morning on a rocking ship—legs wobbly from too many hours in front of a keyboard. I pillaged the fridge and uncovered leftovers from our last two dinners. Eager to rest my weary eyes, I plopped down in the refuge of my recliner (which has seen far better days) and began the adventure of mixing slow-cooked pork loin with the leftover taco meat. I hadn't taken two full bites when a lazy movement in the pasture behind the house caught my eye.

To my bewilderment and surprise, a true indicator of spring had just crawled out of its earthly tomb of the last seven months. With great excitement, I hurriedly placed my bowl of meat on the side table—missing it completely and decorating the carpet with a meaty mess—and rushed to the window with field glasses in hand. To my delight, a drunken yellow-bellied marmot explored the dirt at the mouth of his den with a seemingly perplexed look on his face as to why it was still snowing. The sight brought back memories of the joy I felt when observing the clumsy movements of the marmots in previous years.

Now I recognize I have taken two anthropomorphic liberties in describing this member of the rodent family as perplexed and drunken, but let me explain.

The yellow-bellied marmot (also known as a rock chuck) is a fixture in the mammalian community across Yellowstone's jumbled rock fields, and is perhaps best known for its short, piercing whistle—hence its nickname: the whistle pig. But for those who know a little more about the life history of this chubby, round, long-toothed marmot (try saying it out loud—even their name conjures up a little laughter), this slow-moving critter is also known for its lengthy hibernation endeavors. By the beginning of August, the rock fields that couldn't be passed without hearing loud chirps all spring and summer (there is always at least one marmot known as a "sentinel," who is responsible for warning other members of their colony of intruders) are silent and seemingly lifeless.

It is always a sad hike when walking past one of the numerous marmot colonies once the chattering community has gone silent, because it is yet another indication that summer is nearing its end and fall will soon be upon us. But this sighting on the first day of April of a marmot in his post-hibernation stupor was not a cause for dread; it was a reason to celebrate spring's presence, despite the raging snowstorm.

Seeing the lightly colored marmot reemerging from the underworld filled my heart with joy—not because of the seasonal symbol (which far outweighs some silly East Coast tradition of a shadow and a groundhog) but because of the life-giving resilience of a land I simply know as Yellowstone.

Spring is the time when life returns with a vengeance, and the fecundity of Yellowstone is once again on full display. Nothing in Yellowstone is simple or easy, so spring is no exception. Indeed, we will surely see more winter-like days and raging winds that remind us of darker times; but we will also hear the sweet song of the meadowlark and witness the rising head of a trout, the return of the osprey, and the burnt-orange belly of a marmot sunning itself on the leeward side of a boulder—all giving us hope for the rich days ahead.

For me, this sighting of a yellow-bellied marmot transcended the beginning of a new season and spoke directly to the tireless spirit of Yellowstone. Last summer, while cleaning out my drift boat in preparation for another long guide day on the water, my gangly, pound-rescued Tennessee Treeing Coonhound proudly cantered toward me and dropped a limp and lifeless mound of fur at my feet. Thinking it was just another scrap of winter-killed mule deer (which are numerous in our area), I kept scrubbing the interior of my boat—until the grizzled orange tips of hair caught my eye. To my astonishment, the golden belly and brown body of a yellow-bellied marmot rested at my feet.

Enraged by Tucker's actions and feeling terrible for my lack of diligence in letting him run, I scolded him, with anger rising from deep within my belly. After putting him in the house and sharing the news with my wife, I walked over to my truck to think it through. During a very difficult time in my life, a man who became like my brother took me on a journey and shared with me many of the beliefs and traditions of his Assiniboine–Gros Ventre culture. Still to this day—ten years later—when I find a dead bird in our yard, I heed brother Darrel's advice, wrapping the feathered body in a brightly colored handkerchief and then tying it to a large sagebrush facing west, so that its spirit can fly to the spirit world.

Though one is never to bury a bird in the ground in Darrel's tribe's belief, four-leggeds are different. With a heavy heart, I reached into my glove box and grabbed the bundle of American Spirit tobacco that Darrel said I must always have available for such occasions, and somberly walked to the lifeless marmot. I scooped her body into my gloved hands with care and walked her to a field of boulders, where I had seen her sunning on bright spring mornings. And there, I performed a little ceremony with the tobacco, simply honoring and giving reverence to a beautiful critter that I had grown fond of.

For the selfish thought of my own loss of enjoyment, I had felt guilty when I walked back from that impromptu burial. But later that evening, after returning from the river, as I unhooked my boat from my truck, I heard the chirp of a marmot—the sentinel—making his announcement. And I couldn't help but believe it was another member of the marmot's small band honoring her life with the song of the yellow bellied—a simple song—reminding me each spring that life has returned to Yellowstone.

28

Bliss Pass

It always seems as if a nervous excitement surrounds any multiday backpacking trip, regardless of destination. The thought of leaving behind all that is civilization—cell phones, e-mail, televisions, trucks, and responsibilities—stirs a sense of wonder and free spiritedness that is simply hard to replicate in our everyday lives.

No matter how hard I hike on any given day of a trip, my sleep remains somewhat restless in the backcountry, my aching back and joints never quite adapting to the minimal pad that serves as my bed. Add in the grizzly factor when hiking just about anywhere in the Yellowstone Ecosystem, and shut-eye is a precious resource.

Knowing all of this, one would think there might be a way to slow down my overly active brain the night before my backcountry treks. But with the exception of Ambien, which has been known to cause what my good friend and former Ranger Scotty B likes to call my "Ambien deliriums" (he believed we were being attacked by a grizzly bear when he experienced one of my confused and panicked struggles in a tent at Soda Butte Campground), I've yet to find a way to get a good night's sleep on the eve of a backpacking trip.

Whatever the amount of sleep, when the day finally arrives to hit the trail in pursuit of grand vistas, rugged beauty, and encounters with wild trout, that nervous excitement overpowers the fatigue of a restless night. Plus, when guide work calls, you arrive prepared and ready for whatever the trip may throw at you—your reputation depends upon it.

There are backcountry trips, and there are guided trips to the backcountry. On a regular excursion, whether it be a day hike or a multiday backpacking trip, you can almost always get away with making due should you forget something. When you are being paid the big bucks as a fly-fishing guide, however, you better have your shit together.

Day trips are certainly nothing to bat an eye at, for if you get careless and forget a water filter, first-aid kit, or rain jacket when guiding clients to the second or third meadow of Slough Creek, your client is bound to run out of water, lacerate his shin, or get pummeled by a raging afternoon thunderstorm. But multiday, overnight backcountry trips are another beast entirely.

My first contact with John came in late February. He had read my feature article in the Spring 2009 *Yellowstone Discovery* (a publication put out by the Yellowstone Association), which told of the plight of the grizzly bear during limited whitebark pine crops and forecasted a grim future for whitebark pine in the Yellowstone Ecosystem. He appreciated the piece and kindly took the time to tell me so via e-mail. Following my response (and upon seeing my job titles of nonprofit director / writer / coach / speaker / fly-fishing guide in my e-mail signature), he wrote again, this time expressing his desire to take his wife on a three-day, two-night backpacking trip with an emphasis on fly fishing in the park. While I hadn't led a backpacking trip in over two years due to a bad Achilles, it sounded like a perfect match. So John and I began planning their big Yellowstone adventure.

There is something romantic about the idea of planning a backpacking trip for late July when it is still February. Unless you are a total powder hound, the long nights, short days, cold temps, and rattling winds of winter on the northern edge of Yellowstone National Park begin to wear on one's nerves. Because months still await before the rivers truly begin to thaw, planning summer fishing trips and backcountry forays can act as a natural antidepressant, lending just enough hope to help you through the final days of winter and the unpredictability of spring's fury.

After typing up a mock itinerary for three trips that differed in length and difficulty, I set up a time to speak with John over the phone from his home in Bodega Bay, California. I immediately liked the man. Unlike myself, he didn't use a lot of words or superlatives but was direct, while remaining thoughtful and kind. He made it clear that he had done very little backpacking and that his wife had done none. He was sixty and his wife of ten years was fifty, but he informed me they were fit and willing to endure the hardships of a backcountry sojourn.

One of the things that struck me most in our first conversation of many (John and his wife, Kathy, would later become close friends and instrumental supporters of the nonprofit that I founded, Yellowstone Country Guardians) was John's deep and authentic appreciation for the natural world. This clearly wasn't the same conversation I had shared with others in recent months—conversations about booking a backcountry fly-fishing trip where size and numbers of fish where the main objective. Instead, I felt as if I were speaking with Socrates, the wise man from a motivational book I have read on numerous occasions called *The Way of the Peaceful Warrior.*

It is difficult for some people to transmit their personality over the phone. There are many folks I speak with when booking a trip that make me wonder what I am getting myself into. But John's humble confidence made me curious and enthused at the thought of spending three days in the wilds of Yellowstone with him. Perhaps this trip would be about much more than my getting John and his wife into fish while sharing my interpretive knowledge of Yellowstone's Northern Range.

Far from your typical fish head, with nothing but fat bellies and brilliant colors of wild Yellowstone trout on his brain, John made it clear from the get-go that this would not simply be a fishing trip. He wanted a grand experience that he and Kathy would always cherish. One for the memory bank. Wildlife, birds, ecology, natural history, and hiking were all prerequisites for John. But he still wanted to catch fish; and more importantly, he wanted his wife to catch fish too.

I quickly concluded that Slough Creek had to be part of this trip's equation. I shared with John the three different trips that I had created, their mileage, elevation gain, fishing experience, and quality of campsites and trails. John, a former MVP of the College World Series, clearly had the same ambitious spirit that had won him his prestigious award the year his Arizona State Sun Devils won the national championship—because without hesitation, he chose the hardest of the three trips: we would hike from Slough Creek Trailhead to Pebble Creek Trailhead over the course of three days, with an arduous ascent of Bliss Pass on day two of the trip.

A few months later, while I was speaking in Missoula to students from the University of Montana's forestry department, I met with John at a popular college hangout, the Old Post, for dinner. Though I had just met him and hadn't spent more than a few minutes in his presence, I found myself tense, with a slight tinge of self-consciousness—the way one feels when in the presence of someone important. I figured him to be a guy with some money since he had a second home in Missoula and ran a successful insurance company that he had started from scratch; but he arrived at dinner on an old, beat-up bike, wearing shorts, a T-shirt, and a pair of sandals. He was also covered in paint from working on his home.

Wait a minute; this wasn't what I'd expected. He was down to earth, authentic, and charming, while remaining full of conviction when explaining what brought his wife and him to purchase a small and simple house near the university, in a pleasant but humble part of town—not in the Rattlesnake district, the hipster place to own a home.

He began busting my balls within thirty minutes of our meeting. By the time we were ready to depart, we were already giving big hugs, the way athletes with a common respect for one another do before and after a game—the way I had been with my boys I had grown up hooping with in Seattle. We made the decision that it would be best if I hired help to carry the weight, in order to keep John's pack under thirty pounds and the pack carried by Kathy—whom I had yet to met—around twenty pounds.

Truth be told, John could have easily booked someone who would provide a more plush and comfortable experience; but I could see that John was about relationships and the quality of experience through personal connection, which we had clearly already developed. Compatibility is a powerful factor when deciding on your backcountry mates, be it a leisure or paid trip. I quickly surmised that John didn't have the type of personality to put up with someone bullshitting their way through a guided journey.

Now I had to get creative. I didn't have access to horses, and paying a horse packer to haul our gear wasn't practical, as I would be lucky to break even on the trip if I did.

Time to cash in on the rose ceremony.

PART TWO: THE ROSE CEREMONY

IN THE WEEKS FOLLOWING MY dinner with John, I began acquiring lightweight camping gear to reduce the load I would be hauling to the third meadow of Slough Creek and up over Bliss Pass. Three weeks before our scheduled departure, I visited the old, brick REI in Spokane, Washington, on the same day that I was in town to officiate my first wedding. I had been given the nickname "Rev" (short for "Reverend") years earlier because of my Yellowstone sermons, and I was about to marry one of my best friends and his fiancée, who had attended one of my early sermons and declared that I would be the one to marry them.

If anyone would appreciate my need to journey over to REI to peruse the latest in ultralight cookware it would be my college climber partner and fellow gearhead, Matt. So I suppose I shouldn't have been shocked when I spied him slowly—nonchalantly—sauntering through the bike section of the store just three hours before his big moment. Being somewhat of an ultralight freak, Matt was able to steer me in the right direction, and we picked out some funky, collapsible plates and bowls—along with utensils and cooking accessories—that would surely reduce my pack by a hip-busting three to four pounds. I was on my way.

But even after buying two floorless shelters that I would utilize in lieu of heavy backpacking tents, I still needed to secure the two sherpas.

Summer is a very difficult time to recruit help in the Gardiner area. It's the time many of us work nonstop for four and a half months to make as much of our yearly salary as possible. A lot of the fly-fishing guides I work with hump it out every day from the first of July until the end of September, then purchase their season pass to Bridger Bowl, and sit back and wait for the powder to fly.

Returning from our trip to Eastern Washington through my home town of Coeur d'Alene and then over Lookout Pass (with our soon-to-be-two-year-old napping in the back of my Toyota Tundra), my wife, Crystal, and I were rumbling down the road at eighty mph as I was in reverie about the good old days—the days when I was a teenager and the speed limit on Montana's highways was "reasonable and prudent." I was still stressing about who I could get to help me haul gear for three days in late July when out of the blue, Crystal, who always tries to ease my anxieties, said, "What about the boys?"

My daughter refers to them affectionately as "my boys," and there's never any doubt about whom she's talking: the players on my basketball team. The boys had become a big part of our life—an extended family; brothers to and protectors of my daughter. These were relationships built through hardship and struggle—the kind of relationships that bring you closer to others and would never have been possible without being placed in the right circumstances. I'm a firm believer that there is unmatched power in sport and its ability to connect a group of young men or women in their quest to build character, toughness, resilience, and love while representing their school, family, community, and team. And if it is true that our wealth should be measured not by what our bank account reads but by the friends and relationships we hold dear, then I am a very rich man.

We had recently celebrated graduation at the local high school in Gardiner, Montana. It had been a day filled with reflection and raw emotion. Six of the graduating seniors had played under me for two years, and we shared a glorious final season together. Being the head boys' basketball coach in Gardiner is in many ways like being the mayor in town. There are times of palpable praise as well as times of less tolerable, vitriolic noise. But through it all, I forged relationships and friendships with my boys that I will take to the grave.

When asked what is the most beautiful sight I have ever seen, in light of the countless miles of trails and peak bagging I've experienced, my answer is always the same: the most powerful, memorable, and beautiful experiences of my life have occurred with sweaty, pimply, battle-hardened teens in grungy, musty, dirty locker rooms in small Class C towns across the Treasure State. Together, we shared the unbearable heartache of losing what the *Livingston Enterprise* called "The Greatest Game Ever Played" and the *Bozeman Daily Chronicle* "A Game for the Ages" to our archrivals from the Shields Valley. We shared the loss of my Aunt Susan, who passed away the night before our first divisional game against the Arlee Warriors—the night my three-time all-state player went off for thirty-seven, and one of my captains stepped onto the floor with "Aunt" on his left shoe and "Susan" on his right. A night we would win in dramatic fashion at the buzzer.

Months had passed since that season-ending game—since that final time of sacred bonding in the cavernous locker room at the MAC (Maroon Activities Center) in Butte, Montana. I thought back to late May, when the sun was shining and the temperatures hinted at summer. The gym was packed with community members and family who had gathered to celebrate graduation. It was nearing the end of the highly anticipated event (high school graduation takes on a heightened level of importance in small towns across the rural West, and I imagine, across the country), and the Rose Ceremony was about to begin.

It is a beautiful gesture. I'm not sure who came up with the idea, but the rest of the nation should steal a page from the Gardiner School Book when it comes to creating a memorable graduation, because the simplicity of the rose ceremony inspires a lifetime of pride and affirmation.

Being a small "Class C town" (as we call it in Montana), the number of graduates is relatively small. The size of towns, which spread like chickenpox across the vastly barren and rugged landscape of Big Sky Country, are categorized based on their level of high school basketball, with big cities like Billings and Great Falls representing the AA towns; Livingston, A; Big Timber, B; and the likes of Gardiner and West Yellowstone, C. In Gardiner, where there are approximately 800 year-round residents and a K-12 with roughly 140 students, there are typically between eighteen and twenty-six young hopefuls who graduate in any given year, making the ceremony personal and the closest thing most of these small-town students will experience to walking the red carpet.

After wrapping up the slideshow accompanied by the latest and sappiest of country billboards top hits, the switch for the lights of the gym are flipped with a funky, skinny, elbow-shaped key. And then, as they have for me throughout the season for every 6 A.M. practice, the lights slowly pop and grind, one by one, until the gym is once again relit. Throughout this process, students walk to the five-gallon buckets that sit at the end of each of the two rows of padded chairs that seat the graduates at midcourt throughout the ceremony, and each student grabs four roses.

When I received my first roses two years earlier, I didn't fully understand the significance of this ceremony. But now I was a vet who'd been through two ceremonies, with three dried and fragile roses hanging from my office wall as a reminder.

We knew it was going to be a special and meaningful end to the graduation, because it had been a unique and extraordinary run with this crew of seniors, not just in regard to the wins and losses, but in regard to the culture and family we had built over the course of two long and intense seasons. Though I anticipated roses from certain players, a flood of emotions overtook both Crystal and me as, one by one, my seniors stepped forward with roses, big hugs, and "I love you, Coach."

Each student gets four roses to give to those who have had the most profound impact on their lives. The thorny treasures typically go to Mom, Dad, Brother, Sister, Grandma, Grandpa, Aunt, and Uncle. So when the rose ceremony came to an end, and I held a bouquet of a half-dozen deep-red flowers, my tears ran and my heart beamed with pride.

A month had passed since graduation, and as is often the case, my wife had a brilliant idea. Call on the boys. Cash in on the Rose Ceremony. While a number of my boys were in summer positions with the Park Service, making it nearly impossible to get time off, I began dialing up each of my seniors as we passed through Deer Lodge, Montana, in hopes of finding two willing porters. They had to be strong, fit, and spirited to endure the loads that I would ask them to haul over Bliss Pass. By the time we reached Bozeman, I had my crew.

Colton and Justin were all in. Though they were both skinny as a rail, they had a deep love for the outdoors and life in the mountains. Justin, the local sheriff's son, was six foot four, 170 pounds, lean, sinewy, and an avid outdoorsmen. He spent his summers working for his uncle and grandfather at E.L.K., Inc., performing many of the odds and ends of the shop. More often than not, when I stopped by to say hello, he was either working at the front desk, helping a customer, or attaching leather loops to the end of an elk call. Full of piss and vinegar, Justin is a fighter. I had so much love and admiration for the young man because he brought a swagger and toughness to our team that he seemed to deem his mission. I had defended him against our school administration on more than one occasion when he punched a chair, hit the floor, or kicked a locker in frustration, knowing that his passionate fury was just what we needed.

Colton could run for days; he was the fastest player I had ever coached. What he lacked in offensive skills, he made up for on the defensive end of the floor. When we wanted one of the other team's best guards dogged up the court, we would call on "Zazzy" (Colton's nickname). Much like Justin, there wasn't an ounce of fat on Zazzy. He must have been 1 percent body fat and 99 percent muscle—if that is even possible.

While Zazzy was a smart young man, caring and thoughtful, he struggled with the rigors of Gardiner High School, one of the most respected public schools in the state for its academic standards. This frustrated many of his teachers, as many of them felt he simply didn't care, misreading Zazzy's laid-back, surfer-style aura. When the other kids were running suicides with a zealous fury on their face, hating the coach that they loved, Zazzy just ran with no facial expression at all. Zazzy tolerated school so he could play sports, which seemed to calm and focus his overly active brain.

It was a perfect match; Justin and Colton got along perfectly well, and I often put them in the same hotel room at districts and divisionals in Butte. They didn't say much, they were dedicated to "Coach," they took direction without questions, and they both relished the idea of going on a grand adventure in Yellowstone National Park. Neither of them had ever backpacked in the park or done any extensive hiking in Yellowstone. This is always a shocker to Yellowstone visitors, but few of the local kids have a connection to the 2.2 million acres that is the world's first national park. While teens like Justin grew up hunting on Yellowstone's north boundary and have explored hundreds of backcountry miles outside of the park, the park itself remained a novelty explored by tourists.

Part Three: The Adventure

With less than a week until the arrival of Kathy and John, I scheduled a lunch meeting with Justin and Zazzy at the Sawtooth Deli on Park Street. Nestled in between the chamber and one of Gardiner's finest art galleries, Sawtooth Deli is an anomaly of sorts. The food is creative, diverse, and what you expect to find in a small gateway town such as Moab, East Glacier, Springdale, or Escalante. Its décor is rustic and simple—a reflection of Gardiner itself. And while it is the local hotspot for lunch (from noon to 1:30 on a summer day, you can always count on seeing at least a half-dozen green-and-gray Park Service employees eating a sandwich or powering through one of the daily specials of pasta, Caribbean burritos topped with mango salsa, or wood-fired pizzas), the deli's schedule is sporadic at best. Thus, it is always a gamble. One never knows if the typical fifteen-minute drive down the hill from Mammoth (park headquarters) to Gardiner—made longer with summer tourist traffic and thirty-foot RVs slowly grinding their way down the one-thousand-foot-elevation loss of twisty roads—will all be for nothing.

I suspect that the visitors who really know the park and surround-ing communities enjoy dining at the deli to rub shoulders with the bear and wolf biologists, geologists, and rangers, perhaps to validate their feel-ings as semi-locals. Yellowstone has an almost cultlike following of people like myself who, before working in the park, visited Yellowstone multiple times a year to simply reconnect and refill the spirit.

I'm always blown away by the minimal dining options in Gardiner—to discover there are restaurants that the boys I've coached have never eaten at. Justin is an exception, albeit a limited one. His uncle owns one of the few eating establishments—the Town Café—so even though E.L.K., Inc. is only two buildings down from the Sawtooth Deli, it would almost be sacrilegious if someone from the family were to see Justin's lengthy frame enter the doors of the lunchtime competition. Zazzy didn't have the same loyalty issues with the Town Café, but his mom had worked there for years, and he didn't see any reason to expand his dining experience. He always left the Town fulfilled after a burger and fries, and preferred to keep things simple. On this day, however, the call to explore Yellowstone trumped Zazzy and Justin's usual routines.

I spoke to the boys over lunch, and they hardly said a word. They nodded as if they understood what we were undertaking and seemed to have a good grasp of what I was asking of them. I placed the map on the table and proceeded to go over each day of our three-day backpacking trip. We would get an early start on day one, leaving the house by 6 A.M. After shuttling Justin's redneck truck to Pebble Creek Campground, we would be on the trail by 9:30 A.M., giving us plenty of time to walk the eight miles to the legendary third meadow of Slough Creek. Day two would be the beast. It would be a seven-mile hike to 3P2, our forested campsite on the edge of the upper Pebble Creek meadows. I went over it with them multiple times. It would be a four-mile climb up the pass, gaining approximately 2,700 feet in elevation; followed by a difficult two-mile descent, where we would lose nearly 1,500 vertical feet; and then a half-mile walk to camp.

The math is pretty simple. It all adds up to 6.5 miles, with the missing half mile being the walk from our first night's campsite to the cutoff trail over the steep and arduous Bliss Pass. The last day would be a mellow six-mile hike downhill to our vehicle at Pebble Creek Campground. Straightforward. Simple. No issues. They got it.

Before we departed ways, I looked them both in the eyes, and with a stern coach voice said, "We can't fuck this one up, boys. This is a big trip for your coach. It is a big trip for YCG." I emphasized how this was much bigger than a guided trip, because these folks represented future donors to my organization, Yellowstone Country Guardians. At this point, YCG hadn't yet completed its first program, and anyone writing us checks—let alone those giving us gifts over $500—represented tremendous hope for the future.

I made sure to clear my guide calendar for the day before the trip, knowing it wasn't smart to get home late in the evening, after a long day on the water, the day before such a big undertaking that had so much on the line. The farther you take a client from the trailhead, the more prepared you must be. When you are talking about multi-night adventures, the complexity of the planning and execution of a flawless and successful trip comes down to meticulous preparation.

After making one last stock-up trip to Livingston, I returned to the house just as the asphalt on our walkway began to dry. The entire day had been a disaster. While afternoon thunderstorms and rain showers are a common occurrence throughout July and August, all-day torrential downpours are not. It had rained for nearly eight hours. The sun was just emerging, and the typically hot and dry Gardiner became humid as steam evaporated from the roadways.

Unknown to most Yellowstone visitors, a clockwork-precise phenomenon occurs following any decent amount of precipitation on Yellowstone's Northern Range. What may have been clear, bubbling, effervescent waters minutes earlier on the likes of the Lamar, Gardner, or Yellowstone River quickly becomes a raging, frothy torrent of chocolate milk, leaving the waters unfishable for hours to days, depending upon the quality and severity of the storm.

With the exception of the Lamar, which undoubtedly becomes a muddied mess after the belly of an afternoon thunderhead empties itself on the upper reaches of Cache Creek—a small tributary to the Lamar whose banks and steep slopes were severely altered during the devastating 1988 forest fire, leaving little limbed life, a lack of bank stabilization, and precarious amounts of soil tumbling down into the swift waters of the creek following any substantial downpour—the Yellowstone River is the poster child for post-shower runoff. Not only does the 'Stone receive the 1,300 CFS (cubic feet per second) of average Lamar River flow in July, adding a tremendous turbidity following a rainstorm, but it also receives the approximately 300 CFS (July's monthly average) from the Gardner River, with its glacier-colored water adding yet another palette of lighter sandstone- and shale-influenced runoff to the darkening waters of the mighty Yellowstone.

When I received the call from John that he and Kathy had arrived in town and were checking into the Absaroka Lodge—that I should stop by—I knew the trip was in limbo. I had gone to such great lengths to ensure that this adventure would go on without a hitch, but I hadn't planned for the rapid torrents of desert-colored water flowing through the streets of Gardiner as they arrived at our base camp, nor the ominous flow of the thickening Yellowstone, which they could literally study from their balcony overlooking the river.

Upon opening the door to their room, John greeted me with a sly, almost sheepish smile followed by a big bro hug. He then introduced me to Kathy. She was younger than I had expected. Lean and fit. She more than passed the eye test of whether I felt she was capable of our three-day, twenty-one-mile backpacking foray. She wore a pair of quick-dry pants, a lightweight fishing shirt, and a ball cap, and was clearly prepared for our adventure. Within a few minutes in her presence, I could see what attracted John to her. She had a quiet confidence—a presence, if you will.

As I spoke to John and Kathy about our options and the weather forecast for possible snow flurries above eight thousand feet for the next forty-eight hours (an elevation we would clearly exceed), a palpable nervousness filled the room. They had purchased new gear, and trained in the hills of Northern California and around the foothills of Mount Sentinel in Missoula, but they wanted to enjoy their anniversary gift to one another. Their days of simply enduring a journey for prosperity's sake had passed.

Kathy remained quiet and reserved as I spoke about alternative plans. She wasn't going to do anything she didn't want to do, but I got the sense that this trip was something she was not doing simply for John but for a personal experience, for gratification—a reward of sorts. And this I respected, because it is this same desire to accomplish something bold, new, and memorable that has led me to endure less-than-ideal weather to reach a summit or isolated parts of Yellowstone, and often consumed my restless nights and daytime reveries.

The decision was made: we would remain optimistic. There was no reason to believe any of this rain would alter the water quality of Slough or Pebble Creek. It could create a slight bump in flow and a cooling of temperature that could alter the fecundity of the water's ability to produce willing top-water risers (trout caught on a dry fly for the less aquatically romantic nonangler), but as John had stated from the beginning, this journey was about much more than catching fish. And it was Slough Creek for God's sake! We would surely catch fish.

The trip was on. I called the boys and had them meet me at the house. Within minutes of their arrival, we had spread out all of the gear, food, and supplies to ready for packing. There was a childlike enthusiasm about the boys—an excitement and joy—that was calming and reassuring. I knew at that moment that they would be a perfect addition to the trip. They were so excited to get out of Gardiner, away from their jobs behind a counter and dealing with tourists all day, and it was clear that they had adventure on their brain. One would have thought that we were attempting some harrowing, unclimbed peak in the remote recesses of the Beartooth Mountains. While a three-day trip isn't considered lengthy by backpacking standards, when guiding a trip of this length, the journey takes on an expeditionary feel. As we separated stoves, food, water filters, tent, floorless shelters, pads, cookware, and more, I told them the story of my most recent backpacking trip to the Black Canyon of the Yellowstone, a solo journey in June when the waters were too high to fish and I had simply opted to walk.

Upon boiling the water for my ramen on the first night of my trip, I realized I had forgotten utensils. Opting to use a rock as a substitute, I found the grinding of the granite on my front teeth to be irritating, which then led me to whittle chopsticks out of two small pieces of lodgepole pine branches. Hours later, around midnight, I awoke to water slapping against the side of my tent. I had pitched my shelter at least fifteen feet from the river's edge, but it had been a day in the high eighties, and the snowmelt from the warm temperatures had swollen the river, which seemed likely to swallow me up. I still get the chills thinking about tumbling down the Yellowstone, in the depths of water coursing through the deep canyon walls, under the black cover of darkness while trapped in the nylon shell of my tent. These were the kind of things, I explained to my two volunteers, that can happen on a backcountry trip when not properly prepared or paying attention to your surroundings. I added that I was determined that we would suffer no such embarrassments.

When my alarm went off at 5 A.M. the next morning, July 27, I lethargically climbed out of my bed in my house in Gardiner, on the hill overlooking the northern gateway to Yellowstone, knowing that I must be on point for the next sixty hours or it would be a long three days.

We had packed all three backpacks (mine, Zazzy's, and Justin's) the night before, the boys were to arrive at 5:45, and John and Kathy would follow fifteen minutes behind them. Zazzy arrived sleepy eyed, excited, and on time. Kathy and John arrived five minutes later, ten ahead of schedule (they were both successful go-getter types, and it was clear from my first meeting with John that promptness was something he highly valued). Justin, on the other hand, still hadn't fixed the problem with his alarm that caused him to be late for one or two 6 A.M. morning practices the previous winter.

I had already called him half a dozen times, my optimistic mood quickly transitioning to an obsessive anger. Where the hell was he? I ordered Zazzy to run down to his house, but just as he was firing up his beast of an old Ford pickup, I called Justin's home phone and woke up Scott, his father and Park County Sherriff, who was off that day. Scott (a vocal advocate of my efforts with and support of Justin as his basketball coach during his junior and senior seasons—and a highly valued asset, as I had my fair share of detractors across the community) promptly dealt with the situation, and Justin's red-and-white Chevy pickup, complete with its mismatched door panels, rumbled up the driveway less than ten minutes later. I'm still not sure if Justin was fully awake or if he thought I was going to make him run for every minute he was late (a common cure for late players), as if he had missed the first minutes of another basketball practice rather than the epic backcountry trip I had planned. Either way, I needed him to step up his game—and fast.

The drive to Pebble Creek, where we would drop off Justin's truck as a shuttle rig, was electric. The temperatures were cool (in the midforties), there was an autumn-like chill in the air, and the Lamar Valley was full of life and vigor. The bison were rutting, their guttural moans and bellows echoing throughout the valley floor, and there remained a succulence to the grasses and cottonwoods. We watched a lone coyote snatch up a roadside Uinta ground squirrel that had suffered a fatal end after being run over by an early morning wildlife watcher, most likely en route to get a glimpse of the wolves. And a pair of sandhill cranes gingerly stalked the tall grasses in search of insects and seeds, seeming to enjoy their summer haunts after the long flight from their wintering grounds in the desert Southwest of New Mexico.

It was a perfect introduction to the Northern Range. In fact, it would have been a shame if we had driven straight to the trailhead, for one cannot help but become enamored and inspired by the rich biodiversity and grandeur that abounds in the Lamar Valley in late July. While the meadows of Slough Creek have much in common with the vastness, vistas, and venerability of the Lamar, the trailhead itself is a dry desert filled with horse trailers, trucks, and stock.

I wanted to minimize our time in the parking lot while being absolutely sure that we had packed everything. I can't count how many times I have jogged back to the truck from the first big hill on the trail for something I had forgotten in my haste to stake out one of my favorite fishing pools while leading day fishing trips to the second meadow of Slough Creek. I was committed to making sure that no such bush-league actions took place at the onset of our three-day trip to calm any anxieties that John and Kathy may have had about our pilgrimage to a mecca of Northern Rockies trout fishing.

I locked the truck, as well as the side and back of the canopy. At last, after months of planning and preparation, we were ready to hit the trail.

I tossed a can of bear spray to Colton and Justin, then saw John struggling to attach his bear spray. John had carried bear spray on his hikes in Glacier National Park and throughout northwest Montana, but he was using a new pack and couldn't quite weave the holster of the spray through the waist strap of his backpack. Without hesitation, I reached to help him as I have with dozens of clients in the past, quickly feeding the woven black holster tag through his waist strap and cinching it tight. Then disaster struck.

At first, it was just a loud hissing sound. Then I watched the orange cloud of bear spray slap Justin square in the face.

The poor kid immediately began waving his arms frantically, as if he were under attack from a hive full of bees. Despite the weight of their backpacks, Zazzy and Kathy managed to duck and dart out of harm's way, avoiding any direct contact with some of the most potent stuff on earth. The spray—which could last up to eight seconds—continued to discharge, as the strap remained tight over the can's release lever. Stunned and confused, John and I both reached for the can on his right hip. With his left hand, John aptly diffused the situation by reaching under his right armpit and violently ripping the strap, releasing the pressure on the release valve and immediately stopping any further discharge of spray.

But the damage had been done. I've spent thirty minutes rubbing my eyes, coughing, and shaking my head after a small whiff of bear spray; at 2 percent capsaicin, bear spray is like pepper spray on steroids. Justin had just received what had to be a three- to four-second facial shot of the stuff. He was fucked. Whether it was the burning of his retinas or the sudden shock factor, he was squirming and flailing like a fish thrown on the riverbank to die. And I knew it wouldn't be long before John succumbed to the fire-like sensation that would soon be circulating throughout his nervous system; but for the time being, he remained calm.

I quickly threw down my pack, reached in the top pocket for my keys, frantically unlocked the back of the canopy, and reached for a gallon jug of water we had just used to top off our Nalgene bottles. Coughing and hacking that deep, guttural choking sound, Justin's body responded the only way it knew how in its attempt to rid the toxic chemical from his system. And he was caked in the stuff. We feverishly poured water on Justin's face, in his eyes, and down his throat. His old, tattered, blue-and-white-checkered Western shirt with pearly buttons bled the rich orange of dried bear spray and was already beginning to burn his skin, though he didn't yet know it.

Fuck. The trip was over before it started. I would surely be driving Justin to the Mammoth Clinic and then have to calmly explain to his parents why his eyes and throat felt as if the devil himself breathed fire into his face.

And then another scenario unfolded. Perhaps I had underestimated the toughness and resolve of one of the true fighters I have coached—thin framed but scrappy as all hell, Justin, who never shied away from a good fight, had helped to inspire toughness in our team for the last two years—because Justin seemed to be bouncing back instead of taking the turn for the worse I had anticipated. It actually appeared he was going to be okay.

Now I had to attend to John and Kathy. Kathy was stoic. There was no doubt that she had gotten a nose full of spray simply by being on the periphery of the massive discharge. But she didn't say a word. Bound and determined to make this trip still happen, at one point while standing behind Kathy and John, I shook my head and slashed my throat with my index finger, silently ordering Justin to calm down. We would take care of him. It was clear the shot hadn't hit him as squarely in the face as I had thought, and his cowboy blood would allow him to endure twenty-four hours of suffering if that is what it took.

Justin and Colton took the water and began walking off in the distance, simply to calm the situation, while John and Kathy appeared stunned. Even though John's breaths through the ordeal had to have been laced with capsaicin, he hardly coughed or said a word about his discomfort. Instead, he felt awful about what happened to Justin. He had taken the safety cap off the can of bear spray, and I hadn't noticed. So when I went to strap the can onto the pack, instead of tightly securing to the bright orange safety, the strap went directly over the release valve as if it were a thumb forcefully discharging the can in the face of a vicious encounter. It was my fault, not his.

At this point, John seemed solely concerned for Justin's welfare. Then we looked at John's right arm and noticed that it was saturated with spray. When the can began to erupt, he had instinctively dropped that arm, his forearm receiving a good portion of the spray that had still hammered Justin—three feet away—directly in the face. John's instincts had saved Justin from the full-powered core shot blasting from the can.

Though John's skin must have felt as if he had a first-degree burn, he continued to reach for and peek in Justin's direction as we cleaned off his forearm with water and an extra T-shirt. Still coughing, Justin had calmed down, and Colton gave me a thumbs up. I looked at John and Kathy, and told them to start hiking because we had fish to catch.

For the first time, and with some hesitation (John is a solid six foot two with an iron square jaw, large hands, and the body of an athlete twenty years younger), I got firm with John, telling him that Justin would be fine and that we would catch up. Off he and Kathy went. As they rounded the first bend in the trail, I ran over to Justin to check on him. Upon seeing me, he released all the profanity in his vocabulary (and having spent much of his youth in a locker room, that's saying something). Angry and confused as he was, it was still a relief to me to see he wasn't going blind or in respiratory failure. He simply had a cough and burning eyes, and felt as if his chest and arms were en fuego. We could deal with this. Truth be told, most other teens would have demanded a trip to the doctor, but not J. He was stoic, proud, and loved his coach. He and Zazzy had both said they would walk through fire for me, and now, Justin really had.

• • •

THOUGH RELATIVELY MILD BY MOUNTAIN standards, the climb to the first meadow of Slough Creek has, on more than one occasion, made me concerned about the cardiovascular health of a client. Still shell-shocked from our incident in the parking lot, we hammered out the climb in a sort of confused daze. And John and Kathy had marched out at a quick clip, as we saw Bison Peak before ever making contact with them. It wasn't until the last downhill section leading to Plateau Creek that we finally reconnected.

Without saying a word, Justin threw his pack to the ground like a fifty-pound bag of rolled oats, and with the wobbly legs of a hiker wearing a heavy pack for the first trek of the year, he scrambled to the deepest pool in the ankle-deep creek to submerge his entire head, still trying to put out the fire. Kathy simply smiled and began a short conversation with Colton; she could read that he was a difficult book to open, but in a short time, he had connected with her, nodding and showing tremendous respect and courtesy, even though he preferred silence. Meanwhile, John saturated his handkerchief, dripping water over his face and into his eyes in his attempt to rid the traces of capsaicin, which clearly remained a nuisance.

John must have wanted to show me that he and Kathy were up to the trip, because their pace leading to the midway point of day one was relentless. I knew it was not a speed they would keep up, but in comparison to the two men I had hiked with into the second meadow earlier in the week, who had staggered over the final hill, legs nearly giving out under the weight of their burgeoning bellies, John and Kathy's zeal and tenacity was welcome relief after what could have easily been a disastrous end to a highly anticipated adventure—before even leaving the parking lot.

In his mischievous way, Colton seemed to be getting a kick out of Justin's constant itching, deep breaths, and sighs; Justin's skin burned like hell. Just before arriving at the creek, he had said, "Coach, my skin feels like it is on fucking fire. I need to get to some water." Not fully comprehending his pain and suffering (something so true to our condition as humans; as heartfelt as our desire to sympathize may be, we can never fully understand the depth of another's pain), it wasn't until I saw Justin dipping his head in the creek like a mallard, stretching out his neck and letting the pearls of water drip down his back and over his shoulders, that I truly began to appreciate how uncomfortable the first four miles of the hike had been for him. He described it as a small forest fire spreading over the surface of his skin, igniting each tiny chest and arm hair, sending a pulsing heat wave through the roots and deep below the skin's surface.

We decided I would hike ahead with John and Kathy while Colton and Justin stayed behind, so Justin could continue to bathe in the cool waters of a small creek fed directly from the last remaining patches of mountain snow kept cool on the north-facing slopes of the ten-thousand-foot-plus peak of Mount Hornaday. I made sure to lead in order to slow down the pace, as I didn't want John and Kathy to burn themselves out on day one. As fit and strong as people ten and perhaps twenty years younger, John still had the bones and joints of a sixty-year-old ballplayer; and I knew the stiffness and pain he would wake with the following morning after hauling a pack eight miles, fishing all afternoon, and sleeping on the hard ground.

As one nears the tree line separating the second and third meadows of Slough Creek, a sense of wildness overwhelms and lifts the spirit. Slough Creek Trailhead itself is a forty-five-minute drive from the bustling headquarters of Mammoth Hot Springs and includes a bone-rattling, two-mile dirt road, which only adds to the ruggedness and beauty of the trip. Now we had hiked just under eight miles and were approaching some of the most pristine waters on one of the region's most storied fisheries.

From the time you reach the expansive opening of the first meadow of Slough Creek (after hiking two miles through a somewhat thick forest of lodgepole, aspen, and Douglas fir), the breathtaking grandeur that unfolds before you like a child's picture book seems to increase in magnitude with each hurried step. There are certain streams, creeks, and rivers across the West that inspire a pilgrimage among devout followers of the religion that is fly fishing; Slough Creek is one of them.

Perhaps as a reminder of how blessed I am to live in a wild, remote, and mostly unspoiled landscape, where it is still possible to find relative solitude while in pursuit of trout, I've kept a photo on my desk that one of my best friends from college took the previous fall. It was from a trip to Colorado's Dream Stream. I had flown into Denver with the mission of campaigning for Barack Obama in what we believed to be an important swing state. I had discovered an interest in politics eight years earlier during my freshmen year at North Idaho College, after the presidential election appeared to be stolen from Democratic candidate and environmental activist Al Gore due to a-few-too-many hanging chads. I had campaigned on some level, national or state, every two years since, and this was a monumental election.

While I had admirable intentions of walking door to door as I had in previous years, urging voters to do their homework and vote for "my guy," I had also brought my fly rod, waders, and a handful of bugs. Though I failed to knock on a single door during that three-day trip to Colorado, I did manage to meet, befriend, and release dozens of wild brown and rainbow trout on the tranquil October waters of the Arkansas River. But this wasn't until after a highly anticipated trip to a small section of meandering meadow water on the famed South Platte.

They called it the Dream Stream, but it quickly became a nightmare for me. The parking lots were full. And there were barbwire fences everywhere, as if to fence in the oversized, leaping brown trout, making it feel like a country club for fly fishing. We walked the stream for roughly a mile and found an obsessive, determined angler anchored in every hole on the small section of public water. Having grown up fishing the waters of Montana, with perhaps the most progressive stream-access law in the country, fishing in states where the water and river bottoms are owned by individuals makes me queasy.

We never wet a line that day; the whole scene was simply too much.

This legendary fishery had been hyped to the point of being spoiled, ruined, tainted. The fishery itself may still be in fine shape—this I don't know—but the quality of experience had been diminished to the point that I would much prefer the opportunity to cast to eight-inch cutthroat on the small waters of streams like Pebble Creek than to compete with yahoos for the chance at a twenty-six-inch brown trout from Eastern Europe. Call me a purist, but the quality of the experience still reigns supreme.

In that picture sitting on my desk, I'm standing atop a ladder to climb over the barbwire fence, in a rush to get to the vehicle—wanting to get as far from the crowds as quickly as possible. And I stopped just long enough to smile at the camera, broken-down rod in my left hand, big thumbs down on the other.

You may wonder what this side story has to do with our journey to Slough Creek; let me explain: Though it was still early as we walked through the second meadow, there were at least a half-dozen anglers stalking the banks of the slowly meandering water. I could sense a bit of angst from John that grew with each angler we passed. When you hike four, six, or eight miles into the backcountry, it is with supreme hope that you will have the water all to yourself. Unless journeying through the frozen grasses of early October with a box full of blue-winged olives—or chasing behind Ben Jewell from Parks' Fly Shop in early July, when the water is still too high for any normal angler to fish unless you are willing to throw deep sink tips, stripping back an oversized woolly bugger (he always catches fish by the way)—the chances of having a day up Slough Creek to yourself are about as good as hitting a royal flush playing video poker at the Town Bar in Gardiner. It can happen, but don't count on it.

I had prepared John by telling him to expect to see other anglers during our two days up Slough Creek, but I could see the same concern in his eyes that I felt in my heart when walking the banks of the Dream Stream. So, I began to pick up the pace in hopes of staking out a stretch of water in the third meadow that would surely yield an afternoon of tight lines and fishing bliss.

Just as we approached the sign for 2S4, our campsite for the night, the boys caught up to us. Everything was falling into place. I gave them the responsibility of setting up John and Kathy's tent and our three-man floorless shelter while I began preparing a quick lunch of dried salami, cream cheese, slices of French bread, dried fruit, and bagged granola. We took our time rubbing off the aches and pains of our first eight miles on the trail, then rigged the rods and geared up to fish.

By Slough Creek standards, it was like Grand Central Station. Two horse-drawn wagons passed us, en route to the Silver Tip Ranch just beyond Yellowstone's north boundary; and we could see wall tents set up across the creek at 2S7, whose occupants had been packed in by horses. The Park Service's Northern Range weed crew was camped out a quarter mile upstream at the Elk Tongue Patrol Cabin, and they had undoubtedly been pounding the shit out of the nearby holes. Truth be told, while its beauty is perhaps unrivaled by any other Yellowstone stream of comparable size, and while there remains an aura or charm that surrounds the simple name "slough," there are much wilder fisheries and experiences in the park. Still, it is the hardest place in Yellowstone to reserve a backcountry campsite; we had made our reservations months before, at the beginning of the scheduling season. And getting one is almost the equivalent of winning a lottery, which adds to the mystique of the third meadow.

Three of the four prime holes within earshot of camp were occupied, so we got back onto the trail and began walking toward the north boundary and Frenchy's Meadow. As a guide, you never want to let on to your clients that you are concerned or losing confidence when the fish aren't biting. Pretend if you must, because the minute they sense you have lost your mojo, all hope is gone.

Knowing this and also recognizing my concern that we'd find my next series of primo holes occupied, I began to integrate my interpretive knowledge of the area into the walk (this always has a major calming effect on clients, because it shows you really do know the area and that you aren't faking it). I had already shared a little of the Silver Tip Ranch history—a 1913 homestead of G. Milton Ames named for the abundance of grizzlies in the area—but I had saved the story of old Joseph "Frenchy" Duret.

Frenchy had homesteaded a small piece of wilderness paradise four miles north of the Silver Tip Ranch and was a legendary character for reportedly killing upwards of 250 bears, both grizzlies and black, while living along the banks of Slough Creek. Frenchy's wanton pursuit of any member of the *Ursus* family unlucky enough to cross his path eventually caught up with him, however. On June 12, 1922, Frenchy Duret came to an abrupt and violent end when a trapped grizzly became enraged, and in its wild fury to break free, fatally mauled the man responsible for hundreds of bear deaths throughout the valley's floor.

Just as I was finishing up my story about the homesteaders a few miles to the north, we hit a sweeping bend in the river, and the weight that had been pressing against my chest, restricting my breath, and making my pack-less walk harder than it should have been, quickly lifted as I peered into the depths of two of my favorite holes, which appeared to be virgin and untouched. After a long day with many obstacles, it was 2:30 in the afternoon, and we were ready to fish.

While I hadn't yet observed John cast a fly (after years of guiding, I've grown to receive little solace when someone tells me they are competent with a fly rod in hand), he had the look and feel of someone who was self-reliant on the water. This wasn't because he was decked from head to toe in the latest and cleanest lines of the most recent Simms fishing catalog, or that he was equipped with the seven-hundred-plus-dollar Winston Boron IIx fly rod with a flashy Galvan reel; it was instead the way he walked, the way he gently grasped the cork of the rod in his left hand, and his observant and patient study of the barely moving waters of the third meadow that led me to conclude John would be okay on his own.

The fish become less spooky, educated, and particular the farther you walk up Slough Creek, and the third meadow was where my wife, Crystal, caught her first seventeen-inch trout on a fly rod—a feat accomplished by a number of my clients who have been audacious enough to attempt a day hike (eighteen miles round-trip) to this fly-fishing paradise. But it remains a test of precision and grace. It is also where an angler can experience a high enough level of frustration to cause him or her to regress to the chuck and duck of a spinning lure.

Despite being the common method used by novices fishing the first meadow, it is highly unadvisable to cast from the high banks on Slough Creek. This can certainly be a hard urge to resist. After spotting a pod full of fat-bellied, sixteen- to twenty-inch trout, or that one lone shark of a fish cruising the flats, gobbling up every aquatic insect in its path, I, too, have succumbed and cast from the bank four feet above the river. Even though I always advise against this with anglers, once I leave them to fend for themselves while I get the less experienced of the group settled and into their first fish, I will return to find them inevitably spooking every fish within eyeshot, throwing thirty feet of line from the high, crumbling bank while cascading loose dirt into the water and casting their shadow over the water's surface—putting down every fish that inspired this spastic behavior in the first place. And while I had confidence in John, I made sure to send him in the direction of three holes where he would be forced to cast from the gravel bar, keeping his profile low and his level of stealth high.

One of the great joys of fishing and the great challenges of guiding is the unpredictability of each endeavor. I felt confident that this afternoon would be solid. It was a warm 70 degrees with bright skies, clear water, and good flows. But I've been up to Slough on similar days where a dramatic drop in overnight temperatures—or an incoming storm that changes the barometric pressure—has wreaked havoc with the fishing. So a little bit of swagger is fine, but the minute that confidence isn't matched with humble grace, the river will turn off like a light switch; and the water that once compared to an aquarium full of oversized cuttys will quickly appear totally devoid of fish.

Perhaps I am naïve, or simply too spiritually connected to the waters I fish and the finned friends I pursue, but I believe karma is an important quality when hoping to connect—if only for a moment—with one of our planet's most mysterious and beautiful creatures. The life of a trout remains an enigma to all laymen, with the exception of the dedicated angler. Are there fish heads, anglers, and guides with nothing on their seemingly trout-sized (size-of-a-pea) brain who chase only the big "hogs," hooting and hollering with a total lack of respect for the graceful and fluid creature they pursue? Yes. Does this bother me? Deeply.

"Hog" is the term most commonly used for a big, fat, "trophy" of a trout in the fishing community. I've always found this more than a little disturbing. Nothing against pigs; I like to believe that I have respect for all life (even though I think bacon complements almost any dish). But comparing one of the cleanest, most lovely creatures on our planet—a heavily spotted, deeply colored, stealthy shaped, muscular, and breathtaking species that represents God's greatest art—with any other animal, even a cute and cuddly, albeit slightly dirty pig, seems indefensible.

Though I hadn't spent much time with John and had just met Kathy the night before, it was clear they were good people, with reasonable and even admirable intentions, and I desperately wanted Kathy to get to know a few Slough Creek cuttys. Being late July, we had boxes full of drakes, PMDs, ants, crickets, beetles, and hoppers. I started Kathy with an oversized rubber hopper with a peach body, and it immediately attracted the interest of a handful of fish. While we had five good eats in our first hour on the water, Kathy quickly learned that she couldn't use the same hurried hook set with these slow, deliberate cuts as she had all summer long with the feisty, spirited rainbows of Rock Creek, twenty-some miles east of Missoula.

While I yearned for the moment when Kathy would gently cradle the belly of her first Yellowstone cutthroat in the palm of her hand (while keeping the trout's delicate gills immerged in the water), the fact that the fish were eating gave me great confidence that this would become a reality. John had warned me that Kathy was relatively new to the art of fly fishing, but she clearly had a focused and determined spirit that remained teachable and thirsty to learn.

No matter how many times I fish or guide on Slough Creek, I'm always shocked by how slow the deep water moves. When the wind is up and ripping, the creek appears to be flowing upstream, waves suspending your fly in place, allowing for no natural drift or chance at fooling an unsuspecting trout. But this is one of the great beauties of fishing Slough. The water moves so slowly, regardless of whether you are fishing a shallow riffle or the more common deep, curving pool. And the Yellowstone cutthroat rises so methodically—almost sluggishly, really—making for the ultimate dry-fly-fishing experience. Nothing is more visual.

Perhaps this is part of the Yellowstone cuttys defense mechanism. As a young man who grew up fishing our family waters deep in the high-mountain forests of North Idaho for the equally gorgeous and enigmatic westslope cutthroat trout, I've always taken offense when anglers claim that cuttys are easy to catch. This would be like me telling someone who attended Montana State University that it is somehow a lesser or easier degree to receive than one from Missoula's University of Montana (even if this is the opinion commonly held by loyal Grizzly alum). And yes, my reverence for the cutty runs deeper than it does for any other member of the finned community (with the much-maligned mountain whitefish not far behind), because of both my familiarity with the species and its classification as native, which can't be said for the rainbow, brown, or brook trout in Yellowstone National Park. Therefore, I love to see the cutty rise deliberately, taking its sweet time when deciding whether to contribute to our silly endeavor of catch-and-release fishing, tricking angler after angler too quick on the trigger—anglers who violently yank the fly right out of its soft, luscious mouth.

Kathy's patience, lack of frustration, and commitment to her craft paid off tenfold throughout the afternoon as she landed a number of Slough Creek cuttys of varying shapes, sizes, and colors. But it was her final fish of the day that I will always remember.

We had continued to work downstream, away from John, whom I'd left to himself, confident that he, too, was meeting trout willing to cooperate by softly sipping his #12 Chernobyl ant. Kathy and I crossed the creek for the fifth or sixth time, in an attempt to approach the upcoming run from below its outlet and sneak up on the handful of fish that had no doubt suspended themselves in the belly of the feed line.

I had caught fish in this run before, and while it didn't require a long cast, it did demand a modest upstream reach followed by a flawless and subtle mend, in order to receive that perfect drift that would stir up a fish. The ankle-deep water spilled over a gravel bar twelve feet wide and then sped up as it approached the head of the run. Once there, the water deepened and appeared to slow down as it ate away at the five-foot bank of soil, which would occasionally and without warning crumble into the run's deepest portion. We stood in a section of knee-deep water, the liquid directly in front of us moving upstream, eddying away from the main current. It was tricky, but with an accurate cast, well-executed mend, and a slightly high stick (to keep the line from circulating in the water and moving upstream), it was very fishable.

As I worked with Kathy throughout the day, giving instructions to shoot more line, land the fly with more grace, gently mend the line without creating a stir, wait on the hook set, she hardly said a word. But it was clear she was listening, because whether she executed the following cast properly or not, she deliberately and methodically worked through what I was asking of her in her mind. And then, with the determination of a child stubbornly attempting to tie their shoe for the first time, she proceeded to make progress with each focused movement.

After a half-dozen casts, she was dropping the fly in line with the current with no hint of it being attached to a leader or line—a drag-free drift, as we like to call it in the fly-fishing world. As the fly righted itself and began to float through the meat of the hole, I whispered to her, "That's it." Within two seconds, the massive head of what looked like the biggest cutty we had yet seen rose, drifted under, and then refused the bug. We let the artificial hopper continue its drift so as not to spook the water, and then repeated the cast. Just like shooting a free throw, the muscle memory of doing it thousands of time kicks in when it is time to ice the game from the line. Kathy's lifting and lowering of the forearm became rhythmic and graceful, and she repeated the cast two more times, neither of which elicited a response.

Just before she prepared to make a fourth cast into the pool where she had seen the massive hulk of a trout, I grabbed her bright-orange line in my left hand and her rod in my right, gave the tip of the rod a slight twitch, and let the line filter through my left hand until the peach hopper slapped the crease between my thumb and my index finger. We let the water calm down for a few minutes while I spoke to her about needing to give the trout a different look. This time, I tried a smaller, more natural-looking terrestrial that had always caught fish—if the client was able to track the fly's brown-and-tan body on the water's surface. With the fading sun falling to our backs, the lighting was as good as it was going to get. Now seemed the perfect time to bust out the old Rainy's hopper.

The first cast with the new bug inspired a rise similar to the one that had made us aware of his presence—deliberate, methodical, and with intention. But at the last moment, the line closest to us began to move upstream in the eddy, tightening the leader and creating just enough tension to cause a slight drag. That was all it took. Another refusal. On the second cast, he rose again, but it was only out of mere curiosity—or so it seemed, because there appeared to be little conviction in his action this time.

We spent the next fifteen minutes changing bugs. Our next two selections of a black beetle and a pale morning dun didn't inspire so much as a look; maybe he was done feeding for the evening. It was the time of day—post hopper productivity and pre-evening hatch—when things slow down. I decided we would try one more very natural-looking hopper with a tan body, ribbed thorax, knotted red legs, and a piece of turkey feather acting as its wing.

Once again, we let the waters calm down. We had only seen one riser in the time since we last observed his uninspired inspection of our earlier offering. As I rubbed a tiny drop of Poo Goo (a silicone gel that helps the bug to float) on the dubbing of the bug's underside, Kathy looked at me and said, "This is the one. I just have a feeling."

Certain women seem to have a magic about them—a sixth sense, a knowing. But women's intuition here? Not in the fishing world. This was my church. I was the Reverend, and Kathy was just a member of the congregation. Or so I thought. But she was in the zone now; she could have made that cast with her eyes closed. And she put it right in the heart of the feed line. Though we hadn't seen the trout in over twenty minutes, his dark torpedo of a shape remained etched in our minds. Kathy executed the mend and high stick with grace and fluidity, and just as the fly entered the bubble line, out from the darkness he came. With the same purposeful intention of the first encounter, he slowly but steadily surfaced toward the bug. For fewer than two seconds, he hovered under the most natural-looking artificial fly I had left in my box. Then, with a seductive and simple slurp, he gulped the legs, and Kathy gently set the hook. The fight that ensued is not relevant.

There is something mystical, spiritual, sacred about gently cradling the belly of a Slough Creek cutty in the palm of your hand. For a brief moment, all else is lost but the magnificent beauty and connection with this mysterious member of the water world. While our bodies consist of roughly 70 percent H_2O and we cannot survive without it, a river, stream, or creek without the presence of finned populations seems lifeless. Slough Creek thus represents fecundity and biological diversity at its finest. That moment, when that fish rests still in your hand, is what absolute serenity must feel like. In the blink of an eye, we intimately connect with something far more perfect than we can ever dream of being.

Kathy marveled at the deep golden color of the cutty's lavish belly; the blackened dots spreading from head to tail, perfectly balancing symmetrically from one side to the next; the phosphorescent sheen radiating from its lateral line and the deep orange slash paralleling its lower jaw. The fish was indeed a symbol of aquatic perfection, and we could not help but be humbled.

As we watched our friend depart, I noticed that other fish were beginning to rise at the tail end of the pool, but I didn't even need to ask; Kathy was done for the day. While hours of good fishing still remained to be had, she was fulfilled. Relishing the experience, we stared at the hole for a few minutes, then began to work our way upstream to John.

We found him in a hole only a few hundred yards above where we had last seen him. The fishing must have been good. As we approached him on a broad, dry gravel bar, he delicately placed his hopper on the major seam in the run he was fishing. It was a long, flat, slow-moving stretch of water with a riffle thirty feet above where he was currently casting. He had a look of focused content—he had most certainly caught fish. This was the first time I had seen him cast, and I was impressed. I always enjoy watching a good lefty. And it doesn't matter whether it is the stroke of a southpaw shooting a jumper, throwing a football, swinging a bat, or casting a rod; a good lefty is something special.

John's stroke was short and quick, with a steady pace and a seamless transition from back to forward cast. I imagined it was a less polished version of the stroke he had used to swing a baseball bat and win such prestigious honors in Omaha, Nebraska, forty years earlier, as a standout at the College World Series. While his cast looked good, it was clear by the number of risers and the lack of interest in his offering that the trout had switched their focus. I went over and sat down near the end of the run to observe until I figured out what they were eating.

PMDs emerging in the film. While it would be difficult for anyone to see, let alone the eyes of someone in their sixties (I can't wait for John to read this; he will love all of the sixty-year-old references), I tied on a size 18 PMD cripple and doctored it up with floatant. I instructed John to approach the riser he had been working from upstream, because the angle and lack of flow might get a more natural drift. Within three casts, John had gotten a fish to eat once, but the take was so subtle it was almost imperceptible. On the fourth cast, John (bent over in stealth mode) saw the delicate take and, with a sharp snap to his left side, set the tiny hook in the lower mandible of a beautiful, fat, and lively cutty. With that, we called it a night.

I felt such a sense of relief as we sauntered back to camp and I listened to John and Kathy's shared stories of fishing bliss in the shadow of the pass that would be our obstacle the following day. But that was tomorrow. Today had been a success. Now I simply had to prepare a good and hearty dinner, let the boys tend to the fire, and try to get some rest.

We stayed up later than we should have with the day we had ahead of us. It turned out that Mitchell, my three-time all-state player, and his brother Sam were working for the weed crew nearby. At six foot seven and 240 pounds, Mitch is a big (what we in the coaching world call our forwards and center), and commands a presence even if his shy, warm, and polite personality says otherwise. He and Sam had walked the few hundred yards from the Elk Tongue Patrol Cabin to hang out around our blazing inferno of a fire. Justin and Zazzy are both pyros, and Justin made sure to pack a small pop bottle full of gasoline. There were a few times when I thought the fire bantering was getting a little out of hand, but it was an awkward situation. Mitchell is like family—a little brother of sorts—but I also didn't want John and Kathy to be uncomfortable around four teenagers on our first night in the wilderness. They seemed to enjoy the company, though. And John has a knack for starting up conversation, always adding words of wisdom when speaking with young men.

Though John and Kathy turned in early, and I eventually had to tell Mitch and Sam to go back to the cabin to keep the noise down, I think John and Kathy enjoyed the plethora of basketball stories shared around our bonfire. The debacle in the parking lot seemed a fading memory— one I hoped they would soon forget.

Temperatures dropped to the midthirties that night—a cold night by July standards. In an effort to save as much weight on our hips and shoulders as possible, given the brutal nature of Bliss Pass, Justin, Colton, and I had opted to share a cramped, three-man floorless shelter. I knew sleep was going to be limited on this trip regardless of my sleeping quarters, so the weight savings seemed to make the most sense. Our shelter was a small tepee of sorts, with a four-foot aluminum pole in the middle and ultralight stakes at six different points where the apron of paper-thin fabric met the ground. In the case of rain or snow, it would keep us dry, but it allowed for bugs and other small critters to explore our snug confines.

At one point, around 2:30 A.M., I heard one of the boys drop a loud and sudden f-bomb. I looked up just in time to see Colton violently fling the back of his right hand across his face as if trying to swat a hornet buzzing in his ear. A small mouse or vole, attracted to his warmth and perhaps the salty nature of his post-hike skin, had scurried across his forearm and hand, which rested across his cheek. Though small and harmless, there is nothing appealing about being awakened to tiny, sharp nails scampering across your bare skin. The disturbance didn't cause Justin's tired body to stir, however, and Colton quickly resettled in his bag and was back asleep in a matter of minutes. I let loose a little giggle and promptly wrapped the top portion of my sleeping bag around my head, bringing my hands into the bag's warmth, hoping to get another three hours of sleep.

I rose early the following morning. Fog lifted from the creek and hung above the valley's floor, the moisture adding to the already cool temperatures. With its embers slightly smoldering from the night before, I rekindled our small fire—both for warmth and morning ambiance— and began preparing breakfast for the crew. I had been nervous about this day since I booked the trip, knowing the grueling nature of ascending Bliss Pass and hoping I wasn't in over my head. But I also felt confident; we had a good plan. I had two young, strong, able teens who felt indebted to their coach, and we would just need to take our time getting John and Kathy over the pass.

Being a fly-fishing guide has been romanticized throughout the West, but it really isn't a very glamorous job. We may work in glorious settings, but the work itself, which remains relatively simple, often carries a stressful burden of unrealistic expectations. While 90 percent of my clients are accepting, understanding people, there are those we take on the water who feel a certain degree of entitlement—that somehow the $450 they have spent assures them a predetermined number of fish. No matter how good the fishing is, there will almost always be a slow time throughout the day, and you can only hope you are not guiding the client who earnestly and repeatedly cries, "Here, fishy-fishy!"

The vast majority of the stress I feel throughout a day of guiding is from expectations I put on myself—hoping, wanting, and yearning to provide a quality experience, while knowing the cost of my services remains out of reach for most and significant for the rest. This was the most expensive of any of the trips I offered, and thus, the stress-induced anxiety called for a short wander, alone, to the creek that inspired the journey.

It is easy to become consumed by work when leading a trip to the backcountry (there is no escaping this when one's responsible for clients in a wilderness setting), but I still try to sneak away—even if only for a minute here and there each day—to take a few deep breaths and fully appreciate my surroundings. On day trips, this often consists of sneaking behind a willow to urinate. Unless the fishing is red hot or a client needs constant attention, I will usually walk much farther than necessary to find a place to relieve myself. But those few minutes of silence and solitude, where I escape to perform one of the most routine of life's practices, provide time for precious meditation. The simple ability to take a moment to observe and listen to nature's rhythm—the pulse of flowing waters and mellow call of the ruby-crowned kinglet—allows reflection and rejuvenation that keeps me grounded.

On this morning, after a short walk to the expansive gravel bar (which was growing bigger each week as the flow of water continued to decline with the melting mountain snow), I returned to camp and began boiling water. Just as breakfast was ready, John and Kathy began to stir. To my surprise, they were up and ready to begin the day within minutes. The boys, on the other hand, needed a little prodding before emerging. But once awake—though far from alert—they quickly helped pump water while performing many of our other morning duties.

Breakfast went well. Bellies were full but not bursting. The eggs were warm. The cocoa and coffee were hot but didn't scald the tongue. The weather forecast called for snow in the mountains, and the morning had that autumn kind of feel, but it wasn't so cold as to make us overly uncomfortable. We hadn't traveled with waders (I never haul the bulky GORE-TEX suspenders and boots to Slough Creek unless it is a cold day in October), and wet wading would be numbing. Kathy announced that she remained fulfilled from an afternoon of what she called the best and most productive fly fishing of her life, and wanted to save her energy for the big climb. There was a nervousness permeating the group—not overwhelming but still palpable.

I instructed John to get ready to fish while I pulled the boys aside and reminded them of the plan. They had heard it half a dozen times. They must have felt like they were back in the basketball program, at districts, preparing for a big game and listening to yet another repetitive pregame talk. Much like I had done fifty times in small, grungy locker rooms throughout western Montana, I instructed them with urgency and intensity, as if it were the first time I had ever spoken the important words that represented the difference between triumph and failure.

The boys appeared to be listening, but they had heard my "day two" lecture enough times that they could probably repeat it themselves. I instructed them to break down camp while I took John downstream and then be on the trail by 10 A.M. We would follow four hours behind, begin the long slog up the pass, and meet them at the summit. By giving them a four-hour head start, I figured they would have ample time to hike the four miles up Bliss Pass, the two miles down the other side, and the half mile from the stream crossing to camp. Once there, they could take a short break, set up camp, hang their packs, and hike back up the nearly 1,500-vertical-foot climb to the top of the pass to wait for our arrival. From there, they'd take John and Kathy's packs and follow us back to our campsite, nestled in the forest beside the hurried waters of Pebble Creek.

It was a brilliant plan. It would be a hard day for the boys to be sure, but most accidents occur on the way down, not the climb up; and the downhill portion of Bliss Pass, descending into the upper meadows of Pebble Creek, represents one of the steepest and most slippery descents in the entire park. John and Kathy's legs would be wobbly after hauling packs up the pass—albeit lightened packs, as I'd send heavy loads with Justin and Colton, adding at least ten pounds each to their fifty-pound packs and keeping another five for myself. Reducing their burden by giving their packs to the boys would allow John and Kathy to take their time navigating the loose trail and repetitive switchbacks that accompany the downhill portion of the planned evening.

While not thrilled about the idea of climbing Bliss Pass twice in the same day, the boys didn't say a word—and I think they somewhat relished the challenge it presented. By 9:30 A.M., I gave Colton and Justin a big hug, John and Kathy wished them luck, and we began our walk downstream to the pocket water a quarter mile from our camp. When we left, the tents were still erect, and the food, hung in stuff sacks when unattended, remained on the ground but still attached to forty feet of thin nylon rope limply laid over the bear pole (which stood twenty feet in the air, spanning the length of two lodgepole pines).

As we rambled along the bank, high above the creek, I warned John that the fishing would be slow. I couldn't remember a good day up Slough Creek on a cool morning, especially following the first cold evening of the summer and a low-pressure system. But the day before had been memorable, so any top-water action would be icing on the already frosted cake.

To my surprise, the fishing was excellent. Though the smaller, more realistic-looking hoppers that had been so productive yesterday didn't interest them, the thick foam body and ridiculously bushy post of the #10 chubby Chernobyl inspired a dozen spirited cuttys more lively than their cousins residing in the meandering meadow water from the day before. Unlike the slow, deliberate takes that we experienced the previous day, when each trout had ample time to make up its mind after a thorough inspection of our offering (because of the still nature of the meadow), these Yellowstone cutthroat ate and fought more like rainbows, darting from behind large glacial boulders and charging out of the fast-moving, deep water that makes up the short section of riffle and pockets separating the second meadow from the third. And the steady action kept our bodies warm, even though all feeling in our feet and ankles had long since disappeared.

Satisfied and content, despite losing a strong-willed fat boy in the last of the four holes we worked over the course of three hours, we felt a joy and happiness that only a fruitful session of fly fishing is capable of generating. And even though John was the only one to personally experience the strength and vigor of multiple eighteen-inch trout in the swift and heavy waters of upper Slough's mini canyon, we all walked back to camp bubbling with glee after an unexpectedly memorable morning of fly fishing.

When we arrived at camp, I was pleased to see that all but the snack pack—in which I had put lunch for the three of us—hung from the bear pole and that the tents had vanished. I had calculated that it would take the three of us four hours to ascend the pass and another hour and a half to get to 3P2, our destination for the evening. Given that time frame, we were right on schedule. It was an hour past noon, which gave us an hour to pump water, get into our hiking gear, and gobble a trail lunch before beginning the big climb.

In hopes of escaping the mosquitoes, which had become a nuisance while gearing up for our hike, we decided to shoulder our packs and walk the half mile to the cutoff trail for Bliss Pass to eat lunch. Dropping our packs, we found a log and ate a hearty lunch of dried salami, cheese, dried fruit, and M&M's. It was 2:05 P.M. when we officially reshouldered our packs and began the ascent that, for me, had inspired more than one sleepless night.

Immediately out of the valley floor, the four-mile climb tests the strength of one's thighs under the weight of a heavy pack. The steep slope and large steps start from the get-go, acting as a warning signal to those still debating whether to attempt the 2,700-vertical-foot elevation gain to the top of Bliss Pass. As I stretched my hip flexors, still stiff from our relatively mild eight-mile hike the day before, I wondered who would have left a single aqua sock at the foot of the climb. We had seen it the day before, en route to our fishing destination in the third meadow, and it remained in place today. The black water shoe sat precariously atop the sign signaling the route to Bliss Pass, making it an impossible marker to miss.

John and Kathy held up well. While I started by identifying birds and wildflowers along the trail (the wildflowers were at the height of their glory season), there came a point when the meadows were so full of balsamroot that I no longer needed to impart any naturalist wisdom, for the sea of gold overwhelmed the senses, making all else less relevant. It must have been roughly three miles into the climb, after 2,000 feet of elevation gain, when John started to question when the steady onslaught of a hike would come to an end. Though it started as a little friendly bantering, there came a point when his ball busting made me question myself. Had I been irresponsible as a guide to offer this itinerary—one that included such a brutal and relentless climb? Was it the weight of my pack or just a lack of backpacking in the previous year? Somehow the climb seemed longer and more sustained than I remembered.

After what seemed like the longest three and a half hours of hiking in recent memory, we reached the long ridge walk to the crest of the pass. Though the weather had cleared, making for a warm and beautiful afternoon, the wind picked up as we neared the pond that rests in the saddle of the pass, cooling our sweat-dampened shirts. We took a break to have a snack and put on our windbreakers.

I knew we were nearing the point where the steep descent would begin, and I was surprised there was no sign of the boys. I had attempted calling them over our handheld radios every thirty minutes during our long slog up the pass—with no success. Now I figured we must be close and was puzzled that I still couldn't elicit a response. That said, the cathedral of mountains that entombed us on each side could easily block radio transmissions. Though John and Kathy clearly relished taking our first break, free of the weight of their packs, I began to wonder where the hell the boys were. After an hour of sitting, snacking, and staring into the deep blue abyss of the sky, I suggested that we better get moving before we stiffen up. The descent was going to be hard enough as it was, and it looked like John and Kathy would be hauling their packs for at least a portion of it.

These are the times in guiding that I kick myself for opening my mouth. Why had I told John earlier in the day about my new plan to have the boys hike back up the pass to take their packs for the downhill? This hadn't been part of our original plan; it was going to be a surprise. But now I had set myself up for failure. Had I kept my mouth shut, there would have been no disappointment when the boys failed to meet us at the pass; instead, once they finally connected with us, it would have been a welcome reward. Now that John and Kathy were expecting it, they would be frustrated. (When you don't carry a weighted pack regularly, regardless of how well it fits, you develop painful pressure points that you never knew existed.) They would feel as if they carried their packs a mile longer than agreed upon once reunited with Colton and Justin.

Truth be told, John and Kathy handled the more than twenty switchbacks and rapid descent with grace. Kathy slipped and fell on her backside once—the fall lessened by her pack—and didn't utter a word of complaint. Watching his wife go down brought out the hothead in John, however (something all great athletes and ballplayers have bottled within), and with the tone of a principal inquiring as to where the two knuckleheads notorious for skipping class had gone, he asked, "Where the hell are the boys we hired to help haul our fucking gear?" While there was no doubt in my mind that John was hurting, he remained stoic and didn't mumble a word about his own aching back. He simply wanted to take care of his bride of ten years, whom he clearly loved as intensely as he had the day they married.

We made it through the worst of the downhill with nothing more than a few slips and Kathy's one fall, but as we began descending into the spruce, fir, lodgepole forest, I really began to fret. Not long after beginning our steep descent off Bliss Pass on shaky and tired legs, I became frustrated with the kids, wondering if they were sacked out and chilling at camp, leaving us to fend for ourselves. We had now descended all but a few hundred feet of our 1,500-foot trek and could hear the hurried waters of Pebble Creek.

The sound of the rushing waters slowly and methodically eroding the rocks for whom their waters were named should have been cause for celebration, symbolic that our struggles of the day where far behind us and that it would be a lesser downhill from here on out. But the closer to the creek we moved, the more concerned I became. The two-way radios I had bought before the trip for an incident such as this advertised a range of up to sixteen miles. I assumed this massive range must have been for the plains of eastern Montana, and since we spent the latter part of our climb and our entire descent surrounded by the massive rocky outcroppings of Cuttoff Mountain and Barronette Peak, I had given the radios the benefit of the doubt. But now I could draw a line from the point where we stood to our campsite at 3P2 on the edge of the meadow (I had originally planned for us to stay at 3P3 until someone recommended 3P2 as having more flat spots for multiple tents).

When we saw the blue-and-white tents set up at 3P3—the campsite a half-mile upstream of our destination for the night—we should have been jubilant, knowing how close we finally were to our campsite. Instead, I had this nagging feeling that something had gone very wrong.

As we arrived at our stream crossing just below 3P3, I made one final call into the radio: "Unit 2, unit 1, do you read? Unit 2, unit 1, do you read?" A deafening silence was the only response. I could feel the desperation in my voice, which by now, I didn't attempt to hide from John and Kathy.

We took our time taking off our boots and slipping into our sandals. Though we didn't say much, we all sensed that trouble loomed.

My Chacos were ten years old, had been rethreaded two times, and the soles were as slippery as a bald tire with 100,000 highway miles on its treadless rubber, making them loose and comfortable. After tying my boots' laces with a quick overhand knot, I slung them in the carbineer hanging from the top strap of my backpack and began the shin-deep crossing, which promptly cooled and relieved my achy feet and sore Achilles.

For a fleeting moment, I felt a slight sense of peace. I don't know if you can feel peace and truly lose yourself in a moment when anxiety is coursing through your body, your stomach tightened and chest heavily weighted, but as short as that distraction was, I can still feel the sudden surge of rushing water pulsing against my ankle and calves years after the event. I remember briefly closing my eyes, with my back to

John and Kathy, and taking a deep breath, relishing in the tingly, needle-pricking sensation dominating the ball of my foot and the tips of my toes. I'm not sure there is anything more soothing—more therapeutic—than moving water.

Though my sunglasses remained on the brim of my sweaty Simms fishing hat, I opened my eyes and peered into the knee-deep hole just upstream, in search of a perfectly camouflaged Yellowstone cutthroat—and not of the fat and opulent Slough Creek variety, but instead, the more humble and middle-class Pebble Creek strain. Knowing there was little chance of finding a cutthroat without my polarized-aided eyes this time of evening, with the fading light and lack of shadows, I continued to gaze deep into the hole, welcoming the distraction and brief sense of hope that the water and its fine inhabitants were able to provide.

Once we were all across the creek, it was a short, ten-minute hike to camp. I didn't even attempt to use the radio on our walk through one of the most beautiful and lush meadows of upper Pebble Creek. If Justin and Zazzy hadn't answered my pleading call when we first arrived on the waters' edge, they were unreachable. As we neared the tree line and our campsite for the night, I gripped the radio tight and talked to myself, lips moving the way you see crazed fans at SEC football games praying that the other team will miss the winning field goal—in some delusional hope that I somehow had any control over the situation.

The sight of the rusted metal sign etched with "3P2" brought a sense of dread, not triumph. There was a teasingly long 100-yard walk through the lodgepole forest from the trail to the bear pole, fire ring, and tent locations for the site, and as I had feared from the time we began our descent—a fear that grew more ominous with each forward step—I could see the site was untouched. Empty. No sign of the boys.

"Fuck."

For the first time, I allowed my frustration and concern to show. Not a very professional response to our quandary. I didn't know what our next move would be. Our fate was in the hands—or more accurately, the feet and packs—of the boys, and I had no idea where they could be. I thought I had executed a perfect game plan, but it seemed to have completely backfired. I had sent the tent, floorless shelter, food, stove, and cookware with the boys. All we had were our pads, sleeping bags, snacks, and a water filter.

It was already 7:30 P.M., and we had less than an hour and a half of daylight left. Frustrated and dismayed, John looked at me and said, "We are hiking out." But this wasn't even an option. We had a six-and-a-half-mile hike to the truck—the majority of which we would be hiking in the dark—and I didn't think my clients could walk another four hundred yards. John and Kathy had just put in the most intense day of hiking they ever had, burdened with packs. We weren't going anywhere.

Where the hell could the boys be? There seemed to be only two possible answers: they had either taken the left fork and continued on to 3P4 from the junction with the creek; or they had taken the right, and in their tired daze, walked right past 3P2 and on to 3P1. Either way, we were in a bad situation, as both sites were nearly three miles from our location.

Not having much in the way of options, I decided the best move was for me to jog up to 3P3 to see if the hikers occupying the most picturesque site on Pebble Creek had seen the boys. Tired from a long day's work, I don't even remember the feelings that coursed through me as I ran in my sandals in my search to discover the boys' whereabouts. This had suddenly gone from a well-executed and well-planned trip—one where we controlled our own destiny—to a journey of hope, which was perhaps better than despair at this point and time.

As I neared the campsite on the knobby outcropping overlooking the meadow and massive monolith of Cuttoff Mountain, I slowed my pace and gathered my breath before entering the hallowed grounds of someone else's backcountry site. When it comes to backpacking etiquette, walking into another group's campsite is right up there with taking a shit within eyeshot of the trail, leaving your white ribbon of TP fluttering in the wind. I expected to be met with a "What the fuck do you want?" kind of stare upon my arrival, but instead, adding to the bewildering nature of my evening, the Turner family welcomed me as if they had been expecting my company.

I had never seen anything quite like it in the backcountry of Yellowstone. There were two adults—a well-groomed, fit, and polite businessman, and a beautiful, equally fit and hospitable woman, both in their late forties—with three golden-skinned teenage girls that had the look of club volleyball players. Two tents had been staked and tautly lined out, with duffel bags and a cooler full of food. There was no sign of horses, but someone had to have packed them in. Or maybe this guy was some executive with Citibank who had connections to the administration, and they had broken every rule in the Park Service book to fly him in. I didn't know and I didn't really care; I just needed answers.

After introductions, Ed, the father of one of the teenagers and husband of the beautiful and seemingly content woman, shared the story of their upheaval from 3P1. They had been packed in the previous day by a horse packer from Cooke City, but soon after getting settled, a large group of Conservation Corps volunteers arrived, stating that they had reserved the site. After a heated debate, Park Service personnel arrived and escorted the Turner family to the site they had originally wanted (everyone who knows Pebble Creek wants 3P3), and that was that.

Having listened to his family's ordeal patiently, I proceeded to share my own predicament and asked if they had seen two teenage boys pass through the area—which caused the girls, who were clearly out of their element, to suddenly perk up. They hadn't seen any sign of Justin or Colton, leading me to believe that the boys must have passed through and headed northeast to 3P4 before the Turners arrived at camp. But why, then, hadn't they journeyed back up the pass? There is no way either of these two young men would hang me out to dry. Something had to have happened.

Regardless of the boys' circumstances, I knew they had enough food to get them through a week in the backcountry. Plus, Justin had grown up hunting in the mountains just north of the park, so I didn't see any reason to start worrying too much about them. Not yet anyway. Instead, I needed to focus my attention on John and Kathy. If we still hadn't heard from the boys by the time we reached the trailhead the following day, I would have to contact park dispatch and Justin's father—but this was still a long way off. Right now, I needed to get my clients shelter and food.

Twenty minutes after my arrival, the Turner's sent me packing with an armful of food; a bag with a stove, matches, and fuel; and a tarp that would have to act as a lean-to for John and Kathy. I would simply have to go old school and sleep beside the fire, hoping it didn't get too cold overnight. When I arrived back at camp, John and Kathy had calmed down, resigned themselves to what we were facing, and displayed their typical character by simply accepting the situation. I told them all about my encounter with the family at 3P3 and my failed attempt at securing one of their tents for the evening. While Ed couldn't have been more generous, offering me more than we needed, he'd made it clear that he wouldn't be lending me a tent. I had inquired after noticing that the tent the girls were sleeping in appeared to be a five-man car-camping shelter, and the Kelty backpacking tent that Ed and his wife shared looked to be at least a three-man. But a man has to draw the line in the sand of generosity at some point, and the tent was clearly that line.

We were better off than we had been thirty minutes earlier, but it was still far from ideal. I tried to remain upbeat and provide distractions, but John and Kathy were concerned about the boys. Hiding my own growing concerns, I assured them that the boys would be fine. They were grown, able, and fully equipped. I didn't want any idle time, so I tinkered with the stove until I figured it out and got some water boiling while John worked on building a fire. The next project was what concerned me most. While I had been a ranger in the park and was still an avid outdoorsman, fishing guide, and backpacker, I am an admitted gear head—not a Boy Scout. And now I had the task of erecting a lean-to with a tarp that seemed much too small.

After wrestling with the loud piece of six-by-six-foot plastic for twenty minutes, I somewhat securely fashioned a small A-frame shelter, believing that this design would provide more shelter from what looked to be a cold evening than the traditional lean-to, with one side unprotected. But make no mistake about it, the combination of a lack of holes in the tarp and the minimal amount of rope made for a meager shelter, the sight of which knotted up my stomach like a sponge being tightly wrung.

Shortly after its completion, John—who had helped in its construction—walked over with Kathy to inspect their accommodations for the night. It had been a beast of a day; they were tired, sore, and achy; it was their anniversary; and they had paid a hefty price for this trip. I could see the disappointment in their eyes, but they didn't say a word—they didn't have to.

I looked at John and said, "I will be right back." He asked me where the hell I thought I was going. My back to him, I responded, "To get you a tent," as I fled camp with grand and heroic aspirations.

Ed had already said no—in the light of day—but now it was dark, and I knew I had to give it another try. At least I would demonstrate to John and Kathy that I had done everything in my power to make this right. As I ran through the forest and into the darkened meadow, basking in the light of a nearly full moon and a brilliant display of stars beginning to illuminate the transitioning sky, I did so in reverie. I couldn't help but think of the times in my life where I had been rejected by a girl playing hard to get who later succumbed to my passion and doggedness. Would my doggedness pay off tonight?

Perhaps I should have turned on my headlamp in my haste to leave camp, or simply paid more attention to the half-mile trail that I had already traversed three times in the previous hour and a half, but my forward progress abruptly came to an end as I found myself face down, mouth full of dry trail dust and dirt. My right pinky toe had caught the edge of a root and sent me flying. Next thing I knew, I was writhing in pain, rolling on the dry, hardened earth and wondering what could possibly go wrong next. But this was not a time to feel sorry for myself, so without looking at the damage done to my smallest of toes, I continued on the trail, running with the gate of a battle-tested marathoner, still aching from hauling a fifty-pound pound pack up and over Bliss Pass.

Though I had eight minutes to adequately mock talk what I would say to Ed, initially enjoying the solitude of my evening trail run prior to delaminating the soft skin attaching my pinky toe to my foot and having to carry on in teeth-gritting pain, I failed to do so. Before reentering his camp, I found a fallen tree and sat down on it to rehearse, deciding to beg Ed, if need be, for his smaller backpacking tent.

When I arrived, all lights were out. There was no sign of any living human being—as if they had abandoned camp. It had only been dark for fifteen minutes. I couldn't believe they weren't sitting around a campfire roasting s'mores. Hell, I hadn't eaten anything since we left the Bliss Pass cutoff near Elk Tongue Patrol Cabin, and I was starving. Nothing sounded better than a burnt and gooey marshmallow squeezed tightly by two rich pieces of milk chocolate sandwiched between two dry, crispy graham crackers, and now I couldn't even fulfill that simple fantasy.

With that feeling of uncomfortable dread we have all experienced before asking a question that will likely yield an answer we don't want to hear, I quietly—almost sneakily—walked through the Turners' camp to the smaller of the two tents. As if at someone's front door, I "knocked" on the flap, my hand brushing against the nylon surface, a sound indiscernible from the breeze.

"Hey, Ed, are you awake?"

"Michael, is that you?"

"Yes, Ed. I'm so sorry to bother you, but I need to talk to you for a moment if possible."

I stepped about ten feet away from the tent to give the couple privacy, as I could hear them whispering. Though they couldn't have been in their sleeping bags long, Ed appeared sleepy when he stumbled out of the tent, probably worn out from his ordeal earlier in the day with the Conservation Corps, made worse from an afternoon of fishing the prolific waters of upper Pebble Creek.

"What do you need, Michael?"

He could immediately see that I was uncomfortable bothering him again, disturbing his night with his wife. I sensed that this was his trip, something he desperately wanted to do, and that the girls (who may or may not have been enjoying themselves) were there to appease his need to get away from his busy life in Denver—to find a simpler, more peaceful existence through hiking and dry-fly fishing in a place of solitude, away from the masses.

Now here I was hassling him again. Disturbing his peace.

"Ed, I know this sounds crazy and perhaps a bit outrageous, but I really need one of your tents."

He met this request with a blank—Are you stupid?—kind of stare, and followed his confused facial expression with a repeat of what he had said earlier: "Michael, I'm very sorry about your predicament, but we've done all we can for you. We are not giving up one of our tents."

Determined and desperate, I followed, "But Ed, I'm fucked without a tent. You have to understand how big this trip is for me. These folks, who are celebrating their anniversary, have paid a lot for it, and they are not the pretentious, rich type of folks. I could see the disappointment in their faces when I showed them their shelter for the night. I really appreciate all you've done for me, but this trip is so important."

I had told him earlier about my history with the Park Service in Yellowstone National Park and about my founding of Yellowstone Country Guardians to show him that I was legit, hoping he would find me worthy of help. And though he seemed genuinely concerned about my situation, he was unmoved by my plea.

"You see, Ed, these folks are not just clients, they are donors to my organization. And I think they could be big donors for us down the road."

He remained patient, but I could see my time was running out.

"Michael, I really do sympathize with what you are dealing with, but we simply aren't going to give you one of our tents."

"Ed, I really can't leave here without one of these tents."

"I don't know what to tell you, Michael. You are going to be sitting out here all night then, because it simply isn't going to happen."

I wasn't getting anywhere asking for him to simply give me a tent. He was certainly a kind and generous person, but his philanthropic altruism had run out. I needed to get creative. I had to give him something in return.

"Ed, I see you are a fly fisherman."

"Well, yes. That is one of the reasons why we are up here. This has become a yearly tradition for us. I know the fish aren't mighty here, but as I shared with you earlier, places like Slough Creek simply don't appeal to me. I would much prefer to chase trout in a setting like this."

"I couldn't feel you more, Ed; I'm the same way. The solitude and the experience means much more to me than the fish size. But let me ask you, have you ever been on a guided float trip in a drift boat on the Yellowstone River?"

"No, Michael, I have not. I've always wanted to fish from a drift boat but simply haven't made it happen yet."

"Well, Ed, I'm a fly-fishing guide, and a full-day guided float trip on the Yellowstone River, which includes lunch and bugs, is worth $500. I will give you a free guided day on the 'Stone if you give me this tent."

It was clear that I had finally touched a chord because, for the first time since I had rudely dragged him out of the warmth of his tent, his eyes perked up.

"Sold."

"Are you serious, Ed?"

"Dead serious."

This was by far the biggest catch of any fly-fishing trip I had ever guided. I could hardly contain my excitement. And while I felt terrible for interrupting his family's hard-earned vacation, I received solace knowing they still had three nights ahead, and that the five of them could surely squeeze into the oversized car-camping tent for just one of them. Still, I walked over to the bear pole forty feet away when Ed went back into his tent to tell his wife about the deal he had just struck.

If she was furious, she sure didn't show it. She did try to convince me to bring John and Kathy up to their site so they didn't have to break down and reset their tent again after doing so twice earlier in the day. But a deal is a deal, and I was taking the tent to 3P2.

Within ten minutes of striking the deal, we hurriedly stuffed the tent, poles, fly, and stakes into a large thirty-gallon trash bag; and after giving both Ed and his wife big bear hugs—and assuring them I would be back the next morning with all of their gear—I was back on the trail, en route to John and Kathy with good news. I carried my prized armful of loose and awkward tent with forearms and palms toward the stars, as if carrying something much heavier than it was. I did not run; I was tired. My body ached all over, and my toe felt as if someone had violently hyperextended it in an act of vengeful fury.

My sense of relief that I had secured a worthy shelter for my clients who had become much more through our time and memorable experiences together lightened the load of my scrambling brain and released the anxiety that had tightly gripped my chest since we began our descent into Pebble Creek. For the first time since arriving at the summit of Bliss Pass, a big smile spread across my face. I imagined the dismay and confusion that some poor red squirrel must have experienced, having watched me frantically rush up and down the thin ribbon of dirt path with a fierce scowl on my face, and now, minutes later, as if I had just won the lottery, seeing my pearly whites glow in the light of the moon—bleeding a different, perhaps more palpable (if not mentally troubled) aura from my spirit. I hope this bipolar behavior isn't considered animal harassment, but it would have been disturbing for any onlooker—be they two- or four-legged—to observe my madness.

As I once again neared the forest leading into the cold and empty confines of our campsite, my thoughts turned to the boys. I had successfully secured a tent for John and Kathy, but it would undoubtedly be a torturous night sacked out beside the fire, shelter-less and wondering what had happened to my trusted sherpas. While I was confident they would be okay, I deeply dreaded the long walk out and then the walk into the trailer of Ray and Darlene—the Pebble Creek Campground hosts, whom I had known for over seven years—to ask them to make the call over the radio that two Gardiner teens were missing. The bear spray incident was a simple mistake that we worked through and had added to the mystique of our trip; but this was a disaster.

I knew John and Kathy would be relieved—and perhaps a bit blown away—when I walked into camp with a tent, but I also suspected it would elevate their worries for Justin and Zazzy to another level. That is the way it works. While we were all worried about the boys, we also had concerns about our own situation. And now that three of our collective's needs were met, our concern for the boys would surely reach a more feverish pitch.

My worry reverie was interrupted within three hundred yards of the spur trail to our campsite, when—for the first time since we'd passed a father talking to his daughter while we were trudging up the relentless shoulder of Bliss Pass—the crackling of radio static burst from my handheld.

I dropped the tent to the ground and frantically unzipped the left pocket on my chest, scrambling to grab the pear-shaped two-way radio. In my haste, it slipped from my hands and fell on top of the garbage bag. Though my rational mind knew the radio must lie at my feet, I felt for its plastic case feverishly, as if fearing it would sink into the abyss if I didn't find it that very second.

Once in my hand, I pressed the call button and practically shouted, "Unit 2, this is unit 1. Do you read?"

Within two seconds, I received a response: "Is that you, Coach?"

I tilted my head to the heavens and took a deep breath. It was them. They were alive and, in light of the lack of range of our handhelds, they had to be close.

"Where the fuck are you guys?"

"We're on top of the pass, Coach. You don't even want to know what we've been through today."

It was Colton. He could hardly speak—he sounded exhausted. Who knows what he had endured? At that moment, I just wanted them to get their asses down as quickly as possible.

"What the hell are you guys still doing up on the pass?"

"It's a long story, Coach. How far are we from camp?"

"Not far. It's a two-mile walk down the pass, and then we're half a mile from the stream crossing. I'll walk you through it over the radio, but get your asses down here. Now. Just don't rush and hurt yourselves. I just gave away a $500 guide day for a guy's tent, and I'm going to go give it back to him."

"Okay, Coach. We're in bad shape. We're tired and hurting, but we'll be down soon."

I clutched the radio tight and threw my right arm triumphantly into the air, as though Colton had just hit a deep three at the buzzer to win us a game. Elated, I couldn't decide whether to run down to 3P2 to tell John and Kathy the good news or head back to 3P3 to return Ed's tent—and in the process, regain a day of paid wages. I opted to jog back to 3P3 before Ed and his wife got too cozy.

Though my back ached and my Achilles burned, the discomfort of running with an armful of tent didn't matter. It had been a horrendous and dramatic three hours, and now everything was coming together. This time when I entered the Turner camp, I did not hesitate. I ran down the spur trail leading to their tent and hurdled a downed lodgepole, desperate to catch them before they fell asleep.

They had heard me scurry into camp, because Ed yelled my name before I uttered a word.

"Ed, I've got great news. I just received a call from the boys. They're on the top of the pass and will be down soon, so I won't need your tent after all."

"That is great news, Michael. I know you were really worried about your boys—we all were. But you can keep the tent for the night."

"That's really nice of you, Ed, but we won't be needing your tent. I'm happy to stick around and help you set it back up."

"That won't be necessary, Michael. That tent is already sold for the night. We won't be needing it. We will see you in the morning."

Though he couldn't see my look of bemusement, Ed seemed to know I was about to speak again. Before I could say another word, he added, "It's been a long day. We are going to get some rest. Goodnight, Michael."

How could I argue? Though we no longer needed the tent, their willingness to part with it, along with all of the other supplies they had offered us, warranted my giving Ed a day on the river.

While walking the trail between 3P3 and 3P2 for the seventh time in a little over two hours, I called the boys and told them to take their time.

"Well, boys, I couldn't get the guy who sold me the tent to take it back, so I'm out $500. I'm going to go set it up for John and Kathy, so take it easy coming down the pass. I will be waiting for your arrival."

This time Justin responded, "We're really sorry for fucking this up, Coach. See you soon."

My sense of relief—just knowing they were okay—vastly outweighed the frustration I felt. But I couldn't help wondering how the hell they had messed up this day so badly. I felt what I imagine any parent feels when their teenager misses curfew. Upon their arrival home, there is that sudden gasp—that moment of relief that takes one's breath away—followed by a flood of frustration, and then, often, anger that the child you love so intensely could put you through so much worry and despair. There was little doubt I would share my frustration with Justin and Zazzy, but the truth of the matter is that, in the end, it all had worked out.

When I arrived in camp, John and Kathy had concerned and distinctly disappointed expressions on their faces. And they were huddled around the campfire. I hadn't realized how cold it had gotten.

"I have some good news."

Silent, John looked at me with a fatherly glare, as if to say, "This better be fucking good."

"After some negotiating, I was able to get a tent from the folks at 3P3."

John simply smiled and gave me a nod of approval, while Kathy let out her first good laugh since she tricked that chubby cutty on Slough Creek. "That is very impressive and resourceful, Michael. Good job!"

Having seen the lean-to that would function as her sleeping quarters, she had likely been dreading the ten hours of darkness ever since. Now I sensed that both John and Kathy were content. The evening was still salvageable—and this felt good.

In my absence, they had cooked up two of the freeze-dried meals that Ed and his crew had given me after my first charitable mission to their campsite. I plopped down beside Kathy on a log close to the fire to warm my tired, aching legs.

After a few moments of satisfied silence, I nonchalantly added, "Oh, and I heard from the boys."

"What?" Kathy cried. "Where are they?"

"They were up on the pass and working their way down. That's why I was gone so long. I finally got the man from 3P3 to give us a tent after I offered him a complementary guide day on the Yellowstone. And then, when I heard from the boys at the top of the pass, I went back to return the tent; but he insisted our transaction was final."

Though John remained silent, I suspected—or perhaps just hoped—that he was impressed by my finding them a tent in the middle of the backcountry. He had displayed the same resourcefulness in his baseball career and in starting his own business, and I sensed that he appreciated my dogged, unrelenting efforts to make them comfortable. All was not lost. Perhaps this would even prove fruitful for my nonprofit organization. If things went well, I'd been thinking about asking John and Kathy for a donation to support our youth fly-fishing program. But any solid businessman like John wants to ensure a return on their investment. Seeing I could hustle a guy out of his tent this deep into the wilderness might convince him of the return he'd get—in the form of an inspired next generation of river guardians.

Each conversation I had with the boys over the radio, instructing them how to reach our campsite, seemed to perk up John and Kathy more. When Justin and Colton radioed to say they'd arrived at the stream crossing, John decided to walk up trail to meet them in the meadow. I, on the other hand, opted to stay with Kathy beside the fire. The boys were okay, and I found myself feeling more and more frustrated about what they had put us through.

Ten minutes after he left, John returned, shouldering Justin's backpack, with Zazzy and Justin lagging behind. They staggered into camp like two punch-drunk boxers returning to their corner after receiving a pummeling in the twelfth and final round of a fight. Neither boy said a word. Their moans and stiff movements spoke for themselves.

While John and Kathy expressed concern, I tried not to look at either of them. I felt awful that they were in so much pain, but I was pretty sure I wore the same look on my face that my team saw on the rare occasion they failed to show up, leading to our getting an ass kicking on the floor. This time it wasn't for lack of effort; I knew that just from looking at them. But how on earth were they just arriving to camp at 11 P.M. when they had left 2S4 thirteen hours earlier?

For the first twenty minutes, hardly a word was spoken. John and Kathy remained openly sympathetic, though I have to say, John seemed to silently enjoy the boys' anxious expressions when they glanced my way. They both looked like ghosts—faces gaunt, pale, and lifeless.

At one point, Justin began writhing in pain, "Ah, fuck, my legs." He was cramping up. John rushed to his side with a Nalgene full of water, encouraging him to stretch. After Justin's spasm subsided, Colton finally dared to tell their story.

They'd left camp right on time, just a few minutes after 10 A.M., spry and in good spirits. But when they reached the sign leading to Bliss Pass, with the lone, black water shoe perched atop, they kept walking north. After three miles of flat trekking through the third meadow of Slough Creek, they reached the park boundary. I had never said anything about leaving Yellowstone. I had told them half a dozen times that the day's hike would consist of seven miles, with a four-mile climb, a two-mile descent, and a half-mile walk to 3P2. That only leaves a half-mile to dicker with, but somehow, throughout all their walking on terrain I hadn't described, this escaped them. In hindsight, I realized I should have walked them to the cutoff, but this never crossed my mind.

Colton explained that once they arrived at the park boundary and saw the sign that they were leaving Yellowstone National Park, they noted that the sign also said that the Bliss Pass Trail was three miles behind them. This didn't make any sense. How could the Bliss Pass cut-off be three miles to the south when they had just traveled those three miles? They concluded that someone must have turned the sign around—that Bliss Pass was three miles to the north—and they continued their trek.

As they told the story of walking past the legendary Silver Tip Ranch and into the heart of Frenchy's Meadows, for a fleeting few moments, I actually found myself envying the boys. I have studied the map of the sprawling meadows north of Silver Tip countless times but have never placed eyes upon their wild waters. The boys went on to say that it wasn't until they began losing the trail, with it forking in a multitude of directions without any signs indicating destination, that they began to question their route of travel. By their estimation, they hiked another five miles beyond the park's boundary before deciding to turn back and retrace their steps.

When they arrived back at the luxurious Silver Tip Ranch, they ran into a gentleman with a fly rod in hand and asked if he knew where Bliss Pass was.

"Well, sure I do," he said. "It is three miles south of here, right behind the Elk Tongue Patrol Cabin."

"Holy shit, Zazzy," Justin apparently responded. "We have fucked this up big time. Coach is going to be fuming."

"Let's just move," Colton declared.

As Colton shared the epic nature of their day, he seemed intent upon capturing the limited but intense dialogue that took place over the course of their twenty-plus miles on the trail. Any frustration I'd felt was melting fast, but I still remained pretty much silent.

By the time they reached the sign with the aqua sock on top, warning them of the four-mile climb still to come, they dropped the sixty-pound packs they had needlessly hauled sixteen miles and waited while Mitchell and Sam pumped them four fresh bottles of water. There had apparently been some discussion of Colton and Justin setting up camp at the Elk Tongue Patrol Cabin with their former teammates, who had just finished a day of spraying weeds in the third meadow. Justin was beginning to cramp, and his legs were screaming at him to stop—and the hardest part of their day had yet to begin.

"Coach is going to kill you guys," Mitchell warned. "You have the tents, food, and stove. And it's supposed to get really cold tonight. You better get to Coach for real."

That was it; they knew Mitchell was right. Like Mitch, and perhaps more so than any of the other six boys who had given me a rose at the recent graduation ceremony Justin and Colton, felt an intense loyalty to me. There was no way they would quit.

Justin's legs worsened with each grueling step, and on multiple occasions throughout the climb, he informed Colton that he was done; he was going to pitch a tent and call it a day. This was not like Justin at all, so I can only imagine the pain he must have been in to reach that point. Truth be told, Justin's pack was heavier than Colton's or mine, and the added weight must have taken a toll. But Colton responded by telling him that stopping wasn't an option.

"I don't give a shit how bad we're hurting," Colton had told him. "We're going to keep fucking walking until we make it to Coach."

Neither John nor Kathy seemed bothered by Colton's profanity when sharing the fierce debates and conversations with Justin. While I continued to act pissed, I could not help but be moved by their desire not to let me down.

"The pass just wouldn't end, and then when it got dark, it felt like we had hiked forever. Justin was hurting so bad, I really didn't know how much farther he could walk. But then we heard Coach over the radio, and I knew everything was going to be okay."

This was just another reminder of what I've always said: there is unmatched power in sport. Team sports build bonds and forge relationships that wouldn't otherwise be possible.

After John and Kathy retired to the comfort and relative warmth of their tent, I instructed Colton to help me pump water. Justin couldn't even move, and while Colton walked as if every muscle and joint in his body were so fragile they were on the verge of breaking, he followed without complaint.

"Coach," he started, as we headed to the pump, "I know we fucked up. But we were hurting so bad. Justin had to stop every twenty-five yards. I told him we would quit if it were anyone else waiting for us, but there is only one person on this earth that we were going to keep walking for, and you're that person."

Then, tears welling in his eyes, he added, "I'm really sorry, Coach."

While only twelve years older than Colton, I felt more like a father than a big brother at that moment. I stopped pumping the water, looked him in the eyes, and told him how much I loved him, even if he was a knucklehead. It was a simple but beautiful moment under the blanket of darkness, with the moon and radiant stars softly lighting the rushing waters tumbling by our campsite. Within minutes Justin limped his way over to the creek and we, too, shared a big embrace—similar to those long, strong hugs we would share after a heartbreaking loss to our rivals from Shields Valley or Twin Bridges.

Exhausted, we hardly said a word while setting up the floorless shelter and John and Kathy's backpacking tent. Kathy had turned in early and John wasn't far behind, climbing into the tent that I had "purchased" from Ed and set up while the boys were descending from the pass. I needed a good night's rest, and while I had made amends with the boys, I wasn't ready to be tightly confined with them in a small shelter if I had the option of spreading out in a tent of my own.

For the first time in weeks, I slept hard. We all did. It was sometime just before 8 A.M. when I finally began to stir. My body screamed with every movement. All of my joints were stiff and achy beyond anything I could remember. I knew John and Kathy would be hurting too, and the boys would be a mess. While limping to a small lodgepole to relieve myself, I decided that we would take our time that morning.

It had been a cold night. While it didn't snow, temperatures dropped into the midtwenties and our tents glistened with frost. The only parts of my body that didn't hurt were my hands, but after building a fire and exposing my skin to the below-freezing temps, they too began to ache. It was a slow morning. Even John and Kathy—early risers usually—had trouble getting up, choosing to rest their sore and tender bodies on Ed's 2-inch thick Therm-a-Rest pad as long as possible. I've found that those who rise early at home rise even earlier in the backcountry, for the lack of comfort forces them to stir earlier than usual. So I knew they were hurting when my watch read 8:30 and they still hadn't emerged from Ed's tent.

The boys could have slept all day. Surprisingly, Justin was the first to rise, stumbling out of the tent in his Levi's and battle-worn cowboy button-up. Though he walked with the gait of a bull rider the day after taking an inhumane beating, the good night's rest had done wonders for him. He no longer looked as if he might keel over and die at any moment. We didn't say much, but he gave me a devilishly sly smile as I handed him a warm bowl full of peach-flavored oatmeal. (I don't know what it is about the peach oatmeal; I wouldn't touch it at home. But in the backcountry, it is a must.)

Colton was last to rise, and in typical Zazzy fashion, he smiled, nodded at everyone, and then went about eating his not-so-hot oatmeal. Though I made sure to remind the boys of the trouble their getting lost had caused us, I didn't need to say much, because John took care of that with tactful humor and just the right amount of ball busting. Each time one of us reminded them of the epic nature of their mistake—and equally heroic recovery—they would simply close their eyes and lower their heads, which they slowly shook from side to side, embarrassed grins on their faces.

The boys were ravenous, so I ordered them to eat the last of the breakfast while I walked the trail between 3P2 and 3P3 one last time. It was a brisk but perfect Yellowstone morning. There wasn't a cloud in the sky, nor a hint of wind. And the dark, monolithic outcropping of Cuttoff Mountain soared high into the blue abyss, ominous and dark in comparison to the light and welcoming sky.

There is something magical about the early morning hours in the backcountry of wild places like Yellowstone. The cool crisp air. The anticipation of what the day has to offer. The reawakening of the landscape. I felt deeply content while walking up the trail I had traversed seven times the night before, overwhelmed by a sense of peace that I have only felt on summer mornings such as this, deep into the backcountry. The angst and frustration of the night before had passed, and I was fully immersed in the moment, keenly observing one of the most scenic and welcoming meadows in all of Yellowstone.

Pebble Creek sang her song, accompanied by a choir of mountain chickadees, dark-eyed juncos, Clark's nutcrackers, and ruby-crowned kinglets. I felt selfish leaving the crew at camp while I enjoyed my own mini saunter through one of my favorite sections of trail in the park— a half mile I now knew more intimately than ever before. There is something intimate, perhaps even romantic, about walking alone on a trail in a wild landscape before the sun has melted the water droplets clinging to a meadow full of knee-high grasses, with a handsome babbling creek meandering through the heart of the painting. I could not help but deeply feel a warm and comforting connection to the meadow separating 3P2 from 3P3 as the morning light gently bathed its succulent vegetation as I walked, the folded tent in my arms and pressed tightly to my chest.

The wilderness is a teacher. And perhaps the greatest lesson that the raw and rugged terrain of Yellowstone's northeast corner taught us on this journey was the importance of hope and the significance of a new day. Remain as determined, persistent, and adaptable in life as you are in the backcountry, and the dawn of a new day can yield wondrous treasure.

When I arrived at the Turners' camp, everyone was awake, alert, and ready to start the day. Ed was already preparing to hit the water, itching to put yesterday behind him by getting to know dozens of Pebble Creek's finned residents. Our encounter was brief. While not complaining, the girls appeared lost, not knowing what they would do to occupy their day. Ed's wife was kind, warm, and insistent that I simply leave the tent; she didn't want my help setting it up. It would give her and the girls something to do.

Ed, who was clearly anxious to hit the water, extended his right hand and said, "I'm glad we could help you last night, Michael. I'm off to the water. I look forward to fishing with you later this fall."

"I can't thank you enough, Ed," I replied earnestly. "Your generosity is deeply appreciated and was certainly unexpected. I, too, look forward to reconnecting on the Yellowstone in the months ahead."

And that was it. Ed picked his way through the sagebrush and downed timber, resolute to spend a morning knee-deep in the waters of Pebble Creek. I spent a few more minutes talking with the girls, answering questions about bears, thoughts of which had clearly kept the teenagers from sleeping soundly throughout the night, and then began my short walk back to camp. As I walked through the middle of the meadow, I watched for a moment as Ed hurriedly cast his fly into a riffle ten feet upstream. He must have sensed me watching because, without taking his eyes from his fly drifting through a short riffle, he simply lifted his left arm and waved good-bye. He had come for solitude, and now he was ready to enjoy the meadow that he had expressed such open affection for— by himself.

When I returned to camp, the boys were sitting beside the fire, having already taken down each shelter and packed them in their bags. John and Kathy were fishing, as I could see the tip of a rod and the unfurling of a fluorescent line waving over the water's surface. Everything was back to normal—as it should be. Yesterday's drama was behind us, and the fact that John and Kathy still desired to fish meant the trip hadn't been a total bust.

After dispersing the fire and pouring water on the fuming coals, we began our six-mile walk downhill to Pebble Creek Campground. We kept John and Kathy's rods rigged up to fish any good-looking holes during our multiple stream crossings to the valley floor. Not much was said as we walked to our final destination. It was a silence inspired by both fatigue and contentment. Enjoying temps in the upper 70s, we walked with our heads down, focused on each grabby tree root, determined to stay upright.

Before our second stream crossing, I hesitated, studying what looked like a perfect pool—by Pebble Creek standards. Within minutes I spotted what appeared to be a short but stalky cutty, suspended in a knee-deep hole that was protected by a downed lodgepole pine. It was idyllic trout habitat but would make for a difficult drift. John volunteered Kathy for the job and we proceeded on our knees, remaining low so as not to spook our friend.

Though the cast was not flawless, it was good enough, and without hesitation, on the first drift, the cutty exploded out from under the cover of the downed log and ate our #16 coachman trude. With few places to run and the strength of a five-weight rod designed for bigger water and fish, any Pebble Creek trout should be landed quickly. Kathy escorted him into the slack water from which she cast, and I slid the net under his belly. Without touching his slimy body, I slid the hook out of his upper lip, and we all marveled at what appeared to be a twelve-inch male cutthroat—big for Pebble Creek. There was a slight chill in the air, as the sun had not yet reached this thickly forested section of the creek, making the water feel cooler and adding to the perfect water quality for a native Yellowstone cutthroat. And while we spotted another slightly larger-than-normal trout just downstream, at that point, we were all content to simply walk.

Shortly before noon, we reached 3P1, just three miles from the parking lot, and while we had intended to keep trudging to the truck, the day was too sublime. We were still attempting to put yesterday behind us, so we decided to stop for lunch to savor our last encounters with the creek.

The fishing was what you would expect from the untouched waters of Pebble Creek. Lunch was modest but filling. We were in no rush to leave the last of the meadows that dot the six miles from 3P2 to the trailhead. Though we had pumped water before leaving camp in the morning, our aching muscles screamed for hydration, and we were almost out of it. So John and Kathy began to slowly work their way back to the trail while we topped off the last of the water bottles.

Minutes after disappearing over the hill, they reappeared—not panicked but with alarm on their faces.

"There's a big female grizzly with three cubs in the meadow, not far from the trail," John announced.

While the opportunity to observe a grizzly in the backcountry, away from the hustle and bustle of the park's roads, is something I usually relish, my mind swam with thoughts of liability as I recalled the debacles that pervaded our journey.

"Okay, this is exciting," I responded. "Let's all group together, and go see if she is still visible."

As we crested the hill, we spotted her—a large grizzly grazing in the meadow fifty yards away. Brown, with hints of blonde and silver highlights, she was a beautiful and magnificent specimen. While I have spent countless days in close proximity to bears (mostly black but certainly grizzlies as well), working as a Bear Education Ranger and managing bear jams along the park's roads in the field, there is just nothing—for me—that matches the experience of encountering a grizzly in the wild.

Though I know they are there and they remain on my mind, it is not often that we have the opportunity to closely observe a grizzly bear while walking through Yellowstone's backcountry. I didn't have to say a word; John and Kathy knew this was significant. And the boys, who grew up on the edge of the park but had grown somewhat numb to the magic of Yellowstone (like most local youth), remained still and awestruck by the strength and size of the animal before us. Perhaps being inspired and humbled are much the same, because our proximity to this most authentic symbol of wildness certainly captivated us and stirred feelings from deep within.

Minutes after our arrival, the sow began raising her nose in the air, sniffing for the new scent drifting her way. While bears have arguably the keenest sense of smell of any land mammal in the world (approximately seven times that of a bloodhound), the belief that they have poor eyesight is a common misperception; bears rely heavily on all of their senses. Once she captured our scent and began scanning for our whereabouts, she stood on her hind legs, plantigrade, and made direct eye contact with our group. With eyesight comparable to that of humans, she took a good look at us, and just as I would expect from a good mother bear, dropped to all four legs, vocalized a warning to her cubs, and ushered them into the tree line 150 yards away.

What I will always remember most about our encounter was the last image before she lumbered through the timber and out of sight. After shepherding her three cubs of the year to the safety of the forest, she stopped in a small opening on the edge of the meadow. Once there, she turned and stared in our direction, with all three cubs between her front legs, fidgeting, likely wondering why their mother rushed them so abruptly from a lush meadow full of dandelion and starchy biscuitroot—newfound delicacies they were just beginning to enjoy.

The mother bear knew that humans were trouble and appeared to be using this encounter as a teaching opportunity—one far more important than helping the cubs discover which plants to consume and where. The biscuitroot wouldn't be going anywhere, and the edible wildflowers would remain viable for weeks to come. This lesson took precedence for the grizzly mama.

Though I could have stared into her eyes as long as she would stay, a few minutes after the lesson started, the cubs' patience began to wane. And as is often the case when young and without focus, the play started up with the slightly smaller of the three tackling the sibling standing directly in front of their mom. All three cubs frolicked back toward the meadow, but the female grizzly quickly put a stop to their shenanigans, hurrying them out of sight, deep into the secret confines of the forest.

I didn't know whether it was simply luck or karma, but a gift had been bestowed upon us. While far from melancholy, the mood up until that point was not entirely content. John and Kathy had hoped to see wildlife, and while our drive through the Lamar the first morning of the trip had produced a Serengeti-like number of wildlife sightings, it simply is not the same as meeting a charismatic member of the megafauna on his or her turf.

We had encountered four grizzlies—a female with three cubs of the year; one of the few females with three cubs throughout the entire Ecosystem that summer, after a dismal whitebark pine crop.

Once back on the trail, the final three miles seemed longer than they actually were. It had been a grand experience, we were all hurting, the bugs were biting, and everyone was ready to call it a day. While mystical in its own right, the steeply sloped forest of the final miles somehow seemed less wild—more black-bear habitat than that of the grizzly. Though I don't remember any of the words spoken during the final hour and a half on the trail, I do recall a satisfied silence radiating from each of us with each forward step. When we finally arrived at the trailhead sign, we snapped a multitude of photos to commemorate our journey.

We all walked at our own pace through the Pebble Creek Campground to Justin's tired and battered redneck truck, spread out like a proud troop of soldiers having accomplished what we had set out to achieve. For the first time since the night before, a slight tinge of anxiousness overwhelmed me as I hoped Justin's truck would start, remembering the times he was late to practice when her engine failed to ignite.

Knowing this, Justin walked ahead, dropped his pack on the tailgate, and went straight to the driver's door, where he jumped into the seat of the raggedly upholstered truck, popped the clutch, and revved the engine.

The last of my worries had vanished. Just as I reached the truck, Colton ran up from behind and with a toothy grin said, "Coach, thanks for bringing me on this trip. I will never forget it. This was the trip of a lifetime."

"Zazzy," I said, emotions beginning to swallow me, "it was my pleasure. I wouldn't have wanted it any other way."

Unlike the final day of a vacation, boarding the plane on the Garden Isle of Kauai when a flood of saddened emotions overcomes your senses as you yearn to be back at day one, what we all felt upon gazing at the northern face of the Thunderer was a sense of relief. The trip complete. The memories would last a lifetime. It had been as magnificent and unpredictable as the terrain we had traversed—at least in our minds and perhaps, more importantly, in our hearts.

Each and every one of us had worried about whether we were up for the adventure, whether we could truly pull it off. Now that we had, a bond had formed. We started the journey as an odd mixture of individuals, but as is often the case when accomplishing something worthwhile as a group, we had become a team—a family—if only for a moment. It was a perfect ending to a less-than-perfect trip.

Colton and I rode in the back of the pickup; Kathy sandwiched between Justin and John in the cab of the truck. I don't know if Kathy and John had ever ridden on the bench seat in the cab of an old Western pickup, but as they had throughout most of the trip, they remained unfazed, maybe even relishing in the rarity of their experience.

A powerful medicine comes from hardship after struggle has been endured. While none of us would have wished for the challenges presented during our backcountry sojourn, to a man and a woman, we wouldn't change a thing.

As the evening light dimly spread across the landscape, I observed the Lamar Valley for the first time from a new perspective. Having never driven through the valley in the back of a pickup, I felt immersed in the summer air rushing past my skin and the bison rutting up a storm of spiraling dirt, sending their guttural moans throughout the valley floor. Yellowstone's grandeur never disappoints, always showing itself in new and profound ways to those open and seeking its wild spirit.

As we passed one final band of bison, we pulled over, turned off the engine, and silently gazed into their deep and mournful eyes. Awestruck by their regal grace and stoic presence, I reflected upon the grandness of our adventure. Bliss Pass was a beast of a climb, Slough Creek a temple of a fishery, and Pebble a lovely treasure of simple beauty and wildness. I have often said, "Just the word *Yellowstone* has something sacred to it."

Now John and Kathy, Colton and Justin fully understood the depth and meaning of this spirited landscape. And once again, the wildness of Yellowstone had touched and inspired my own wild heart, leaving me satisfied, immensely grateful, and physically and emotionally exhausted—but already aching for more.

Such is the magic of Yellowstone.

29

Hoodoo Equinox Storm

Yellowstone Country is perhaps, on many levels, no different from any other large tract of wilderness when it comes to executing a foray into the backcountry. There are trips and then there are adventures. In my overly analytical mind, a trip is a getaway—an escape to the mountains, desert, ocean, or river; whereas an adventure more often than not represents a longer stay, with many uncertainties and a certain degree of childlike anticipation and enthusiasm. Our mid-September journey to the Hoodoo Basin represented the latter.

Maybe it is the mentally and physically arduous eighty-plus-hour weeks that I have been putting in the last few summers, the lack of weekend and vacation time, or simply the wild splendor of shouldering a pack with sleepless nights and adventure on the brain; but any extended walk in the backcountry seems to pump a little something extra into my blood, adding that lively bounce to my step—even when weighted down with a heavy pack.

After another long guide day in the field, I returned home hungry and exhausted, and still needing to pack for the next day's journey. The life of a guide in Montana amounts to a chaotic four months of family upheaval—a marathon of sorts. I hadn't made the time for a personal backpacking trip of any length (one that I was not leading) since my preguide days. As a result, my minimalist packing skills were a bit rusty, to say the least. But I managed to dust them off, assemble everything I needed, and by 2 A.M. on the eve of our boots hitting the trail, I climbed in bed knowing I was in for an adventure. A nervous excitement filled my active, sleepless mind.

The window for a non-ski-aided backcountry adventure in Yellowstone is short—and made even shorter this summer by historically high snowpack and river flows. It had been too long since I had been able to take a few days away from my nonprofit organization, guiding, and speaking engagements that had come to consume my life. Now I was about to journey into the heart of some of Yellowstone's wildest country with a friend and mentor by my side—someone with as deep a sense of place in my beloved Yellowstone (a place that speaks to the meaning of sense of place to so many) as anyone I know.

I met Nathan Varley in 2001, on a cold winter day, while exploring Yellowstone's Lamar Valley with my wife. We were newlyweds on Christmas break from North Idaho College, and we had come to observe wolves in the morning and ski in the afternoon. I was immediately attracted to Nathan's quiet confidence and willingness to share his knowledge with an eager-to-learn college student who was not one of his wildlife-viewing clients for the day. While I have shared this with Nathan since (as he now serves on the board of directors for Yellowstone Country Guardians, my nonprofit), his kindness and can-do attitude when I told him about my goal and dream of becoming a ranger in Yellowstone was an early catalyst for helping me believe it was possible.

Yellowstone is full of magic and power; but its ability to inspire people to dream big—and to make those dreams come true—may very well be the greatest gift "Wonderland" has to offer. While I had seen it on the map and heard rumors of its wild and eerie charm, the seed of my need to visit Yellowstone's mysterious Hoodoo Basin was planted during one slow day working the Visitor Center desk with another Yellowstone dreamer and longtime summer employee, Terry Ward (who, in later years, became a dear friend and supporter of my next Yellowstone dream—YCG).

"Need" may seem too strong a word for some who wish to visit certain places, but for a lover of Yellowstone, there are a few places and trips that are on the "Need to See/Do" list. Walking the length of the Bechler River from Cave Falls to Lone Star Geyser, exploring the Thorofare, and summiting Eagle and Electric Peaks represent a few adventures on just about every Yellowstone dreamer's checklist. And while I have experienced many of these adventures (some on multiple occasions), there is something about the Hoodoo Basin—call it a gravitational pull, if you will—that I have never been able to get off the brain or perhaps the heart.

In some ways, it had almost become an obsession. Every summer, I'd tell myself I was going to take some time off the water, away from guiding and the daily grind of putting people into fish, and YCG's exhilarating but exhausting River Guardian Fly Fishing School. And then every October, the guide season came to a close; YCG's fall program loomed; and before I knew it, the mountains and passes were once again locked up in a restless state of sleep as winter took hold.

But this year would be different. Call it fate (or maybe bad luck), but just before our move to Livingston the last week of August, I injured the tendons in my right wrist. After rowing for an entire day on the heavy waters of a river that shall go unnamed (as my father and I selfishly refuse to share the love and passion we feel for this wild Wyoming fishery with the rest of the world), my wrist was in bad shape. So we cancelled day two of our annual float so that I could put my wrist on ice until the next day, when I had to row for an eight-hour guide trip on a blustery day on the Yellowstone River. That was all she wrote. My guiding from a drift boat had come to an end for the year, I was in a cast, and it was time to get creative.

I realized there was no better time to make my Hoodoo dream a reality. Take a negative and turn it upside down. So I called the bearded man who had inspired me in the Lamar Valley ten years ago and who has become one of my best friends—a brother of sorts—to ask what he thought of taking an adventure to Hoodoo Country. Never one to pass up an opportunity for Yellowstone backcountry adventure, Nathan jumped on board immediately. But, typical of the life of a Yellowstone guide, the calls for trips kept flooding in, and both Nathan and I spent the first three days of what was supposed to be our Hoodoo adventure leading wildlife tours through the Lamar. Bound and determined to still make it happen, we plugged away, gave our clients all we could, and then we carved out a window of time—three days and two nights—to get ourselves unplugged from the chaos of a Yellowstone summer and plugged in to something a lot more primeval.

And now, on the 13 of September, I awoke to a cool but bluebird day, excited to finally be on the road. The Paradise Valley was radiant, and just two weeks after making the big move fifty-one miles to the north, I rolled into Gardiner (my home of the last ten summers and seven years) with a big grin on my face—only to be one-upped by the look of mischievous delight on my boy Nate's mug.

Nate is known for a lot in the Yellowstone community. His PhD in ecology and thirty-plus years of Yellowstone history, mountain goat and predator-prey studies, and solo experiences in the wilds add to the lore. Yes, he has climbed more than eighty peaks in the Yellowstone Ecosystem, has pounded out thousands upon thousands of backcountry miles, knows the edible berries and Latin names that go with them, and brings a uniquely Nathan vibe to any trip or adventure. And while this all greatly enhances what he adds to a backpacking journey into the mountains, his unfailing ability to create magic in a pot with his gourmet backcountry meals makes him indispensable, especially after a grueling climb over a steep and unforgiving pass.

Though we knew our time was limited, we acted like schoolboys fresh off a reading of Jack Kerouac's *On the Road*. It didn't matter that a five-day saunter had been shortened to three; we were living in the moment, rolling through the valley filled with guides, clients, and wolf watchers with a sense of peace that we were "off"—taking time off from guiding and off on our own adventure.

Traveling with Nathan has a calming effect on me, and while my excitement at what awaited literally pulsated through me, a quiet joy overcame me on our four-hour drive to the trailhead. After an unhurried stop at Buns N Beds in Cooke City, where Jan, the owner, kindly cut my bunless hamburger into small pieces after watching me struggle in my cast, we slurped the final drops of our milkshakes, said good-bye to civilization, and journeyed through some of my favorite country in the world.

My great-great-grandpa pushed cattle up the Chisholm Trail into Wyoming; and my roots run deep, with three generations of Wyoming and four generations of Idaho, Montana, and Wyoming history in my family. The drive from Cooke City to Cody, the Clarks Fork, Sunlight Basin, and Dead Indian Pass have always ignited my fascination with place. And whenever we get a weekend to go throw up a tent with our three-year-old, my wife and I seem to find ourselves out along the banks of the Clarks Fork or North Fork of the Shoshone—a rugged and wild country shaped by a violent volcanic past some fifty million years ago.

I'm not quite sure what it is about that big, remote, wild Absaroka Country that resonates so strongly with me, but whenever I'm in that northwest corner of Wyoming, I feel something deep within my core—an internal compass that differs from how I feel in other parts of the Ecosystem. Perhaps my family ties and the area's sheer remoteness explain it. The landscape is so vast, unoccupied, desolate, and full of wild enchantment—rugged country that has not been yuppified like so much of the Rocky Mountain West.

While Nate and I were tempted to start at the Lamar River Footbridge Trailhead inside the park, beginning our hike in the parking lot where we'd set up scopes for clients all summer long—with hordes of people around us—simply didn't have the same appeal as twisting through the Sunlight Basin for over an hour on a dirt road en route to Painter Cabin. Having driven past the turnoff to the Sunlight Basin road dozens of times in my truck and on my road bike, I could hardly contain my enthusiasm as we began bumping our way down its long dirt road.

This would be Nathan's third or fourth trip to the Hoodoo Basin, so he knew of two pretty stoic stream crossings we would have to make with the truck to reach the unofficial trailhead. With water and steam spewing out of the tailpipe as the hitch ground against the steep embankment of the creek, it wasn't easy as pie; but we hooted and giggled jubilantly as we inched closer to shouldering our packs. It was getting late in the afternoon, and we had a solid ten-mile hike—most of which was vertical—to reach our designated campsite for the night. So we pushed a little farther than we likely would have otherwise, and finally gave up when the road narrowed to more of an ATV track than a passageway for a full-sized vehicle—which then necessitated backtracking, clearing brush along the way.

Finally, we found a small pullout large enough for my truck—one we had passed forty-five minutes earlier. We shut off the engine, and listened to the songbirds and hurried waters of Sunlight Creek as we put the finishing touches on our packs. Then we hit the trail.

The first few miles are a gentle amble through a thick, almost Pacific Northwest–style forest transitioning from lodgepole to spruce and fir. The berries were abundant, and we enjoyed the sweetness of currants and *Vaccinium* (by way of whortleberries and huckleberries) in plenty.

Soon after our first creek crossing, the gentle stroll in the forest gave way to a steady and steep climb, which continued for several miles until we reached the park's east boundary, on a big sprawling ridge overlooking what I firmly believe is the wildest section of Yellowstone.

The Thorofare receives more acclaim than the Hoodoo Basin for being the most remote region in Yellowstone, as there is a point near the southeast boundary, not far from where the Thorofare Ranger Station is located, that is farther from any road than anywhere else in the lower forty-eight. However, the lack of human presence, combined with the sea of mountains dominating the Hoodoo Basin (the trifecta of Saddle, Hague, and Little Saddle Mountains, surrounded by the ominous Castor and Pollux, Grant and Notch), make the Hoodoo Basin area the most rugged country in Yellowstone National Park—at least in the opinion of this young man, who was wide-eyed and awe-inspired watching the sun set here on another summer day in Yellowstone.

We probably stayed and soaked in the view from the ridge for too long, considering we still had a two-hour, several-mile walk across a big, expansive, and open meadow that tightly hugged the ridge we stood upon. I will never forget that walk on that summer evening in Yellowstone. Here I was, away from everything that always seemed so consuming in my life, with little on my mind but the raw and inspiring beauty that extended as far as I could see as I walked with a backcountry messiah of sorts. Several times between the ridge and camp, we lost the trail under the now deepening and darkening sky—additional indication this was not a heavily traveled trail. I couldn't have been happier.

If Nathan had not been to this site in years past (a site he spoke of glowingly) or been so observant, there was no way we would have found 3M7. After an hour of walking in the dark—seven hours after setting out on foot; and fourteen hours after leaving the comfort of my house, wife, and radiant little girl—we finally reach base camp. And while there was no place I would rather have been at that moment—perched above the goblins that represent the Hoodoo Basin, which we would start exploring early the next morning—my mood (and angst) quickly shifted when, after pumping water for the evening, I discovered a fresh grizzly scat, full of whitebark pine seeds, dead center of where we would have liked to set up our floorless shelter for the next two nights.

I have often spoken of the "night factor" in Yellowstone Country.

While I don't think about grizzlies much while hiking by day, for some reason, they become all too present in my head when I am getting ready to crawl into my sleeping bag at night. This had the makings of another restless and sleepless night with grizzlies on my mind. But first I would be treated to one of Nate's backcountry culinary delights.

Being that guy who typically opts for the light, quick, and easy freeze-dried backpacking food, I was more than a little impressed when Nate busted out the thawed elk meat to add to our creamy pasta with freshly cut red peppers, which I had diced while wondering why we were sautéing elk—of all critters—within ten feet of where a grizzly had recently shat his stomach full of seeds. But these thoughts slowly wafted away with the smoke of our fire as my body warmed and my taste buds celebrated what would have been a notable dish at any restaurant in Gardiner—a five-star meal. I climbed into my mummy sleeping bag, my belly warm and full.

While Nate (who was empty-handed when it came to bear spray) slept like a meat-drunk dog that night, I actually slept better than I had anticipated. It was clear that change was on the wing. We'd gone to bed on a beautiful summer evening only to awake to the first day of fall—things change that quickly in Yellowstone. The day that was supposed to bring sixteen hours of off-trail hiking in our attempt to summit the hard-to-reach Indian Peak quickly morphed into an adventure of another sort. The temperature had dropped thirty degrees overnight, now ranging in the mid- to high 40s; and the sky, which hovered around us in a claustrophobic, fog-like stupor, clung to the mountains and threatened to rain, holding little promise for a day among the peaks

Knowing our time was limited before the storm descended upon us, we hurried down to the Hoodoo Basin for my first look at the goblin labyrinth that had haunted me for nearly a decade. Knowing we would be back to the basin later in the day—and still dreaming of summiting Indian Peak—we forged ahead to the ridge of Hoodoo Peak, where we got our first good look at the massive outcropping we were going to attempt to climb. I'm a huge believer in trying to make the seemingly impossible possible, but climbing Indian Peak was clearly not possible in one day. So we regrouped, looked at the sky (which was getting darker, lower, and more threatening by the minute), and opted for a summit of Hoodoo Peak followed by a dash to Parker Peak.

By 11 A.M., we stood on the summit of Hoodoo. Short of breath after hustling up the steep slopes of the 10,563-foot peak, a quick celebratory hug and a photo was all the time we had before the already nasty winds whipped into a raging torrent. Finding shelter from the wind on the leeward side of the summit knob, we took in some calories. The fog and rain continued to roll in until visibility was barely twenty feet. Wet, cold, and restless, we began our slog down the southeast ridge of the peak, abandoning Parker Peak in hopes of finding a shorter and less exposed route to camp.

After an hour and a half of scurrying down steep talus and meandering through wet grasses, we found camp, made a quick lunch to warm the bones, and by 1 P.M., were forced to seek refuge in our floorless tarp of a shelter. It wasn't until 5 P.M., when the storm started to lighten up and my antsy desire to explore the goblins became too much to resist, that we finally emerged from our sleeping bags and decided to saunter down to the hoodoos. Still feeling restless and ready to explore, I took off ahead of Nathan and spent thirty minutes alone, feeling inspired and empowered to be navigating through the maze of hoodoos—an eerie and unforgiving landscape—with the throbbing of my heart as my only company. And throb it did.

For a few mesmerizing hours, we climbed and slid and discovered goblins and hoodoos that we liked to imagine had never been seen before. Though this surely wasn't the case, for a dreamer and Yellowstone romantic, these thoughts of grandeur only added to an already amazing experience. While dark clouds and dampness lingered over the basin, muting the browns, greens, and oranges, something about the Hoodoo Basin felt alarmingly alive on that first evening of autumn.

The final morning of any long-anticipated adventure or trip always brings a little weight to my heart; I typically find it difficult to leave a setting so remote, rugged, and wild. But all night long, we could hear the storm brewing, and feel the condensation and wind pounding our tent. By the time we awoke, early on the morning of September 15, wet and heavy snow had accumulated around the skirt of our shelter. We were cold and damp, and itching to get moving.

While we slept, it had snowed five inches. Looking to the north, camped in the shadow of Hoodoo Peak, we watched clouds race violently across its summit. Breaking down camp in these conditions is a finger-numbing, unpleasant process. After lighting up the stove one last time, we began the damp slog through the meadow and up to the pass. Though cold and wet (I was wearing grocery sacks over my socks in my trail-running shoes, which had let in so much water the day before that my heels were scorched with blisters), we still yearned for adventure.

We knew the hike out would be messy and muddy; we only hoped that a horse crew hadn't traveled the trail before us. But who else would be crazy enough to be in these mountains in the midst of what we now called "Equinox Storm?" After a long, two-hour march to the pass, we ditched our packs and summited an unnamed 10,000-foot peak—just for prosperity—and then we began our arduous and slippery walk back to the truck.

The weather remained fickle most of the day, but we still carried the smiles on our faces that adversity and challenges bring to a grand and memorable adventure. At one point, during a short window, the clouds parted, giving way to a brilliant blue sky made even more striking by the fresh snow delicately sprinkled atop the cavernous peaks of the Absarokas. We broke for lunch and rested for over an hour beside a swift little stream. We barely said a word the entire time, lying on our backs and relishing the sun's gentle warmth on our only exposed flesh—our necks and cheeks.

We felt fulfilled, but at the same time, still hungry. The journey had filled our spirits but had not entirely quenched our thirst for adventure. But it is my hope that, as long as my legs keep working and my back supports a pack, this thirst will never be quenched.

A beautiful friendship that has been growing, transforming, and changing like the dramatic seasons of Yellowstone was strengthened by this journey; that is the power of sharing adventure, hardships, and challenges—it brings out the character and resolve in people. And while we were perhaps a little disappointed that we didn't get to spend the entire time pushing ourselves physically in search of another view from another summit, I don't think either of us would change a thing about this truly epic three-day adventure.

By the time we climbed back in the truck, the rain started to fly again. I turned on ESPN radio to hear how Boise State and the Pac-12 teams fared through the course of the day, but our silence—which seemed so natural along the stream—now lacked the same sense of contentment. Not wanting our adventure to end, nor ready to return to the hustle and bustle of the world, I wanted to relish the final hour of dirt road we still had left to travel—so I switched the radio off.

After the last of the stream crossings—whether purposefully or not, I still can't say—I took a little pressure off the gas pedal. I think Nathan recognized that I was not driving out as fast I had on the way in, but he didn't complain; he simply gave me that big glorious grin, and we began talking up and planning our next adventure, and the one thereafter.

• • •

THE JOURNEY TRULY IS THE destination. The conception of, planning for, and anticipation of an adventure are, in many ways, every bit as important as the adventure itself. What would life be without the ability to hope and dream? Despite crappy weather and a trip cut short, Nate's and my Hoodoo expedition exceeded my hopes a hundredfold. Perhaps this is the ultimate gift of adventure. In a challenging world that too often shatters our grandest and most noble aspirations, the execution of a long-planned adventure provides the spirit food and creative nutrition to keep us dreaming of the endless possibilities that unfold at our feet when venturing deep into wild country.

In the end, perhaps our reason for running rivers, climbing mountains, and carrying heavy loads into the backcountry surpasses the expansive vistas, surge of adrenaline, and sense of accomplishment one inevitably experiences in pursuit of wild encounters. The more I journey into wild places, the more I come to believe that these moments of unmatched empowerment represent our effort to become intimate with our higher self—to reconnect with our core mission—and if we are lucky, to continue dreaming of all that we can one day become.

Acknowledgments

Life ain't all roses and applesauce. It's a grind filled with heart-ache, struggle, and challenges—but also with love, friendship, and adventure. Yellowstone Country abounds with much of the latter. I must say, no matter how hard things get, when I step outside and look around at the cathedral of mountains that surround our valley of sublimity—the pulsing rivers breathing life into the land around us, and the glorious smile and dancing feet of my daughter, Kamiah—I can't help but realize that I've got it pretty damn good.

There are so many people who have touched, impacted, and inspired my Yellowstone journey and the pages filling up this humble collection of essays. This book is a tribute to all those who have fought for wilderness, wildlife, and our last wild places. To the legendary authors who have inspired me to write and strive to become a passionate voice for the places I love: Ed Abbey, Aldo Leopold, Rick Bass, Terry Tempest Williams, Doug Peacock, and David James Duncan. To Mike Mease and the frontline warriors who tenaciously represent the Buffalo Field Campaign, enduring relentless winter winds, blizzards, and sub-zero temperatures in their fight to stop the senseless slaughter of Yellow-stone's wild bison, I give thanks.

Yellowstone is often described as a "people's park," and for more than a century, it has inspired families from all over the globe to visit the extreme northwest corner of Wyoming. My annual childhood pilgrim-ages to Yellowstone did more than connect me to the power of the natural world; these journeys deepened my bond to the people nearest and dearest to my heart: my family.

I've often asked, "What would life be without Yellowstone?" I could just as easily ask, "What would life be without Mom?" I really don't believe this book would have ever been possible without the coaching, mentoring, unequivocal support, and love of my mom. Leaving behind her life as a lawyer to pursue her passion as a writer, my mother has woven stories that shed light on the issues and places that matter most to our clan. There is no thank-you that would ever be enough, so in the two most beautiful languages I know, I say *mahalo* and *Ayóó ániínishí*.

To my dad, best friend and partner in trout-related pursuits, my gratitude runs as deep and long as the rivers that haunt our winter reveries. Thank you for believing in my dreams and standing by me, always willing to endure the most daunting of storms.

If not for my Grandpa Chris and Grandma Isabel, I would not have my generations of Wyoming roots and pride in where my family comes from. To my Uncle Wayne, who has been such an important figure in my life, your love for our ancestral Wyoming is an inspiration; thank you for being the rebellious crusader that you are. And to my authentically beautiful sister, Ashley Ryan, and my precious niece, Mira: thank you for your love. Your commitment to an equally wild Glacier National Park and your home of East Glacier are a testament to the gravitational pull of place.

To my literary agent, friend, and fellow dreamer, Alan Centafonte, you truly are the "Centa Man," as you do the work of one hundred men. You are my champion. Without you, the dream of seeing this book in print would not have been possible. You have provided me with one of the most important gifts a person can ever bestow upon another: hope. For that—and so much more—I thank you.

To my editor, Jen Weaver-Neist: from our first three-hour conversation spanning the distance between my home office on the banks of the Yellowstone to your home waters along the shores of the Columbia, I sensed you were a kindred spirit; and I realized I had struck gold with you as my editor. The editorial process of a project this personal can be overwhelming, but you made it joyful and meaningful. For that, I extend my most heartfelt gratitude.

I couldn't be more blessed or grateful for the people at Graphic Arts Books, who have been an absolute dream to work with. Doug Pfeiffer, Kathy Howard, Angela Zbornik, and Vicki Knapton, you are the best team in the business. Thank you for believing in this project and for giving me the opportunity to join the GAB ohana.

To my exceptional friend, officemate, and by-default mayor of Livingston, Montana, Brad Bunkers, you are a creative maestro—a guru of everything graphic-arts related. Thank you for everything! Your unwavering support, love, and friendship are gifts I treasure; and your cover design for this book is bomber, my brother. I'm both humbled and honored to have one of Tom Murphy's brilliant photos featured on the cover of this book. There is no person in the twenty-first century who has a deeper connection to Yellowstone than you, Tom. Your generosity of spirit is a blessing to the Yellowstone community.

Nathan Varley and Linda Thurston, you are two of the most generous, unique, authentic, and beautiful souls I've ever known. Working for you has been a dream, and being your friend is an honor. Your foreword to this book is a gift I will forever cherish Nate; thank you, my friend.

To three of my cherished mentors—Tom Roy, Steve Hoffman, and Tim Christie—I am honored and grateful every day for the wisdom, gifts, and friendship you have bestowed up me. I once wrote, "I never believed in heroes until I met Tom Roy." Tom, you have been a beacon of supreme wisdom and unwavering support. Steve, your passion for life, raptors, and conservation is unparalleled; thank you for always believing in me. Tim, your friendship, love, and sage advice is a gift. To the three of you, I gratefully bow my head and say thank-you.

To my environmental studies nature-writing professor at the University of Montana, Phil Condon, thank you for igniting the spark and serving as the conduit for me to write. To my Park Service family, Brian Suderman, Carol Shively, Ellen Petrick, Bob Furhman, John Meyer, Marc Hannah, Jim Williams, Allison Vanlonkhuyzen, Dan Richards, Toby Sauer, Kevin Dooley, and Keith Young, it was always a pleasure and an honor to work for you, learn from you, and serve beside you.

To my friends and outfitters Dale Sexton and Matson Rogers, there are no two men in the fly-fishing world that I admire and respect more. Your generosity in supporting YCG's River Guardian Fly Fishing School enabled us to do what we do. Your friendship is an honor that I treasure.

To Robert and Naomi Gary, I will never forget the dinner at your house not long after Kamiah and I returned from our journey to the Pacific. Robert, you are an inspiration, my brother. To Tom Gauthier and Gary Kane, you are two of the best administrators in the business. Thank you for your friendship, support, and for always facilitating my work with local youth.

To Randy "Doons" Ingersoll, you are the most loyal friend I've ever known. Never has there been a man with a more pure and uninhibited love for Yellowstone. You are a true original—a beautiful soul—and you will always be my family. To Scotty B Black, Matt Larson, and Daniel Claussen, what can I say? Your friendship, support, and presence in my life has been a source of inspiration and a bedrock of stability that I can always count on.

To the Yellowstone Country Guardians board of directors, donors, and most importantly, to the teenagers who breathed life into our organization and vision, may you always keep the YCG fire burning and forever be passionate guardians of our beloved Yellowstone.

Lastly, to my beautiful baby girl, Kamiah, who inspires me each day. There was a time when my passion for conservation, adventure, and Yellowstone blinded me from the vision of becoming a father. And then on a bluebird day in late October—perhaps Yellowstone's most glorious season—I welcomed you into the world. My world has never been the same. My purpose has never been more clear. Now, when I dream of my legs working the way they once did, it's not about bagging peaks, logging miles, or chasing trout. Instead, it's about sharing the place that I love more than any other with the person that I love more than anything on this big, wild, watery planet. You are my source. Providing you with love, goodness, and stability is my purpose. Mahalo, my love.

For a wild Yellowstone. . . .

With nothin' but love,
Michael W. Leach